Stanley Rosen, Evan Pugh Professor of
Philosophy at Pennsylvania State Univer-
sity, is also the author of *G. W. F. Hegel,
The Limits of Analysis, Nihilism, Plato's
"Sophist,"* and *Plato's "Symposium."*

The Ancients and the Moderns

THE
Ancients
AND THE
Moderns

RETHINKING MODERNITY

Stanley Rosen

Yale University Press

New Haven and London

Designed by Richard Hendel
and set in Palatino type by
Tseng Information Systems, Inc.
Printed in the United States of America by
Thomson-Shore, Inc., Dexter, Michigan.

Library of Congress Cataloging-in-Publication Data
Rosen, Stanley, 1929–
The ancients and the moderns.
Bibliography: p.
Includes index.
1. Philosophy, Modern.   I. Title.
B791.R77   1989   190   88–26155
ISBN 0–300–04331–7 (alk. paper)

The paper in this book meets the guidelines for permanence and
durability of the Committee on Production Guidelines for Book
Longevity of the Council on Library Resources.

10 9 8 7 6 5 4 3 2 1

Contents

Preface

In the preface to the second edition of the *Science of Logic*, Hegel refers to "the peculiar restlessness and dispersion of our modern consciousness."[1] In the context, this is a pejorative expression, but a moment's reflection tells us that it has a positive corollary. Restlessness is the superficial manifestation of what Hegel elsewhere calls "the seriousness, the suffering, the patience and work of the negative."[2] And again, activity or making (*das Tun*) is itself nothing other than negativity.[3] To return to the *Science of Logic*, "the ground of Becoming, the restlessness of self-movement, lies in the negative."[4]

For Hegel, of course, restlessness and negativity, although they never disappear, are finally the active dimension, the engine driving the comprehensive and circular concept of the whole. In Hegel's peculiar synthesis of ancients and moderns, the Platonic Ideas or Aristotelian forms unite with the Kantian concept on the one hand and the absolute ego of Fichte and Schelling on the other to provide the wise man in one way, and the ordinary citizen in another, with "satisfaction."

In the late twentieth century, the Hegelian legacy remains only as a distorted and fragmentary memory within Marxism. And Marxism itself has been further "dispersed" by the "peculiar restlessness" of the modern consciousness. Our contemporary sense of our own existence has been indelibly stamped by Lockean uneasiness and the Nietzschean will to power. Modern restlessness today takes on the shifting forms of neuraesthenic aestheticism, an aestheticism of mathematical *technē* and textual playfulness. It is as though the seriousness of Heidegger's endorsement of Being as a "playing child" (Heraclitus' *pais paizōn*), having passed through the unbearable tension of "authenticity" and "resoluteness," is today dissipated into frivolity.

1. *Wissenschaft der Logik* (Leipzig: Felix Meiner Verlag, 1951), 1:20. Except where noted otherwise, all translations are my own.
2. *Phänomenologie des Geistes* (Hamburg: Felix Meiner Verlag, 1952), 20.
3. Ibid., 286.
4. *Wissenschaft der Logik*, 1:157.

The great difficulty of residing in the modern epoch has thus paradoxically culminated in the triviality that nothing could be easier. We
have all become hermeneuts and deconstructors simultaneously, that
is to say, interpreters of a text that dissolves before our very gaze. In
the contemporary idiom, reading has been transformed into writing.
The rejection of domination is accordingly also the exercise of the ultimate domination or rewriting of history, an activity hitherto reserved
for tyrants.

None of this is intended to suggest that history wears its meaning
on its sleeve; nor am I blind to the positive aspects of the contemporary reconsideration of the western tradition. What I wish to defend
is the thesis that it is *difficult* to be a modern. I would therefore reject
the facile assertion, popular in some quarters, of a quarrel between
antiquity and modernity as an opposition between austere nobility
on the one hand and sophistry on the other.

In the first place, the opposition between the noble and the base,
or between philosophy and sophistry, already defines the structure
of antiquity. From this standpoint, there is no difference between
antiquity and modernity. Second and more fundamentally, the path
into the quarrel between the ancients and the moderns takes us into
the question of whether philosophy is possible at all, or whether it
is not simply noble sophistry.[5] If philosophy is *technē*, either mathematical or hermeneutical, then it is merely a species of poetry.[6] The
doctrine of *truth-conditions*, or the definition of meaning in terms of
the laws of logic, is as much poetry as the doctrine of the abolition of
truth-conditions, in an age of "alternative" and "deviant" logics.

We should have learned from Hegel that the names *antiquity* and
modernity stand for the two constitutive dimensions of our conceptual mastery of human existence. To call the first positive and the
second negative is by no means to give the palm to antiquity. But
Hegel's reference to the seriousness, suffering, patience, and work of
negativity are by implication an acknowledgment of the weight he
gives to antiquity. The "first negation" (or negation of the positive
moment) draws on that weight for its own substance. The "second
negation" (or negation of the negation) is neither a simple cancella-
tion nor a simple return to the initial affirmation. In Hegel's language,

5. See Plato, *Sophist* 231b3–8 and 268a9–c4.
6. For further discussion, see the preface to my *Quarrel Between Philosophy and Poetry*
(New York and London: Routledge, Chapman and Hall, Inc., 1988).

the substance of the first negation becomes the subject of the second negation. This means, not that antiquity is replaced by modernity, but that modernity is the self-consciousness of antiquity.

We do not need to be Hegelians in order to draw the moral from this Hegelian lesson. In the postanthropological, postmetaphysical, postmodernist epoch, there is no more substance or subject, hence no self-consciousness, and neither antiquity nor modernity. Accordingly, there is no more postmodernism, since *post-* draws its sense from what precedes it, namely, modernity, which is in turn defined by reference to antiquity.

A genuine attention to the quarrel between the ancients and the moderns is therefore as much an immersion in antiquity as it is in modernity. My next point requires careful qualification if it is not to be misunderstood. The immersion to which I refer cannot be philological or scholarly, if by these terms is meant the return to an objective understanding of the meaning of the texts of ancient and modern philosophers.

There is a fundamental paradox of hermeneutics which may be stated as follows: an objective understanding of a text is a subjective understanding, but a subjective understanding cannot be objective. This does not leave us at the mercy of relativism; a subjective understanding, to continue with the previous formulation, must defend itself against its rivals. It is not by chance that Plato frequently uses the metaphors of war, hunting, and athletic contests to describe philosophical investigation. There is, in other words, a crucial difference between mere playfulness and playing to win.

The polemical use of pure reason, to borrow a phrase from Kant, is something quite different from recourse to this or that ideology of objectivity. Philosophy is not mathematics; the technical accuracy of a philosophical interpretation depends in the penultimate analysis upon grasping the author's intentions, but ultimately, upon the philosophical reappropriation of these intentions. The fact that one man's philosophy is another man's sophistry has no bearing on the intrinsic situation. It belongs instead to the sociological, or better, political domain of persuasion.

There is no such thing as philosophical persuasion, if by this is meant persuasion by the exchange of "objective" or logically valid arguments. One can always find a technical justification for the repudiation of someone else's technical toys. Arguments, if they are not to remain at the professorial level of the seminar room, must rise to the level of the restlessness and patience of the human spirit, that is, to the level of the labor of negativity. But what rises cannot be mere rhetoric or "hot air." We need to master the technical details of a philosophical text, but this turns upon our perception that *all* details of a philosophical text are technical, including the rhetorical structure and the polemical intention. It turns upon a deeper conception of the *technē* of philosophical activity as the unity of theory and practice, that is to say, as an activity that sees with the assistance of its artifacts, but which devises those artifacts in accord with what it sees.

The essays contained in this volume are offered as a contribution to the unending task of restoring the seriousness and difficulty to the obligation of being a resident of modernity. It may be true that Zeus is a playing child; unfortunately, we are ourselves neither gods nor children. I am the last person to speak out against playfulness; let me also be the first to observe that the words of this preface are not free of the danger of pomposity. One must however be prepared to run the risk of pomposity in order to return to philosophy something of the pomp and circumstance without which modernity is mere vulgarity. These essays are accordingly prolegomena to modernity.

Stanley Rosen
State College, Pennsylvania
March 1988

The Ancients and the Moderns

CHAPTER ONE

A Modest Proposal to
Rethink Enlightenment

According to a famous remark by Hegel, the owl of Minerva takes flight only at dusk. Philosophy is in other words a creature of decadence, which is somewhat paradoxically identified as a concealed manifestation of progress. As the conceptual articulation of the development of Spirit within history, philosophy acquires its full voice whenever the completion of an essential stage of this development is about to occur. Philosophy is thus at once the swan song of a dying epoch and the firebird that arises from the ashes of its own corpse. For Hegel, death is reincarnation: This is the plain sense of the obscure doctrine of double negation. What returns, however, is the concept, not history itself. In other words, the contradictions by which one historical epoch is transformed into another are not simply death struggles or birth pangs but local manifestations of an absolute, circular, or comprehensive logical process. By a series of necessary self-transformations, philosophy becomes wisdom.

We who dwell outside the Hegelian circle, "beyond good and evil," nevertheless remain within its shadow. For the advanced thinker of the late twentieth century, the end of modernity, the closure of metaphysics, the death of God, and the arrival of the postanthropological epoch are all signs that wisdom itself has arrived, only now in its true identity as difference. Perhaps we do not understand that the identification of wisdom as difference is merely another formulation of the Hegelian principle of the identity of identity and difference. Nor do we seem to appreciate the irony that the supersession of presence by absence is another form of presence, or what one could also call the enlightenment of *chiaroscuro*.

Hegelian science to one side, our historical experience entitles us to engage in Socratic prophecy. The evocation of the past, like the imagination of the future, is nothing but the dialectic of presence. If

1

this prophecy is genuine, then the quarrel between the ancients and the moderns must be redefined as schizophrenia. There are accordingly neither ancients nor moderns, and certainly no postmoderns, but only simulacra of our fragmented selves: the historical detritus, not of a repudiated absolute ego, but of human possibility.

Lest the reader accuse me of playing with words (as though this were precluded from philosophical discourse), let me shift linguistic registers. We establish the presence of difference by distinguishing this from that, and so by relying upon the identity of this and that. Each "this such" (to employ a sober Aristotelian term) is an identity of identity and difference. The question is now whether this logical truism is also a structural platitude of human possibility. And it seems that it must be so. If, for example, Nietzsche is right to speak of the subject or self-conscious person as an illusory text masking the reality of countless subtexts, this multiplicity of *personae*, even as branching out to implicate other subjective networks, retains its identity as a branching-out point or node of difference.

The identity of identity and difference holds good at both the microscopic and the macroscopic level, in both analysis and synthesis. But what of human history? Is not the serial presentation of macroscopic differences immune to our logical truism? Structure is atemporal, but life is not. Or is this not precisely the point? As even Nietzsche would insist, to live is one thing; to understand life is another. The difference between the ancients and the moderns is undeniable at the historical level. But this difference has no bearing upon the possibility of inner structural identity, especially if that structure, commonly known as human nature, is itself an identity of identity and difference.

From this standpoint, the quarrel between the ancients and the moderns takes on new contours. We tend both to overlook and also to be confused by the fact that this quarrel takes place exclusively among moderns. That it could not have occurred in antiquity in the same terms is a historical contingency which takes nothing away from the capacity of modern thinkers to see themselves in the mirror of the past. If the doctrine of historical relativism were true, there would be no such quarrel because the mirror would be opaque. That we cannot return to the past in no way cancels the fact that we have already been there, and so, as historical beings, are still there. As moderns, we are also ancients. Strictly speaking, it therefore makes no difference to us whether the ancients were also moderns, in the trivial sense that they could not see out through the mirror and observe us discerning ourselves in their archaic visages.

In another sense, the ancients, as paradigms by which we discern our difference, or identify ourselves, are moderns by virtue of participation in the identity of identity and difference. Time does not separate us at this level, it binds us together. With the passage of time, they have become ourselves. Nor could they have done otherwise, from our present standpoint (and there is no other standpoint). The metaphysics of possible worlds has no application here. The "noble simplicity" of the ancients and the "terrible restlessness of the modern consciousness" to one side (after all, these expressions apply to a small minority of residents in each epoch), we look into the restless and innovative souls of the ancient Athenians and the arrogant, expansive, and yet rule-bound souls of the ancient Romans, and we see ourselves.

This is the necessary precondition for any serious reflection upon the difference between the ancients and the moderns. It is the basis upon which the differences that flow from the extraordinary power of modern science can be properly evaluated. Our common humanity permits us to ask: What would the ancients have done had they possessed our knowledge? Arguments from isolated instances of philosophers who warn against the political hazards of unlimited technology may then be countered by the charge of obtuseness or moral baseness. Can it be that Cyrus, Alexander the Great, and Julius Caesar were wiser than Plato and Aristotle on the one thing necessary? Regardless of which side one takes in this debate, it can be held at all only if there is a genuine choice. And this choice can be resolved neither by history nor by recourse to the principle of noncontradiction. We choose only by looking into the mirror.

So much by way of an introductory invocation of the Muses. I want now to argue on behalf of a modified or moderate enlightenment. Underlying this argument is the presupposition that the differences between the ancients and the moderns are contingent, or that there are ancients and moderns in both epochs. Differently stated, I shall take the side of the moderns in their quarrel with the ancients, but on grounds that are not peculiar to the political or cultural configurations of our own epoch. The extreme form of my thesis is that the evidence for modernity may be derived from antiquity. The doctrine of human nature is ancient, not modern. To reject the ancients entirely would be to reject ourselves as well. I can therefore subscribe to Nietzsche's contention that man is the unfinished animal, a contention that is intelligible only if we know what it means to be a man on the one hand and an animal on the other.

———————

The defense of the ancients is today most strikingly formulated by those who call themselves conservatives. (I disregard the expression *neoconservative*, with its self-vitiating implication of radical revisionism, or of making the past "up to date" while at the same time it remains the past.) This defense is articulated as a celebration of prudence, which is itself identified as the aforementioned "noble simplicity of the ancients." It is thereby taken for granted that revolutionary tactics and intricate political strategy, unless they point backward or support the status quo, can be neither prudent nor noble.

I begin with a simple experiment. What would be required in order to restrict the vitiating effects of the Enlightenment by means of the presumed wisdom of the ancients? To some extent this will engage us in the comparison of rivals to the title of salutary myth, but not entirely. Or rather, no myth can be salutary unless there is a natural difference between health and sickness. This difference may also be stated in Kantian terms as one between childhood and maturity, provided we retain the un-Kantian understanding of maturity as noble youthfulness.

If I am not mistaken, the attack on the Enlightenment takes two main forms. The first contends that the natural distinction between the few and the many requires the restriction of passion by reason: the many are passionate, the few reasonable. Passion, if unregulated, will destroy reason and can be regulated only by the rhetoric of religion and patriotism or by the exoteric expression of prudence. Unfortunately, this amounts to the restriction of reason by passion: The divine madness of philosophy must be restricted to the privacy of the thoughts or guarded conversations of the few. The second form of the attack is not motivated by a perception of natural aristocracy but rather by the conviction that reason is self-destructive, as is most evident in the potentially disastrous consequences of scientific technology. The problem here is not that passion negates reason, but rather that reason negates itself. Passion, understood as the desire for self-preservation, or more nobly as sympathy for mankind, is more reasonable than reason. The practical consequence is once more that reason must be regulated by passion.

These two versions of antienlightenment, although they may be distinguished from each other, normally appear together, and in a variety of doctrinal guises. It would undoubtedly be held by more than one conservative that the opposition just stated between reason and passion is an oversimplification and that we require something like the Platonic tripartition of the soul into reason, spiritedness, and desire. Others would object that reason is itself distinguishable as theoretical and practical, and that what we require is the restriction of the first by the second for comprehensive political motives.

I have no intention of denying the pertinence of these and other still more subtle distinctions to the task of acquiring an exhaustive analysis of the human soul. My suggestion is that, in the present context, these subtleties are invoked by critics of the Enlightenment in the service of the following fundamental political thesis: The public expression of reason leads inevitably to the domination of reason by the imagination, which is in turn subservient to passion, and in the extreme instance of passion, to the will to power. One is therefore entitled to infer that on the conservative position, passion is by nature stronger than reason, unless reason is able to devise cunning instruments by which to restrict passion. The chains of passion are forged by reason in the smithy of the passions; unfortunately, in order to fulfill their purpose, they must be worn by reason itself.

Conservatism, in the present sense of the term, is therefore based upon a perception of the limitations or defects of human nature. At the same time, this perception is linked to an ambiguous understanding of nature. Whereas man is the rational animal, he is not sufficiently rational to live in accordance with nature—or more specifically, with *his* nature. From this it follows that either man or nature is irrational or that nature is divided within itself. Nature in the cosmic sense is thus an enemy rather than a friend of mankind. The result is inevitably a doctrine of the supernatural or of a radical split between theory and practice. In this way, man transforms himself from the rational to the active animal. Paradoxically enough, this is also the precondition for the advent of liberalism, that is, of the Enlightenment.

This thumbnail sketch of the progress of conservatism suggests that it transforms itself into its opposite by its own inner rhythms. Let me put this to one side as a preliminary anticipation of my theme. For the moment, I merely note that, according to the conservative, *homo sapiens* (as opposed to some few individual human beings) is the passionate animal, in whom reason is an instrument for the unending process by which we attempt to satisfy our desires, a process in which we must inevitably consume ourselves. The double identity of nature underlies the distinction between the few and the many, as well as the not-so-secret philosophical conviction that the many are to be preserved from self-destruction by the deification of the few. The philosopher returns to the cave as a god or lawgiver; more precisely, he returns in the form of his exoteric traces.

This point must be emphasized in view of the widespread contemporary misunderstanding of Platonism, or of the history of metaphysics as the ostensible domination of presence. To the extent that conservatism and Platonism converge, one must say that the philosopher is present only as absent, either as a divine being who does not know whether his neighbor is a human or a beast, or else as a fallen god who must curtail (not to say abstain from) the pursuit of wisdom in order to tend the herd-animal "man" with a judicious mixture of rhetoric and force. In either case, the Platonic philosopher cannot live within the city as a philosopher. The absence of the philosopher is a direct consequence of the inaccessibility of wisdom to human discourse. In the imagery of Plato's *Phaedrus*, enlightenment is impossible because the soul, described as a winged charioteer leading a team of horses, one good and the other the opposite, is prevented by the ignoble horse of passion from gaining a steady and uninterrupted vision of the hyperuranian beings or Platonic Ideas.

We see here the philosophical version of the Christian doctrine of original sin: The origin as expressed in human existence is intrinsically evil, which is to say that the inaccessibility of the transhuman origin guarantees the defective nature of mankind. The return to the absolute origin is not a purification of worldly or political existence but its transcendence. To be sure, transcendence can take the historical form of limitation, whether by a philosopher king or by a religious community, whether by law or by love. In either case, despite the differences between them, passion sets a bound to reason: "this far and no farther." It is no triumph of reason to insist that the voice of passion is silent and unbounded unless restrained by reason. Such a claim puts a good face on the impotence of reason and reminds us that

Socrates was outstanding among Athenian soldiers in the audacity with which he retreated.

In sum: enlightenment is held to be impossible because, if it is pursued, reason will either destroy itself or succumb to passion. We must now inquire whether the noble preserves itself by accommodating to baseness or, alternatively, itself becomes base. I introduce the distinction between nobility and baseness of spirit because this distinction is fundamental to the articulation of conservatism and so to the critique of enlightenment.

The conservative may argue either that enlightenment leads to destruction or that it allows baseness to triumph. But the question is whether a noble death is not superior to a base life. We have learned this question from the conservative and are entitled to address it to him. To be somewhat more candid, it was Socrates who taught us that the unexamined life is not worth living, just as it was presumably Socrates who first gave a full account of political conservatism. In my opinion, Socrates was, rather than any kind of a conservative, an enlightener who spoke, not just *ad captum vulgi*, but to the circumstances of his day. What we today call conservatism must seek its ancestor in Aristotle, not in Plato. Aristotle does not bring philosophy down into the city, as is evident from his distinction between theoretical and practical wisdom.

I cannot develop this point here, nor is it necessary for our present argument. Suffice it to say that whatever degree of examination we permit of human life has its political consequences. It is a principle of philosophical conservatism that the human soul is higher than the bestial soul, and so too that the adult intellect is higher than the childish intellect. The conservative philosopher cannot remove philosophy entirely from the city without suppressing himself and thereby returning the nonphilosopher to a semibestial condition of herd existence. Not even the Aristotelian distinction between *theoria* and *phronesis* is enough to overcome the fact that this distinction is made in public, in the presence of gentlemen and not merely of philosophers.

Intrinsic to the distinction between nobility and baseness is the necessary allegiance to nobility, and hence, as I would argue, the necessary wish for enlightenment. The blunt realism or pessimism of the ancients is not a populist repudiation of reason but rather a doctrine of necessary compromise. Philosophers must rule because nonphilosophers are incapable of ruling themselves. In Aristotelian terms, the same may be said of the possessors of practical intelligence. The condemnation of passion, in short, is a tacit admission of the preferability of an open to a closed city. Far from being utopians, then, the ancient philosophers were reconciled to the impossibility of the truly best city. A city in which philosophers are shepherd kings is thus a practical compromise or attenuation of the true paradigm of a city in which all men are philosophers.

No doubt many will disagree with the preceding paragraph as an example of forced reasoning. I present it in evidence but will not insist upon it. For some at least it may serve to buttress my earlier suggestion that conservatism transforms itself into radical enlightenment. What no one can reasonably quarrel with is the observation that conservatism requires compromise. The question therefore arises: At what point do we compromise?

We may begin our reply with a brief consideration of contemporary physical science. The most "liberal" progressives today favor the restriction and elimination of all scientific research that may be directed toward the destruction of the human race. It should by now be plain that what we call progressive liberalism is in fact the voice of conservatism, that is, of the critic of the Enlightenment. To express this in a parenthetical manner, fairness to all requires a steady descent into the abolishment of the intellect. The fact is that all fundamental aspects of the natural sciences, whether physical, chemical, or biological, may lead to the destruction of the human race. In the parenthetical formulation, every degree of intellectual superiority is unfair to the mediocre majority.

Whereas no one would argue against the wisdom of attempting to prevent a nuclear holocaust or the biochemical pollution of the environment, not many are prepared to admit that the only secure way in which to protect ourselves against science is to abolish it entirely. I pass by the practical obstacles, as we are here engaged in the discussion of principles and paradigms. Science must not merely be abolished, then, but our security requires that it never be permitted to arise in the future. The machines must be broken and the textbooks burned, but beyond this we require noble lies and philosopher guardians who will weed out and destroy the potential scientists from each generation of children.

Unfortunately, it is not possible to identify with certainty every child whose gifts are potentially scientific; prudence dictates that we destroy *all* children whose intelligence exceeds a certain modest level. But which level? And to the degree that we are successful, will there not come a time when the guardians are themselves too dull-witted to separate the dangerous children from their innocuous brothers and sisters? Even granting the steady deterioration of the gene pool, there may be sports, or exceptions who have escaped attention; there is always the danger of a chance genius who will have concealed his superiority or been concealed by simple and loving parents. Safety requires that *all* children be destroyed: That is the ultimate absurdity of the attack against the Enlightenment.

I must ask the reader not to take refuge at this point in the pious disclaimer that we of course wish the judicious regulation of scientific inquiry and technological progress for the benefit of mankind. Of course. Nor am I excluding the possibility that within a properly enlightened society, rational deliberation will lead to the desired result in a wide range of cases. My point is that this deliberation can take place only within the context of scientific progress and hence by something more than a token or symbolic appearance of the philosopher in the marketplace. It is not possible to extirpate the moral and political dangers of modern science without enacting the very consequences we fear. The example of science is of course not an isolated one; a similar argument holds good for the general relation between theory and practice.

Let us assume that it is within our power to reconstitute political society in the light of the wisdom of the ancients. Science and technology will be carefully regulated in order to ensure a prudent and virtuous existence for the community. Industrial expansion and the proliferation of consumer goods will cease; the free market will be replaced by a state-supervised economy. The luxurious or fevered city, to employ a phrase from Plato, will be purged of its excesses and tempered to an economy of scarcity. The arts will be censored by direct political intervention, at least for a generation or two, during which time a new and comprehensive educational program, designed to produce virtuous citizens, will transform the character of the people.

To continue, patriotism will be buttressed by love of the gods and hatred (or at least fear) of strangers. Sexual behavior will be subjected to strict regulation by law and by custom. In any version of the classical city short of the extreme Platonic paradigm, women will return to their customary role as wives and mothers. The distinction between the few and the many will be reinstituted by a redistribution of property and by restriction of education to the sons of the aristocracy. Old money will be accorded a higher status than new money; the country will be acknowledged as more virtuous than the town. We need not move directly to Plato's just city in order to require noble lies and salutary myths as part of the comprehensive restriction upon change. Nor can the classical polis, whether of an Aristotelian or an extreme Platonic tincture, be maintained without the careful adherence of the few, in all their written documents and public statements, to the myths upon which the city is founded.

This is enough to indicate what will be required; as Aristotle puts it, whatever the law does not permit is forbidden. The reader may prefer the modern political wisdom of Edmund Burke or of (some of) the founding fathers, but these are already compromises with the strict paradigm of classical excellence. There cannot be the slightest doubt that the actual imposition of this paradigm would require the destruction of Western civilization from the fourth, and strictly speaking, from the fifth century B.C. onward.

The contemporary champions of antiquity will protest that they have no intention of such a preposterous application of their paradigm. I intend to deal very specifically with their proposal to use this paradigm as a standard of excellence by which to make judicious corrections in contemporary decadence. But it is far from trivial, and certainly not preposterous, for me to state plainly and simply what that paradigm actually entails of those who would conform to it. If the paradigm is itself absurd, then it cannot serve as a noble or prudent standard by which to rectify our own baseness.

For this reason I insist upon the obvious, which is unfortunately seldom if ever acknowledged by spokesmen for the ancient wisdom. Even the destruction of Western civilization from the fourth century B.C. onward is insufficient and a temporary respite from historical decadence. The securing of the common good will require ever stricter regulation of public life. The preservation of virtue, in view of the radically defective human nature insisted upon by the classical sages, demands the steady transformation of the city into an armed camp, as Aristotle describes Plato's just city. The situation is, I think, even worse than this. In the *Republic*, Socrates assumes that the philosopher citizens of this city will always agree upon its excellence. Socrates implicitly excludes the possibility of effective disagreement and eventual revolution, not by the workers, but by the guardians. Although he does not say so, heterodox thinkers must be expelled from the city along with the politically deviant poets.

And so, by steady stages, we return to the extreme consequences of our initial paradigm. The secure preservation of virtue depends upon tyranny and barbarism. *Not even the ancients were prepared to enforce such an extreme paradigm of wisdom.* Not even the daring Plato permits himself to state with full rigor the implications of his city of philosopher kings. Nevertheless, the truly striking distinction to be drawn is not between the ancients and moderns, but between the philosophers and the nonphilosophers, or at the least between those philosophers who attempt a rigorous defense of political life against decadence, and all those, philosophers and nonphilosophers alike, who sing to a more relaxed Muse.

Since the defenders of antiquity are in any event agreed that it is inadvisable to adopt an extreme paradigm such as the one I have sketched, it is time to turn away from the obvious to consider what the aforementioned representatives of classical wisdom claim is their actual intention: a moderate defense of moderation.

The main conclusion of the previous section is as follows: The relation between theory and practice, precisely on the classical or ancient view, is such that we cannot apply the classical doctrine of virtue as a standard for improving modern moral and political life except by transforming that life beyond recognition, and indeed, in the extreme case, by destroying it. If this is right (and it would certainly be denied by the contemporary "ancients"), then there is something immoderate about classical moderation. That is to say, it is not moderation that is at fault but the attempt to transfer its classical historical embodiment to the modern world. This conclusion illustrates my earlier distinction between human nature and its perspectival modification by historical contingency.

It is not enough to say that we advocate the noble as opposed to the base or the prudent as opposed to the intemperate. In politics, whether world-historical or local, it is always necessary to specify the particular case. What precisely is noble and prudent? Many of us will, for example, admire the measured tones and dignified demeanor of the gentleman; but a society ruled by gentlemen is also one of class distinctions, a permanent leisure class, the preservation of the old ways against corruption by the nouveaux riches as well as by the *vulgus*—hence a return to the economy of scarcity—and so on.

I need not repeat myself. Nor do I need to recommend the extirpation of the gentleman, provided that we are prepared not to go to extremes and thus to live with inconsistency and decadence. But to live in this way requires a closer look at our conception of nobility. At this juncture we seem to be faced with an insuperable difficulty. Nobility is a perception, not a concept. Or—what comes to the same thing— our concept of nobility is rooted in a perception, not in another concept. To employ familiar terms, nobility is a value, an estimation, a ranking, and therefore it is an ambiguous mixture of aesthetic and moral qualities that may be named and understood but that must in any given case be recognized directly.

Even if we could be persuaded by discursive or conceptual analysis of a definition of nobility, we would still be required to apply that definition to the unendingly various particularities of human existence. Agreement here seems to depend upon the same conformity that we have just rejected as absurd and self-negating. An appeal to nobility without conceptual analysis is empty, yet the presentation of this analysis either begs the question or reiterates it: Why is *this* analysis noble?

The adherent of classical virtue may therefore reply to our introductory criticism that we have reached an impasse. I have argued that the effort to apply the paradigm of classical virtue can only be effective if it initiates a process that will eventually destroy itself. The classical sage may reply that what counts is not a long life but a virtuous one. We must run any risk in order to approach nobility. Nor am I able to counter this argument by denying the radical defects intrinsic to the Enlightenment or the strong possibility that it, too, is caught in a dialectic of self-destruction. The question of how to live thus seems to come down to this: how shall we die? Not merely, then, is reason the slave of passion, but life is the *jongleur* of death.

Or rather, this consequence obtains if we take our bearings by the extreme case. If radical conservatism leads to tyranny and radical enlightenment to nihilism, then perhaps it is radicalism that should be avoided. Let us consider the possibility that there is no practical difference between moderate conservatism and moderate liberalism, provided that the emphasis is in both cases on moderation rather than upon conservatism or liberalism. In this instance, differences in the perception of nobility are caused by mistaking theoretical extremism for thoroughness and profundity.

The moderate conservative is cautious about change, which is to say that he accepts a change for the better. But the principle of moderate liberalism is the same, namely, prudent enlightenment. The paradigm of classical virtue is then revealed as at least in part a defensive maneuver against human weakness. The paradigm of modern enlightenment must recognize the claims of its classical counterpart even while observing an implicit deference within ancient wisdom to the essence of the modern claim. To the Platonist, the modern spokesman says: "It cannot be noble to submit to a hostile and tyrannical nature if one has the means to defend oneself." To the Aristotelian, the reply is slightly different: "Your prudent separation of theory from practice is rooted in the immoderate surrender to the tacit Platonic principle that nature is hostile to enlightenment. What you call teleology is, at bottom, subservience to nature."

These replies are obviously nothing more than indications of the direction to be taken by a complete statement. What I intend them to clarify is the contention that classical philosophy in its conservative persona is dominated by conceptions of nobility and of nature that not only proponents of enlightenment, but the ancients in their "modern" or "mad" persona, reject. To say this is not at all to abolish the difference between the human and the divine. In religious language, it is to disagree about the nature of divinity. Let me emphasize that the point is not the power of modern science to modify nature in accordance with human convenience. It is the question of the nobility of our natural response to the hostility of nature, or of the bifurcation within nature itself, which is, as it were, both human and inhuman.

Let me restate this last observation. The disagreement between the ancients and moderns surfaces most dramatically in the case of the mathematical and experimental sciences. This is a story too well known to require retelling. Important as it is, it is nonetheless not the central point of this chapter. Modern science does not produce a new conception of nature; a new or evolving conception of nature produces modern science. To take a simple example: The experiments one conducts are a consequence of what one believes it possible to discover, as well as of what one believes it noble and good for mankind to know.

This last formulation is what concerns me here. Whether classical philosophy designates nature a friend, an enemy, or both, it is not simply motivated by wonder or the desire to know. Wonder and the desire to know lead directly to modernity and the Enlightenment. The contention that the classical sages would have regarded the modern Enlightenment as undesirable is technically correct, but it does not correctly explain why they would have held, or rather did hold, this view. I do not think that this explanation turns decisively upon their inability to conceive of the extraordinary powers of modern science. The spokesman for antiquity is no doubt correct in saying that they would have rejected unlimited scientific progress as ultimately destructive of the good life. The root of the matter is the view that reason is subservient to passion.

At the same time, the aforementioned contention is an oversimplification, because it ignores the intrinsically enlightening nature of philosophy itself, and therefore of ancient philosophy. When Socrates brought philosophy down from the heavens into the cities of mankind, he engaged in a revolution that cannot be concealed by attempts to regulate its dangerous consequences. An undiluted conservatism would have preserved the separation from the city of the sage as sage, or, in other words, the totally esoteric status of philosophy. Clearly Socrates believed that undiluted conservatism is either undesirable or impossible, or both. The Socratic dilemma is how to balance the madness of philosophy with the sobriety of politics. But this is exactly the modern dilemma. We should not allow ourselves to be deluded by the fact that this dilemma takes on a different appearance in different historical ages.

On the other hand, we cannot ignore these differences. Changed circumstances lead to new strategies of action. Revolutions may advance in stages. Thus the inner logic of philosophy may provide a continuity between antiquity and modernity that presents itself as historical opposition. It is therefore no accident that modern philosophy begins with an attempt to emancipate or justify passion. As others have suggested, the moderns raise courage to a higher status than is accorded it by the classical sages. What the contemporary "ancients" do not admit, so far as I can see, is that the modern philosophical courage is not simply that of the *vulgus* or of the imagination of poets, but that it expresses a perception of nobility. Modernity is not grounded in a rejection of nobility; it is grounded in the charge that the ancients lacked nobility. If this formulation is too extreme, let us say that the ancients were not yet in a position to act in accord with their partially concealed understanding of nobility.

I suspect that this formulation, even in its less extreme version, may appear to be intentionally overstated to some of my readers. Let me assure them that I mean it literally. We will never understand classical philosophy, and Plato, in particular, so long as we take our bearings by pious rhetoric, or what one might call the exoteric expression of resignation. Classical playfulness and aloofness or *Heiterkeit* are rooted in despair, and so too is the assessment of the unimportance of human affairs. This should be an obvious inference from the thesis that modern optimism is rooted in courage, or that human life, and so history, become central when nature is transformed into the accessible order of mathematics.

It is not quite true to say that in the late twentieth century modern man has lost his self-confidence, or for that matter his self-consciousness (as is at least recommended by partisans of the postanthropological epoch). On the other hand, there can be no doubt that we are experiencing a crisis of confidence. In my view, the most visible and important sign of this crisis is the contemporary relevance of the quarrel between the ancients and the moderns. I mean by this that the champions of antiquity, after having been relegated to the status of ineffectual aestheticism, are today enjoying a renaissance. As it seems to me, this is due to the extreme rigor with which twentieth-century spokesmen for the Enlightenment banished the ancients from a position of respect.

Positivism in all its varieties, pragmatism, humanistic existentialism, the fundamental-ontological attack against Platonism, and the various ideological celebrations of contemporary science: these are perhaps the most important reasons for the polarization of two extreme factions in present-day intellectual debate. The fact is that a pure or extreme version of the paradigm of enlightenment—when articulated entirely or largely in terms of scientific progress, the mathematicization of human experience, and, entirely inconsistently with these, the extreme emphasis on fairness or egalitarianism and freedom from all forms of domination—leads directly to chaos.

It is this extremism of the moderns that has given a new plausibility to the claims of the ancients, or rather, to a one-sided formulation of those claims that ignores the madness or revolutionary political requirements of philosophy. Ironically enough, in the camp of such defenders of antiquity we must also include those postmoderns who regard themselves as opponents of the Enlightenment, and so too those fundamental ontologists whose love of the origin is a primitivism fueled largely by a fear of modern scientific technology. Antiplatonism is in itself not enough to make one a modern.

What has gone wrong here is not due to the application of a base paradigm but to the thoughtless and extreme application of the correct paradigm. Modernity has created its own caricature and thereby given plausibility to the ancient contention that reason is the slave of passion. I will not attempt to resolve here the question of whether this contention is an exoteric accommodation to historical circumstances or an error caused by a failure of nerve (and so, in my judgment, by a lack of nobility).

I infer from this not that the ancients were right to warn us to go slowly but that the moderns have forgotten their own passion for comprehensiveness. The last great thinker to advocate totality, that is, to attempt a synthesis of antiquity and modernity, was Hegel. Unfortunately Hegel's totality is already scientific and systematic, or rationalist in the extreme sense. Since human life is not a concept, to say nothing of other problems, Hegel's explanation of human life is a failure.

This failure is the direct cause of the nineteenth- and twentieth-century emphasis on finitude. It is also the direct cause of the turn toward scientific positivism. In other words, the decay of Hegelianism may be directly understood as the falling apart of finitude and infinity, or the dissolution of the central Hegelian synthesis. Hence the aforementioned polarization between the "ancients" and the "moderns," or more accurately, the present chaos that is the result of the instability of finitude and infinity when separated from one another. In a certain sense the consequences of the decay of Hegelianism are a vindication of the soundness of Hegelianism.

But only in a certain sense: I come back to the extreme conceptualism of Hegel, which is already due to Hegel's peculiarly modern (not Greek) conception of *logos*. The claim that his logic is complete is also a claim by Hegel to have overtrumped the mathematicians at their own game. This becomes much clearer, of course, many decades after Hegel, in the age of axiomatics. But it is evident enough from a Hegelian standpoint: Mathematics cannot be complete, not because of limitations intrinsic to axiomatization, but because it cannot explain its own significance. Mathematics is not a concept, in the technical Hegelian sense.

Hegel claims that his concept is complete because it contains an explanation of the significance of every fundamental aspect of human experience (and hence of the natural and supernatural, which have no significance apart from human cognitive experience). We do not need to go into the technical details in order to see one point that Hegel has overlooked entirely. There is no conceptual explanation of the nobility or desirability of a complete conceptualization of human experience. Hegel may well explain why human beings desire conceptual completeness, but he cannot demonstrate conceptually the nobility of that desire.

This is not an essay on Hegel; I have introduced him only as necessary to account for our own historical situation. The rejection of the ideal of completeness as represented, for example, by Goethe may also serve to indicate my point. In our time this ideal has resurfaced in the somewhat superficial but not entirely mistaken debate about the two cultures and the plea for their reunification. The solution is not that each of us become both poet and scientist; nor am I implying that the proper resolution of the contemporary crisis is by a new synthesis of antiquity and modernity.

My thesis is rather that there is no resolution to the contemporary crisis, if that means to remove it completely and to revert to the noble resignation of antiquity or the virile optimism of the seventeenth century. Crisis is intrinsic to human existence, ancient or modern. Crises must be negotiated; this is not the same as to eradicate them. And negotiation requires moderation, but not the moderation that is embodied in the paradigm of classical virtue now being pressed upon us by the so-called conservatives.

There is, I have been suggesting, a kind of Gödel's Theorem in human affairs: Every attempt to systematize life or to govern it by a set of axioms rich enough to encompass the totality of experience leads to a contradiction. Because in the present case axioms are consequences of principles or paradigms, the same point holds at their level. It would be fatal to construct a paradigm of moderation that goes to extremes in its indefiniteness: "Nothing too much" is as vacuous as the injunction to "go to the roots." One may arrive at the roots with a bulldozer or a spade; which instrument to use depends upon the circumstances.

This is not to deny that the circumstances of life are illuminated by our principles, it is rather to observe that the circumstances are also obscured by the reciprocal interplay of their shadows in the light of these principles. The apparent aporia of the previous section concerned the supposed impossibility of choosing between conflicting perceptions of nobility on a rational basis. This amounts to the contention that there is a radical disjunction between paradigms and their empirical instances, a contention that seems to be open to the same criticism leveled against Plato's Ideas by Aristotle. If the circumstances do not allow us to choose rationally between paradigms, how can they be instances of these paradigms?

To restate the previous question in an affirmative mode, the aporia arises as a result of two distinct kinds of extremism. The first is an extreme conception of nobility; the second is the tacit acceptance of the extreme sovereignty of analytical or demonstrative reason. To take them in order, I hold first that if an extreme or "pure" paradigm of nobility cannot be applied without disastrous consequences, then that paradigm is ignoble at worst, and at best neither noble nor base. What is ostensibly the moderate application of an extreme paradigm, namely, one that accommodates to the circumstances, is in fact the application of a moderate paradigm—not the application of the extreme paradigm at all but of another.

An extreme conception of nobility cannot compromise with circumstances without debasing itself; conversely, if compromising with circumstances is noble, then our conception of nobility is not extreme. There must be an essential connection between the paradigm of nobility and what lies within human power. If not, the paradigm is entirely irrelevant to our concerns except in a destructive sense. All the more reason why we must know what lies within human power. If the classics were mistaken in their understanding of the subservience of reason to passion, then they mistook cowardice for moderation. One cannot however simply repeat the point with respect to the moderns, because the only way to know the extent of human power is by enlightenment.

I have therefore been arguing on behalf of the premise that modernity is intrinsically more noble than antiquity. But, to turn to the second version of extremism noted above, the greater nobility of modernity does not commit me to the identification of wisdom with demonstrative reasoning. The greater nobility of modernity is not the consequence of modern arguments, but rather of the genuine philosophical nobility of the ancients, as manifested in the revolution instigated by Socrates. I have already criticized the modern heresy of total conceptualization with respect to Hegel. The point deserves repeating, and I pose it in the form of a dilemma. If deductive arguments are themselves noble and base, then there is no noncircular way in which to demonstrate by such arguments the rational superiority of one paradigm of nobility to another. If on the other hand arguments are neither noble nor base, then they have no bearing upon our perceptions of nobility and baseness.

It does not follow from this dilemma that we have no perceptions of nobility nor that we must not employ arguments in defense of these perceptions. I am plainly now arguing on behalf of my own perceptions. But I am under no illusion that these arguments, or others of a greater technical ingenuity, can succeed in transforming my perceptions into logical theorems. Nor would I wish for this result, since it would amount to the destruction, not the certification, of my perceptions.

We can and must do our best to articulate what we take to be the merits of our perceptions. In the nature of things, we must employ rhetorical as well as logical arguments; it even seems to follow that rhetoric is more fundamental than, although it certainly cannot dispense with, logic. That the discursive account of the merits of our paradigms falls within the illumination of these paradigms is a blessing, not an aporia. The desire to achieve a neutral or value-free position from which to evaluate conflicting perceptions of nobility is self-contradictory. Those who wish to push the point to the last consequence will find that one cannot speak rationally without knowing what one is talking about; in this case, as in so many others, *to know* is at bottom what Bertrand Russell would have called "to be acquainted with." And acquaintance arises from perception, not from further talk, which is why enlightenment is indeed indissolubly connected with ontological presence.

The same, however, cannot be said of the ancient wisdom, and on this critical point I am forced to contradict Heidegger and especially Derrida. The fundamental characteristic of the partisans of antiquity is the rejection of the present, a rejection that is rooted in ontology and not simply in *phronesis*. Nobility is defined essentially by human limitation or by the inaccessibility of Being, to put the point in contemporary jargon. By the same token, the postmoderns also reject the present on ontological grounds, namely, because of the absence of Being. My earlier argument that postmodernism is a deteriorated version of the Enlightenment is entirely compatible with the present assertion that postmodernism explicitly rejects the Enlightenment because of theoretical extremism.

Postmodernism is the Enlightenment gone mad. In human affairs, madness takes the role of contradiction in logic; anything follows. One consequence of the madness of theoretical extremism is that an ostensible repudiation of Platonism is itself a version of Platonism, that is, of Platonism as it is, not as it is imagined to be. The extreme rhetoric of enlightenment also emphasizes the future rather than the present, and in a sense that Hegel calls the affirmation of the bad infinite. But I am not in the business of defending the extreme rhetoric of enlightenment. My point is rather that this extreme rhetoric does an injustice to the paradigm of enlightenment.

I must now attempt to state the content of that paradigm, however succinctly. It is always better to know than not to know, in spite of the fact that knowledge may be put to evil use. The early moderns were entirely correct: Knowledge is power. The more knowledge we possess, the more powerful we are. For this premise to make sense, we have to include moral and aesthetic sensibility in our definition of knowledge. I therefore claim that the articulated conception of the Enlightenment by men like d'Alembert and Condorcet, who make mathematics the paradigm of knowledge, is contradicted by their own spiritual adherence to enlightenment.

What we need to learn from the ancients is not prudence or the superiority of temperance to courage, but the intimate connection between reason and the good. In fact it is base to assert that temperance is always superior to courage. The adherence to enlightenment must be modest in various senses of that term, none of them incompatible with courage. Indeed, we put the best construction on classical wisdom when we hold that temperance is the courage of modesty. Still, this is not enough, since modesty is not quite the same as the recommendation to judicious boldness.

In view of the obvious dangers of the Enlightenment, to advocate a modest progress in enlightenment is not modest. The paradigm of enlightenment that I am defending is rooted in the present, not in the past or the future. It is a paradigm that enjoins us to face the present courageously and that makes possible facing the present courageously because it does not define courage as resolution toward the future or as resignation toward the past.

Certainly we must acknowledge the wisdom of the past, where such wisdom genuinely exists, just as we cannot take the present seriously without accepting the inevitability of the future. But if nobility is not present to mankind in its contemporary circumstances, it will not someday be vouchsafed to us as a gift of Being; nor can it be found by parsing the cryptic sentences of the Platonic dialogues. In one more formulation: Nobility is ontologically present, even though there is no ontology of nobility, that is, no complete discursive account of the nature of the noble.

With the preceding clarifications, we may rehabilitate the future to this extent: Except for those who wish to return, not to Burkean England or Periclean Athens but to pharaonic Egypt, there is as a matter of moral certitude only one direction in which to move. The modern paradigm, or what I want to call a modest version of the Enlightenment, is more sensible and more prudent than the ancient paradigm as it is given political expression, and also than the extreme or immodest version of the Enlightenment understood as the bad infinite. One does not need to be a classical sage to understand that infinite progress means the valuelessness of each moment of progress; this point was made by Hegel.

In conclusion, I repeat only that modesty and prudence take their natures from the paradigms they serve or the goals to which they are directed. These natures will differ according as we pursue a defensive policy of resignation or an offensive policy of hope. Hope becomes steadily less utopian as the present improves, and the present improves as our power increases. Although we fully recognize the dangers and obstacles, it is noble to strive for the increase of human power, not in the vain desire to become gods but in the reasonable desire not to be slaves.

I have argued that the conception of antiquity reflected in contemporary defenses of the ancients is much too simple. The portrait of noble simplicity is exoteric, not esoteric. My last remark is intended not so much as a conclusion as a stimulus for further discussion. Whatever the prudential inferences of the ancient sages from the *logos*, it is always the *logos* to which we must attend. In so doing we obey the wisdom of the ancients: *Amicus Platonis; magis amicus veritatis.*

CHAPTER TWO

A Central Ambiguity in Descartes

Modern thought characteristically begins with a self-confident assertion of its novelty, precision, and power.[1] The fundamental justification offered for this tripartite assertion is the application of new mathematical and quasi-mathematical techniques to the study of nature, with the intention of its ultimate mastery. In order to carry through this project, its initiators radically altered the classical conceptions of *theoria* and *physis*. Whereas "theory" was formerly understood as a kind of looking at things as they are, it now came to have a practical, constructive, even creative sense. The contemporary notion of an original theory, questionable and perhaps even meaningless from the classical pagan perspective, is the descendant of the seventeenth-century project to master nature, albeit modified by German philosophies of history and (as in the case of Nietzsche) creativity. The nature to be mastered was no longer the Greek *physis*, or the living and even reasonable center of order in man and the world, but a lifeless and so unreasonable extension in the void, moving in accordance with the laws of mechanics but blind to the rational purpose of the human soul. Nature in the sense of matter was thus sundered from soul or mind in God and man.

In essence, the dualism implicit in the beginnings of modern phi-

This essay first appeared in *Cartesian Essays: A Collection of Critical Studies*, ed. Bernd Magnus and James B. Wilbur, © 1969 by Martinus Nijhoff, The Hague, Netherlands.
1. For some representative passages, see Machiavelli, *Il Principe* (Milan: Feltrinelli, 1960) Opere 1, 123; Galileo, *Dialogue on the Great World Systems*, trans. Salusbury-Santillana (Chicago: University of Chicago Press, 1953), 426; Descartes, *Discours de la méthode*, in Adam and Tannery, eds., *Oeuvres de Descartes* (Paris: J. Vrin, 1897–1910), 6:61–62, 71 (hereafter referred to as A-T); Descartes, *Les Passions de l'âme*, in A-T 2:327 and 1:i; Hobbes, *Leviathan* (Oxford: Oxford University Press, 1947), 518–19; Spinoza, *Ethics*, bk. 3, preface, and prop. 18. See also Gilson's edition of the *Discours* (Paris: J. Vrin, 1947), 176–77; he quotes Descartes's letter to G. Voet (A-T 8:26): "*Sed circa Philosophiam . . . nihil laudabilis est, quam esse Novatorem.*"

losophy is a secularized version of the Judeo-Christian teaching of the separateness of body and soul. Similarly, the rebellion against ancient philosophy and religion may be understood as a moral or political revolution against God.[2] This rebellion is not necessarily equivalent to atheism, but one can scarcely misunderstand the implications of the desire to make man free in the sense of being master and possessor of nature. At least there was no misunderstanding on the part of philosophers, scholars, and religious leaders until our own century. But the disagreement among contemporary scholars concerning the religious intentions of the great seventeenth-century philosophers cannot simply be attributed to a lapse in historical discernment. For the two reasons just indicated, the modern project is unintelligible apart from its Christian origins. Materialism and Idealism in their modern forms both stem from the ambiguous legacy of what we now call Cartesian dualism. If one could prove that Descartes was a disguised atheist, as he was normally regarded prior to the first decades of the twentieth century, and even that he was by intention a Materialist and mathematical physicist rather than a dualist and metaphysician, the ambiguity of his thought would not thereby be resolved.

In my opinion, the dualism of body and mind is not the correct starting point for one who hopes to grasp the ambiguity in Descartes's teaching and thereby in the foundations of the modern world. The first step in Descartes's project as he himself understood it was the development of the mathematical method of reasoning as the basis of a new physics, and thereby the discovery of indubitable first principles.[3] So far as the universal doubt and consequent discovery of the *ego cogitans* are concerned, I shall restrict myself here to two points. Universal doubt means the rejection of everything dubious. This doubt is possi-

2. Consider Leibniz's objections in the *Discours de métaphysique* (ed. Erdmann; Meisenheim/Glan: Aalen, 1959) to the Cartesian doctrine that the laws of mathematics are subordinate to, and so changeable by, the will of God (817, II). "*Ou sera donc sa justice et sa sagesse, s'il ne reste qu'un pouvoir despotique, si la volonté tient lieu de raison, et si selon la définition des tyrans, ce qui plaist au plus puissant est juste par là même?*" If God is a tyrant, it is just to rebel against him. Leibniz, without agreeing that God is a tyrant, well understands that Descartes is a rebel: "*En effet, ceux qui ne sont pas satisfaits de ce qu'il* [i.e., God] *fait, me paroissent semblables à des sujets mécontens dont l'intention n'est pas fort différente de celle des rebelles*" (818, IV). Cf. G. Kruger, "Die Herkunft des Selbstbewusstseins," in *Freiheit und Weltverwaltung* (Freiburg, 1958), 67.

3. Descartes, *Regulae* 4, 9, in A-T 10:401; Descartes, *Principia* 4.206, in A-T 8:328; Gilson, *Discours*, 63, line 31.

ble only if we are able to identify the dubious with absolute certitude. In other words, it is dependent upon the possession of a criterion for absolute certitude. This criterion is not the fact that I am thinking or even that I exist, from which either nothing or everything follows; it is instead the conception of mathematical intuition and the associated notions of evidence, or clarity and distinctness. Second, Descartes himself says, in a letter to Mersenne, "I tell you, between us, that these six meditations contain all the foundations of my physics. But one must not say so, if you please, because those who favor Aristotle would perhaps make more difficulty."[4] This passage cannot be satisfactorily explained by an appeal to Descartes's image of metaphysics as the roots of the tree of science. Such an appeal could lead only to the identification of metaphysics as epistemology. Differently stated, physics is not founded in the dualism of mind and body, but in the nature of intuition, number, and geometrical form.

Of course, no part of the preceding suggestion indicates that the problem of dualism is not central in Descartes's thought. On the contrary, I want to cast some light on that problem as a fundamental consequence of Descartes's understanding of mathematical thinking. Furthermore, mathematical thinking, despite its mathematical character, does not cease to be the activity of the human subject. Despite the central importance of mathematical physics in sixteenth- and seventeenth-century philosophy, the modern project, and especially in its aforementioned self-confidence, may fairly be seen as a new emphasis upon man as agent, and so upon the self in a sense quite different from earlier Stoic or Christian introspective meditations. One need not fall into the anachronism of confusing Descartes for Kant in order to appreciate the extraordinary significance of the *ego cogitans*.[5]

Descartes, precisely as a physicist, had a practical motive: to conquer nature on behalf of mankind. The conquest of nature means specifically the ability to control for the sake of human passions particular natural events, and thus what has subsequently come to be known as history, by means of the mathematical method of reasoning. Before as well as after the substitution of history for nature (and the extension of the domain to be controlled from body to mind as well), the *ego*

4. A-T 3:297–98.
5. Among those who warn us against anachronistic interpretations of Descartes is Yvon Belavel, whose excellent study should be cited: *Leibniz, Critique de Descartes* (Paris: Gallimard, 1960), e.g., 25.

cogitans is the middle term between mathematics and spatio-temporal particulars. Descartes, of course, did not intend to be the father of subjectivity. Nevertheless, I believe that a consideration of mathematical thinking as an instrument of mastery over nature will provide some grounds for justifying contemporary interpretations that stress the role of the subject in Descartes. But the results will not justify a simple or clear-cut expression of Cartesian dualism.

A comparison of the various texts in which Descartes treats the faculties of reason, imagination, and will, shows him to be anything but clear and distinct. There is an ambiguity with respect to the nature of *idea* and therefore with respect to the objective and eternal status of rational order. In general, Descartes maintains that the sciences, or human wisdom, "remain always one and always the same."[6] Thinking would seem to be defined as clear and evident intuition or immediate vision of that which shows itself to us as what it is, "immutable and eternal."[7] It would be possible to question the certitude of the sciences, as regularly defended by Descartes, through an analysis of the status of God as the ostensible guarantor of clear and distinct ideas. For my present purpose, however, it is not necessary to enter into this famous question of the Cartesian circle. I am not concerned with the indubitability of ideas but rather with whether the order they exhibit is made or projected by the human mind.

As Descartes says in the *Discours*, we understand best what we have invented ourselves.[8] This maxim, frequently repeated in the seventeenth century and decisive for an understanding of the difference between ancient and modern philosophy, underlines what one may call the individualistic dimension of Descartes's methodological instruction.[9] One may object that Descartes is referring to techniques for invention or discovery and not to the making of individual or private ideas. That which is discovered or invented must conform to natural laws and be valid for all men. But the same could be said in the case of Kant, Fichte, and Schelling, or of any philosopher for

6. *Regulae* 1.
7. *Regulae* 3; Descartes, *Meditations*, vol. 5, in A-T 7:64; Gilson, *Discours* 43, lines 10ff.; *Principia* 4.206.
8. Gilson, *Discours*, 69, line 21.
9. Cf. Belavel, *Leibniz*, 32.

whom rational order is a consequence of the generative activities of human thought. The issue is immediately evident in Descartes's definition of *idea*, in which he breaks sharply with the Platonic notion of archetype and thereby influences all subsequent use of the term: "by the name of idea I understand that form of any thought whatsoever, through the immediate perception of which I am conscious of that same thought."[10]

By "any thought whatsoever" (*cujuslibet cogitationis*), Descartes means the content of sensation, imagination, the conceiving of pure intelligibles, and also the content of will.[11] In other words, *idea* stands for the form of every product of mental activity and is therefore itself produced by such activity. Even if one were to insist that the conception of pure intelligibles or *entes rationis* corresponds to the Platonic *noesis* of archetypes, it would remain the case that Descartes regards imagined and willed forms as ideas also. But the correspondence between pure intellection and Platonic *noēsis* is difficult if not impossible to maintain. This difficulty may be illustrated in the case of number, the decisive Cartesian example of a purely intelligible entity.

As Jacob Klein has shown,[12] Descartes adopted Vieta's notion of the specific form of number as existing *symbolically*, as a universal concept that can be applied to *any* object, physical or mental. This universal concept, in itself undetermined, can serve as the subject matter of a *mathēsis universalis*: a mathematics of symbols rather than of monads or objects. Having no determinate objects, the Cartesian *mathēsis universalis* deals solely with "order and measure," regardless of whether such measure be sought in "numbers, figures, stars, sounds, or any other object."[13] Nevertheless, although it has no determinate object, *mathēsis universalis* determines order, measure, disposition, or proportion on the basis of a unit abstracted by the mind from its objects. Descartes calls this abstract entity the "pure and simple object" of

10. Cf. *Reply to Second Objections, Medit.*, Def. 2, and Gilson, *Discours*, 318ff. See also G. Kruger, *Philosophie und Moral in der Kantischen Kritik* (Tübingen: J. C. B. Mohr, 1931), 17.

11. *Principia* 1.32. The two modes of *cogitandi* are *perceptio* and *volitio*: "*sentire, imaginari, & pure intelligere, sunt tantum diversi modi percipiendi.*"

12. In "Die griechische Logistik und die Entstehung der Algebra," *Quellen und Studien zur Geschichte der Mathematik, Astronomie, und Physik*: div. B, vol. 3 (Berlin, 1936).

13. *Regulae* 4, in A-T 10:378.

arithmetic and geometry.[14] There are two points to be raised here. First, number considered "abstractly or generally and not in created things" is a mode of thinking, like universals.[15] What Descartes means by "mode of thinking" depends upon what he means by "innate ideas." Second, it seems that abstract number is produced by thought via the operation of imagination upon the perception of extended or material things.

Let us first consider the operation of the imagination, on the assumption that innate ideas may be formed separately or by some process of pure thinking. According to the *Regulae*, the figures or shapes of extension are reproduced in the imagination, and from this "picture" the symbolic idea of number is abstracted. Thinking is thus essentially intuition, namely, a viewing of primary forms and properties of extension through the mediation of the imagination,[16] and not immediately, as Descartes sometimes seems to be saying. Number, figure, and the like are not really distinct from extended bodies but only "imagined" to be so.[17] Order and measure thus seem to be consequences of mind's interaction with nature rather than clearly and distinctly objective or intrinsic properties of a nature existing independently of, and accessible to, the *lumen naturale*.[18]

The inseparability of intuition and imagination is supported by the various passages in which Descartes unambiguously defines rational thought as mathematical.[19] The homogeneous character of rational thought in the various sciences is based upon the determination of order and measure by means of abstraction, which, as we have seen, depends upon the imagination.[20] Even in the *Meditations*, number is

---

14. *Regulae* 2, in A-T 10:365.

15. *Principia* 1.58.

16. Cf. *Regulae* 5, 7, and 12.

17. *Regulae* 14, in A-T 10:445: "*Ut si de numero sit quaestio, imaginemur subjectum aliquod per multas unitates mensurabile. . . .*"

18. Galileo is much more straightforward than Descartes: "Nature did not make human brains first, and then construct things according to their capacity of understanding, but she first made things in her own fashion and then so constructed the human understanding that it, though at the price of great exertion, might ferret out a few of her secrets" *Opere*, (Florence: Barbara, 1890–1909), 1.288.

19. See, for example, *Entretien avec Burman*, in A-T 5:176–77; Gilson, *Discours*, 41, line 4.

20. Cf. *Regulae* 3 and 7: the certitude of deduction rests on memory, and the motion of the imagination intuits each step in the remembering of a complex inference.

considered as a property of corporeal things[21] and then derived from the multiplicity of thoughts. This derivation at least raises the question of whether thinking, as a multiplicity, is not itself to that extent corporeal. But let us deal with the *Meditations* primarily in terms of innate ideas, presumably a more general notion than abstract or symbolic number.[22] The significant aspect of the doctrine of innate ideas, so far as the present discussion goes, is the ostensible separation between imagination, or thought directed externally, toward bodies, and intuition, or thought directed internally, toward itself.[23]

The first passage I shall consider occurs in the *Second Meditation*. Descartes has ostensibly just proved, by recourse to thought alone, that he "is" a thinking thing. He then asks: what is a thing that thinks? and gives his usual answer. Thinking includes all mental activities, among them will, imagination, and sense. If, however, imagination is defined as the contemplation of the figures of body, then the definition of a thinking being includes the conception of body. Why is the suggestion of the possibility that bodies are imaginary in the sense of mental more plausible from the beginning than the alternative suggestion that minds are corporeal? As I have already noted, the multiplicity of thoughts tends to support the materialist hypothesis. But in addition, I cannot say that I am mind or thought without posing body or extension as that from which I am dissociating myself. The statement that "body is mental (imagined in the sense of unreal)" depends upon an indubitable principle or criterion. Descartes, by his own account, has proved only that he is thinking, and not that thinking is conceivable independent from body.

Nevertheless, Descartes insists that some part of himself does not at all fall under the imagination.[24] In order to illustrate the function of intuition as distinct from imagination, he employs the example of how we understand a common thing or body like wax. The significance of the choice of wax is suggested by the fact that, in Aristotle's *De Anima*, it functions as an analogue of *mind*. Since wax is able to receive all forms, it is in a way itself formless. What Aristotle attributes to

---

21. *Medit.* 3, in A-T 7:44.
22. For simple cognitions, see *Regulae* 12, in A-T 10:419ff.; and *Reply to Second Objections*, in A-T 7:135ff. These simple cognitions, called "indubitable" by Descartes, function like axioms in his *mathesis universalis*. For present purposes, they may be subsumed under the discussion of number and innate ideas.
23. *Medit.* 2, in A-T 7:28; and vol. 6, in A-T 7:73.
24. *Medit.* 2, in A-T 7:29.

mind, Descartes attributes to matter: extension is capable of receiving all forms through the rearrangement of its parts. In the example, wax, when melted, does not cease to be wax, and yet we conceive it to be capable of assuming an infinity of forms that cannot be duplicated by the imagination. Therefore, Descartes concludes, extension itself, or any body, can only be grasped through an inspection of the mind (*solius mentis inspectio*) but not through imagination or sensation.

Is the example of wax a fair and sufficient basis for the conclusion Descartes draws? I do not think so; we need merely ask ourselves whether an apple, tree, or cat, if melted down, would preserve its nature while also exhibiting a malleability inaccessible to the imagination. In fact, the malleability of wax is an aspect of its extended form and is being accurately perceived by the senses throughout each of its transformations. After sensing a certain number of these transformations, we may then infer that they are infinite; and this is precisely the way in which Descartes himself develops the argument. Comprehending the nature of wax does not begin with an intuition of extension *solius mentis inspectio* but rather with a series of sense perceptions. What Descartes can establish by this procedure is the Aristotelian doctrine of *sensus communis*, or the link between sensation and thought. So far as his own teaching is concerned, the idea of wax (to say nothing of pure extension) seems to have exactly the status of abstract or symbolic number. The example actually testifies to the dependence of general ideas on the imagination and not to the separate functioning of intuition.

Before turning to ideas of incorporeal things, I would like to pose the following dilemma. Either the content of intuition (and so of innate ideas) is dependent on the imagination, or it is dependent on God. If the former, then intuition is always of bodies, and the regularity of order depends on the creation of artificial abstract form. If the latter, then, since God is primarily free will, natural order (as Descartes allows) is an arbitrary divine creation, subject to equally arbitrary change.[25] Since Descartes emphasizes that man is most God-like with respect to his will,[26] whether we consider the doctrine of imagination or the certitude furnished by the idea of God, there is reason to discern in Descartes a confusion as to the relationship between man's mind and mathematical order. This confusion is apparent in

---

25. *Reply to Sixth Objections*, in A-T 7:412ff.
26. See *Medit.* 4, in A-T 7:57; and *Les passions de l'âme*, 3.152.

the *Fifth Meditation*, when Descartes describes the triangle as an example of an innate idea. He says: "As when, for example, I *imagine* a triangle . . ." (italics mine).[27] But he also claims that the nature of the triangle is "immutable and eternal,"[28] which contradicts the previously cited assertion of the unrestricted power of God's will to alter even mathematical truth.

But let us return to innate ideas of nonextended beings or forms. Ideas, considered as modes of thought, independent of external things, are either innate, adventitious, or "made by myself."[29] General ideas are innate: "for that I understand what a thing is, what truth is, what a thought is, this I seem to have from nowhere else than my own nature."[30] In a letter to Mersenne,[31] Descartes gives some examples of the three kinds of ideas; as we would expect, God and mind are the first to be mentioned among innate ideas. In the present classification, "God himself" is cited as one of the "images of things . . . to which (images) alone the name of idea properly applies."[32] If we bear in mind the previously cited definition of idea as the "form of a thought," it seems clear that Descartes is identifying this form as an *image* or product of the imagination. And in the present context, he goes on to say that ideas, considered solely in themselves as mental forms, cannot be false: "for whether I imagine a goat or a chimaera, it is no less true that I have imagined one than the other."[33]

The distinction between truth and falsehood pertains, then, not to the form, but to the content of an idea. Error apparently arises only in the act of judgment, and the principal error of this kind occurs when "I judge that ideas which exist in me are similar or conformable to things posited outside of me."[34] But one may reasonably ask: if truth depends upon clarity and distinctness, and these are attributes of perceptions or conceptions, whereas the latter in turn are ideas, how can we distinguish between the form and content of an idea, let alone pass judgment on the truth or falsity of the content in question? Furthermore, as Descartes says, judgments take us outside ourselves.

27. *Medit.* 5, in A-T 7:64: "*Ut cum, exempli causa, triangulum imaginor . . .*"
28. Ibid., "*ejus natura, sive essentia, sive forma, immutabilis & aeterna . . .*"
29. *Medit.* 3, in A-T 7:378.
30. Ibid., 38.
31. 16 June 1641, in A-T 3:383.
32. *Medit.* 3, in A-T 7:37.
33. Ibid.
34. Ibid.

In that case, how can I judge, solely on the basis of internal reflection, that any innate idea is true with respect to its content? If, for example, I have an idea of myself as thinking, I know from this only that I am in *some* mind but not that I myself exist *as* a mind.

To stay within myself is to restrict my attention to the form of ideas and hence to images. But to go outside my mind is to enter the world of extension, which cannot be thought except through the mediation of imagination and sensation. Inside or outside, I seem to be dependent on the function, if not indeed the sovereignty, of the imagination. And this problem is independent of the question of whether reliance upon God as guarantor of clear and distinct perceptions is an instance of circular reasoning. This distinction between inside and outside raises another difficulty concerning innate ideas. The form of the idea may be innate without guaranteeing that its content corresponds to an external entity. *Innate* means *inborn*: if the form is born with me, in what sense could the content be eternal or correspond to anything eternal? By ostensibly beginning inside himself, Descartes makes it impossible ever to reach the outside or to escape from the domain of ideas as images. In fact, of course, Descartes begins with the inside *and* outside, as is shown by the very function of the imagination.

It is not my purpose to engage in a detailed analysis of the *Meditations* but only to suggest a certain ambiguity implicit in Descartes's thought. This ambiguity reappears in every fundamental stratum of the Cartesian teaching, and, as I would state it, leads to a dualism that one might with equal justice identify as a monism. Whether one calls this monism Idealism or Materialism again depends upon which side of Descartes's complex teaching one chooses to emphasize. To summarize what I have been saying: Descartes defines thinking and ideas in such a way as to make it impossible to determine whether these definitions lead to a world of mind and matter, or one of either mind *or* matter. In the *Meditations*, Descartes gives a variety of arguments to support the dualist interpretation of his teaching. But none of these arguments is convincing, apart from the reasons I have already given, because (as he says) of the unknowability of the substance *mind*.[35] Thus, for example, granted that there must be as much reality in the cause as in the effect,[36] the substance *mind* may still be the cause of its

---

35. The unknowability of the substance *mind* is contradicted at *Medit.* 6, in A-T 7:18, for example, where Descartes asserts (and more strongly in the French revision than in the Latin original) that he knows *"toute l'essence"* of himself as a thinking thing.
36. *Medit.* 3, in A-T 7:40ff.

own ideas. Either reality means thought, or it means extension. If the first, then matter is in fact mind; if the second, then mind is actually matter. Similarly, the insistence upon the conceptual separability of mind and matter is vitiated by the regular dependence of intuition on imagination.

This ambiguity in Descartes's writings leads me to agree, up to a point, with those who see in him the beginning of modern subjectivity. I do not myself believe that it was Descartes's intention to initiate the doctrine of subjectivity; instead, I regard such an initiation as a consequence of two incompatible goals that characterize the Cartesian philosophy. The first is to identify the structure of nature, and so all of rational order, with mathematical properties of extension; the second is to give man mastery over this order, thanks to the new technique of mathematics. If order is to provide man with certitude and security, it must itself be eternal, regular, and independent of, although accessible to, subjective mental activity. Unfortunately, if man is to be master of this order, it must be subject to his will. The importance of the imagination in mathematical thinking is a preparation for the primacy Descartes gives to the will in *The Passions of the Soul*. Once again: extension becomes accessible to man in abstract thought by means of the imagination. But as a consequence of the function of imagination, the resultant abstract order is revealed as a product of the human mind.

In *The Passions of the Soul*, Descartes says that the functions of the soul are all either active or passive thoughts: "those which I name its actions are all our desires (*volontés*). . . ."[37] Desires are again of two sorts: "for the one are actions of the soul which terminate in the soul itself, as when we want to love God or generally to apply our thought to some object which is not at all material: the others are actions which terminate in our bodies. . . ."[38] The activity of the soul is *willing to think* rather than simply *thinking*, which thus becomes a passive instrument of the project to master nature. The activity of the will is more noble than all other thoughts; its nobility consists in the assertion of man's freedom, and this freedom is the only thing in our nature "which may give us just reason for estimating ourselves. . . ."[39] In fact, says Descartes, free will "makes us in a certain

37. *Passions* 1.17.
38. Ibid., 1.18.
39. Ibid., 1.19.

way comparable to God in making us masters of ourselves. . . ."[40] One is tempted to add that, if man is his own master, he is not subject to the rule of God. However this may be, the will, and not intuition or pure thinking, is preeminently the mark of God in man.[41] Here we see the sharpest difference between the (pagan) ancients and the moderns. The Stoic component in Descartes's description of "*generosité*," the cardinal virtue, is thus modified by the proud recognition of the power man's will has acquired, thanks to the new mathematical physics. Nothing truly affects man but the free disposition of his will or desires;[42] presumably, then, he is unaffected by the will of God. Man may will himself to love God, but he is also free to ignore, or perhaps to hate him. If man masters mathematics, then presumably he, too, will acquire the divine power of will whereby old laws and old bondage are replaced by new laws and an active new freedom.

Cartesian dualism, in its most obvious (and not necessarily final) form, repeats the Christian teaching of the separateness of body and soul. At the same time, however, Descartes follows the Scotist strand of the Christian tradition in an effort to resolve the "separatist" consequences of dualism. The theological doctrine of the sovereignty of will over intellect is intended to explain both the creation of matter and its accessibility to the power of mind. Such a doctrine implicitly argues that, if knowing is distinct from doing, the sovereignty of intellect over will would mean that there is no reason for doing anything.[43] In the case of God, the sovereignty of will over intellect may suffice to explain both the creation of the world and God's power over it. In the case of man, however, there is still a missing link between what he wants to do and what he can do. This link is supplied by the function of the imagination. As we saw in the *Regulae*, the imagination renders the structure of matter accessible to the conceptualizing powers of the intellect. Thanks to this accessibility, the will may carry out its projects, and specifically, the project of mastering nature.

This doctrine, in its origins Christian or theological, leads to the philosophical teaching which for brevity I shall call Idealism. The Idealist

40. Ibid., 3.52.
41. Cf. the discussion of will in *Medit.* 4, in A-T 7:56ff.
42. *Passions* 3.153.
43. For a theological formulation of this argument, see Kierkegaard, *The Sickness unto Death*, trans. W. Lowrie (New York: Doubleday Anchor Books, 1954), 224.

overcomes the distinction between knowing (theory) and doing (practice) by denying the independent status of the intelligible structure of matter, if not of matter itself. That is, intelligible structure becomes a project of mind, understood not as pure reason but as reasoning and imagining will. But the aforementioned doctrine also leads to the philosophical teaching we may conveniently call Materialism. The Materialist overcomes the distinction between knowing and doing by denying that mind is itself independent of matter or anything other than an intelligible structure of matter. Although Materialists are usually atheists and Idealists usually theists, the former also preserve the priority of will and imagination to reason, and so the Cartesian conception of science as a human project.[44] This point may be restated in terms of contemporary mathematics, which, considered as a technique, is presumably indifferent to philosophical questions of the kind now being discussed. Thus A. A. Fraenkel says, with respect to the definition of cardinal number, that the mathematician "is rather concerned with handling the mathematical objects than with exploring their nature—somewhat similar to the chessplayer who does not care what the bishop or the pawn 'mean' but how one operates with them."[45] Nevertheless, mathematical operations, which presumably uncover rational order in its most fundamental and general sense and thereby serve as the foundation for order in the physical sciences, are free creations of the human intellect, according to Fraenkel, whom I cite as a fair example of contemporary thinking among mathematicians.[46]

One does not, then, avoid the problem of dualism in Descartes by stressing the importance of mathematical *ratio* and mathematical physics in his teaching. Neither does one avoid the problem of dualism by adopting Idealism or Materialism in their post-Cartesian forms, since these forms are direct consequences of the Cartesian philoso-

44. To take an example from an atheist and a materialist, see Bertrand Russell, "Logical Atomism," reprinted in *Logical Positivism*, ed. A. J. Ayer (Glencoe, Ill.: Free Press, 1959), 37: "The reason that matter is impenetrable is because our definitions make it so. . . . Matter is impenetrable because it is easier to state the laws of physics if we make our constructions so as to secure impenetrability."
45. *Abstract Set Theory* (Amsterdam: North Holland Publication Co., 1961; 2d ed.), 59.
46. Ibid., p. 2. See also the first edition of the same work, p. 23: "The mathematician, in contrast to the grammarian, abhors exceptions and is in a position to avoid them as his language is created by himself."

phy. Idealism cannot avoid asserting that mind is extended any more than Materialism can avoid asserting that matter thinks. The notion of matter (or energy) is as irreducible a component of Idealism as the notion of mind is an irreducible component of Materialism. Every attempt to perform the reduction of mind to matter or vice versa is based upon the prior distinction between the two. Differently stated, Materialism as much as Idealism rests in its modern form upon the primacy of will and imagination to reason and therefore leads to the same ambiguity with respect to the status of form and order, whether in a mathematical or some other sense.

I do not intend to remove the ambiguity in Cartesianism or to solve the problem of dualism. The most I can hope for is to have plausibly suggested why and how the ambiguity and the problem arose. Nevertheless, I should like to conclude this chapter with the following general reflection. One solution to the problem of Cartesian dualism that has gained special prominence in our time is the phenomenological and/or existentialist conception of "Being-in-the-world." That the solution is not free from internal difficulties is well known to all who have followed Husserl's attempt to overcome subjectivism by a doctrine of intersubjectivity, or Heidegger's vacillation between the view that Being depends upon man and the view that man depends upon Being. In my opinion, there is considerable merit in the attempt by proponents of this solution to remind us of the priority of the world, as lived in ordinary or prephilosophical experience, to all theoretical interpretations of the world. But so far as I can understand them, existentialists and phenomenologists repeat the error of Idealists and Materialists, in varying ways, to be sure: namely, the error of assuming that the defect in dualism lies in unnecessary complexity. Philosophers of these schools all seem to have surrendered to the powerful human desire for unity, a desire that leads, if unchecked, and whether in the service of mathematics or the existentialist revolt against the objectification of Being, to monism. But monism is merely a cryptic, and so ambiguous, form of dualism, which one is always free to interpret either subjectively or objectively, as one sees fit. I do not believe that what we require to escape this problem is a new kind of thinking in the Heideggerian sense, but rather an old kind in a way that is present in philosophers like Plato and Hegel. If dualism is bad because it splits the world into two irreconcilable halves, what we need is not to reduce one half to the other, or to beg the question by talking about the "factic" or prephilosophical unity of the two, but to identify the *third* principle or bond which provides us with what I prefer to call this factic harmony (rather than unity). Dualism must be replaced by trinitarianism if it is to be replaced at all. But that is another story.

CHAPTER THREE

Antiplatonism

A CASE STUDY

The frequency with which the expression "Antiplatonism" is used today suggests that its meaning is well understood. We have become accustomed to the thesis that the history of metaphysics is equivalent to Platonism, and so too that we now dwell in the postmetaphysical epoch. Metaphysics, and therefore Platonism, is accordingly defined as the doctrine that Being is presence, or somewhat more specifically, the presence to the mind's eye of fully determinate and unchanging formal structure. The Antiplatonists further assert that this doctrine serves to conceal Being rather than to reveal it in its true nature. In various ways, and with a variety of qualifications, they are agreed upon the need to "deconstruct" the Platonist conception of Being.

This agreement carries with it the corollary that the truth of Being is not presence but absence, or perhaps better, not the presence of eternal forms but rather the process or activity of which one consequence, but by no means the only or decisive one, is the production of forms. There is, however, sharp disagreement among the Antiplatonists as to the source or nature of this original activity. For introductory purposes, I suggest that the disagreement turns upon whether the human being is the source itself (and if so, in what sense) or the key to the understanding of that source.

A word of clarification is required about the sense of the term *absence* in the lexicon of Antiplatonism. Very generally, it is intended to designate the primacy of freedom from eternal structures, whether natural or supernatural. Accordingly, freedom is understood as the celebration of diversity and novelty, both in the domain of theory and practice. The absence of Being, in other words, is not merely a question of imperfect human understanding; it is also the condition of history and creativity. *Absence* thus has two main senses within Antiplatonism. It refers first to the concealment of Being by Platonic structures, and second to the intrinsic lack of determinate structure in

37

the primordial process or activity by which the world is continuously being shaped and reshaped.

It would be a long and difficult task to decide when Antiplatonism made its first appearance in the history of philosophy. One could even argue that Antiplatonism antedates Platonism, as Socrates suggests in the *Theaetetus*.[1] Much more fundamental is the question of whether Plato was himself an Antiplatonist, given the definition of the term just noted. These are not simply historical questions; rather, they bear upon the Antiplatonist thesis of the historicity of Being. In more accessible terms, if the history of metaphysics is the history of Platonism, then how can it also be the history of Antiplatonism? Are we to believe that all avowed Antiplatonists prior to Nietzsche, Heidegger, or Derrida were in fact unconscious Platonists?

These questions are much too broad to be addressed in a single chapter. They do, however, justify the suspicion that the contemporary discussion of Antiplatonism is far from satisfactory. It is my intention here to take some first steps in the effort to achieve greater clarity concerning the quarrel between Platonism and Antiplatonism by considering a single example. I propose to discuss the case of Kant, who by all accounts is a crucial stage in the prehistory of late modern (not to say postmodern) Antiplatonism. To mention only the most important point, it is Kant who makes canonical the shift from the doctrine of form in the Platonist sense to the doctrine of form as a product of the function of thinking (in the two senses of understanding and reason).

The question to be addressed is then as follows: Was Kant an Antiplatonist? Unfortunately, we cannot address this question without some attention to what is meant by *Platonism*. Whereas we may take our bearings by the preliminary account of contemporary Antiplatonism that I have already offered, this is clearly insufficient to explain Kant's own sense of his relation to Plato. Neither does it cast much light on the question of whether Kant's Antiplatonism is not itself at a deeper level a version of Platonism. Our procedure must therefore be in one sense general and in another specific. We require a comparison between Plato and Kant, but in terms that are both restricted and essential to the thought of both philosophers.

Two further methodological points need to be made in advance. The first is that we must distinguish between Platonism in its tradi-

1. Plato, *Theaetetus* 152d2–e9, 180c7ff.

tional sense and the teaching of Plato as it is presented in the Platonic dialogues. Unfortunately, there is no consensus on the nature of the actual Platonic teaching; some would even deny that the dialogues contain any positive doctrine. This question cannot be resolved in one chapter. For our purposes, this is not a fatal difficulty. It is widely agreed by the contemporary Antiplatonists that the aforementioned distinction exists, or in other words that the Platonism they attack is based upon, or coincides in part with, material in the Platonic dialogues but is not to be regarded as the authentic expression of the meaning of the dialogues themselves.

The most important aspect of the Platonic dialogues, according to Antiplatonism, is the so-called theory of Ideas. For many, if not all, self-professed Platonists, it is also the crucial element of the Platonic teaching. In my opinion, which I have discussed elsewhere in considerable detail, there is no consistent, detailed, and discursively coherent theory of Ideas in the Platonic dialogues.[2] Correlatively, there is no homogeneous doctrine of Being defined univocally as pure form in the sense of the presence of fully determinate structure. In order to achieve initial clarity about the relation between Platonism and Antiplatonism in Kant, it is not necessary to arrive at a final understanding of the Platonic dialogues. All that is required here is to show the unquestioned presence and crucial function of Antiplatonism within the dialogues. To state the point from the other direction, we need to show that Kant was a Platonist as well as an Antiplatonist, or more fundamentally, that there is a common problematic underlying the writings of both philosophers.

Let me emphasize that my intention is quite limited. I hope to provide evidence for the general thesis that contemporary discussion of Antiplatonism and the history of metaphysics, despite its verbal complexity, is based upon a radical oversimplification of the issues. More specifically, I want to argue that Kant neither initiates nor exemplifies a genuine repudiation, or reversal, of the fundamental problem of the Platonic dialogues. This brings me to my second methodological point.

I have no desire to "deconstruct" Kant or to argue that his Antiplatonism conceals an unconscious Platonism. To formulate the point in this way is, among other things, to give too much definiteness

2. See especially Rosen, *Plato's "Sophist": The Drama of Original and Image* (New Haven: Yale University Press, 1983).

and rigidity to the philosophical procedures of Plato and Kant. So long as one adheres to the official understanding of Kant—namely, to the analogue of the traditional understanding of Platonism—it is of course a simple matter to sustain an opposition between the two thinkers, even on doctrines that Kant seems to borrow, in a revised form, from Plato. As soon as we begin to examine minutely the details of the Kantian texts, the result, I suggest, is surprisingly similar to that which follows from a minute examination of the details of the Platonic text. The "official" teaching begins to dissolve in contradictions and aporias and is gradually replaced by a set of fundamental, possibly insoluble, problems.

It is not my view that this results in a "deconstruction" of philosophy or a demonstration of the need to enter into a postphilosophical epoch. Those who advocate such consequences are in my opinion guilty of the fatal error of accepting the traditional, and therefore superficial, understanding of the doctrines they believe themselves to be superseding or clarifying. My own view is rather that what passes as postphilosophical activity is instead a continuation, whether at a high or a low level, of philosophy itself, namely, the deepening of comprehensive problems that cannot be solved by technical devices of any kind. How we formulate the problems will determine what technical devices we construct. The puzzles resolved by these devices are not the problems, but technical surrogates for the problems.

This is the general context within which I ask the reader to consider the evidence and analysis that follow. I shall focus my attention on certain crucial aspects of the Platonic and Kantian treatment of two distinct but related notions: Ideas and phenomena. To repeat, my intention is to show the presence of a common problematic underlying the specific differences between the two thinkers on these points. In summary form, the two main results of my discussion are these: In both Plato and Kant, the root meaning of *phainomenon* applies not merely to the appearances of genesis but also to the domain of Ideas; despite the differences between the Platonic and the Kantian Idea, and with full attention to the shift in both cases from intellectual perception to discursivity, the problem of original and image continues to hold good for Kant as well as for Plato.

I cannot explore the point in detail, but I intend to support the further thesis that post-Kantian philosophies (or antiphilosophies) of language, whether understood as spoken or written, continue to be instances of Platonism in this crucial respect. All discourse is either original or an image of an original. The first alternative is incoherent or leads directly to silence; the second is genuine Platonism. Platonism is thus not a theory or a positive account of the nature of things. It is the articulation and continuous reconsideration of a problem underlying all positive accounts of the nature of things.

Kant's Antiplatonism is closely connected with a strong preference for Aristotle. This preference is expressed in such a way as to reveal a fundamental misunderstanding of Plato's explicit doctrine: Stated with maximum concision, Kant takes Plato to be a Neoplatonist in the decisive respect. I begin with two passages from Kant's posthumously published *Reflections on Metaphysics*, dating from the 1770s. The first:

> Plato stated very well the origin of the concept of perfection. But not of the *notionum*. Plato enthusiast, Aristotle analyst.

The second passage:

> History of the difference between *sensitivis* and *intellectualibus*. aegypter. Pythagoras. Heraclitus (eleatic). Plato (*ideae innatae*) and Pythagoras made the *intellectualia** into particular objects of possible intuition; his school, the . . . academic philosophers, exoteric *sceptice* and esoteric *dogmatice*. *Intuitus intellectualis*, from which everything derives.
>
> **intellectualia vel quoad obiecta vel formam cognitionis*[3]

Aristotle, the codifier of logic and the categories, the exemplar of careful conceptual analysis, is finally superior to both Plato and the members of his "Pythagorean" tradition of mathematical enthusiasts. Plato and the Platonists engage in mathematical "enthusiasm" (*Schwärmerei*), namely, the claim to possess an indirect intuition via copies (*ectypa*) of the mathematical objects and Ideas directly intuited by divine understanding. "The philosophy of Aristotle is in contrast work," the work of conceptual analysis.[4]

---

3. Kant, *Akademie Ausgabe* (Berlin: Walter de Gruyter, 1968), 17:555f., nos. 4447 and 4449. For discussion, see H. Heimsoeth, "Plato in Kants Werdegang," in *Studien zu Kants philosophische Entwicklung* (Hildesheim: Georg Olms Verlag, 1967).
4. *Von einem neuerdings erhobenen vornehmen Ton in der Philosophie* (1796) in *Akademie Ausgabe* (Paperback edition, Berlin: Walter de Gruyter, 1968), 8:391 n. and 393. The term *Schwärmerei* is applied directly to Plato as well as to Platonism.

Two points require special attention here. First, the *ectypa* or intellectual perceptions of the human intellect are copies of originals that, as I shall later indicate, are in Kant's reading of Plato not merely intuited but produced by the divine intellect. Second, whereas Kant denies the possibility of intellectual intuition, he explicitly and regularly advocates the view that Ideas (and Ideals) are produced by reason (*Vernunft*), and that concepts applicable to objects of experience are produced by the understanding (*Verstand*). As human intelligence is an instantiation of the transcendental ego, Kant as it were both secularizes the Platonic divine intellect and in effect suppresses the ancient distinction between divine and human production.

All other considerations to one side, it follows from this that for Kant, regardless of whether one is capable of thinking God's thoughts, there is a decisive substitute. We produce the intelligible world; in this sense, we are gods. At the same time, however, *intelligible* means here the conceptual structure of the world of appearance (the phenomenal world). The noumenal world is not intelligible in the scientific sense that descends to us from Aristotle. This is not to say that there are two entirely distinct worlds, as we shall shortly see. But it cannot be denied that, as an accommodation to human cognition, the phenomenal world is, in a peculiar but real sense, an ectype or image of a cognitively inaccessible and hence absent archetype. Kant never claims that the phenomenal world is itself an original; he is not, or does not wish to be, an Idealist.

I am not yet in a position to do more than entertain what will strike some readers as an obscure suggestion. I agree that the suggestion is obscure but will try to show that the fault is Kant's, not mine, or rather that the obscurity lies in the nature of things. We may best continue by turning to a brief exposition of the role of intuition in Kant. This will cast light both on Kant's Neoplatonist reading of Plato and on the problem of the original and image in Kant's own doctrine of Ideas.

In the *Critique of Pure Reason* (hereafter abbreviated as First Critique), Kant begins his exposition of the transcendental aesthetic with the following paragraph:

> In whatever manner and by whatever means a kind of knowledge may relate itself to objects, intuition [*Anschauung*] is that through which knowledge is immediately related to those objects, and to which all thought as means is directed. This takes place however

only insofar as the object is given to us; and this in turn is however possible only, at least for human beings, insofar as the mind
[*das Gemüt*] is affected in a certain way.[5]

Kant goes on to say that objects are given to us by sensibility, the
unique source of intuitions, which however are thought exclusively
via the understanding (*Verstand*), "from which concepts originate"
(*entspringen*). There are two "pure" forms of sensibility, and hence of
intuition: space and time.[6] These forms are pure in the sense that they
belong neither to the objects of appearance nor to things in themselves
but are subjective conditions of sensibility, that is, conditions for the
perception of objects by human beings.[7]

Whether space and time are themselves acts or pure objects of
intuition or both, the fact remains that for Kant, they are sources of
a priori synthetic knowledge that applies exclusively to objects as appearances and not to things in themselves.[8] Similarly, categories, or
"pure concepts of the understanding which apply a priori to objects
of intuition in general,"[9] are conditions for the thinking of sensuously
encountered objects, or appearances, and are not properties of things
in themselves.[10]

I interpose the observation that Kant's assurance concerning the
restriction of space, time, and the categories to appearances does
not seem to rest upon any conclusive arguments, nor could it, given
the complete unknowability of things in themselves. This assurance
contradicts Kant's contention that we cannot know how beings other
than those like ourselves may think.[11] A second observation: Human
intuition requires that the object be "given" to the mind. It is nevertheless, according to Kant, a "necessary maxim of reason," that is,
a "heuristic, not an ostensive concept," that we proceed in our re-
flections *as if* the totality of things, hence of things in themselves, is

5. Kant, *Kritik der reinen Vernunft* (hereafter abbreviated as *KrV*; Hamburg: Felix Meiner
Verlag, 1956), B33. Translations of passages from the *KrV* are modifications of the Kemp
Smith version.

6. *KrV* B36.

7. Ibid., B36, B42, B49, B51f.

8. Ibid., B55–56.

9. Ibid., B105.

10. See especially Kant's discussion of the "transcendental philosophy of the ancients"
in *KrV* par. 12, and in particular B114.

11. Ibid., B43.

directly intuited by "a self-subsistent, original, creative reason."[12] For a mind of this sort, intuition would be identical with production.[13]

Nevertheless, as is evident from Kant's entire doctrine of synthesis, the human intellect produces its own objects. More specifically, the same function that unifies the representations of intuition also unifies the representations of the judgment; the same function produces and epistemically cognizes the object of scientific experience.[14] Whereas it is a heuristic concept or regulative Idea that God produces the totality of things in themselves, it is for Kant a truth of transcendental philosophy that human beings produce the world of experience or of appearances.

Kant's refutations of Idealism serve to underline the point, already implicit in the distinction between appearances and things in themselves, that there is a relation between these two dimensions that I have previously designated as one of original and image.[15] To repeat, this is not to say that Kant posits two distinct worlds, of which one is the reflection of the other. The produced or apparent is the result of the accommodation of the noumenal to the transcendental ego. Presence, so to speak, is an image of absence. This initially obscure formulation has a good Kantian justification. The noumenal world presents itself to us by absenting itself behind a veil that we ourselves cast over it. The veil (the transcendental ego) enables us to produce a knowable surrogate for the original that is neither a pure original nor a "photographic" copy. We may therefore suggest that the world of appearance is the specification of the set of rules known as the transcendental ego, or an image of the noumenal world as modified by that set of rules.[16]

It is now time to give a more precise account of Kant's terminology with respect to appearance. In this terminology, "appearance" (*Erscheinung*) has two senses. I shall refer to these as the *objective* and *subjective* appearance. The objective appearance is the object as constructed and known by the operations of the transcendental ego. It

12. Ibid., B698–701.
13. Ibid., B138f.
14. Ibid., B104f.
15. See especially *KrV* Bxxxixff. and B274f.
16. For reasons of economy, I shall not discuss the transcendental synthesis of the imagination and its resulting schemata. It should at least be noted that the sense of "image" (*Bild*) latent in "imagination" (*Einbildungskraft*) is also not that of a reflection or copy of an original, but rather of a specification of a rule. See *KrV* B179f.

is the same for every person, that is, the object of the science of physics.[17] In Kant's official terminology, the word *phenomenon* refers exclusively to the objective appearance.

In accord with this usage, the noumenon or thing in itself is what Kant calls a *Verstandeswesen* or mere entity of the understanding; in other words, it is the thinkable but unknowable correlate to the knowable object, or in my terminology, the original of which the phenomenon is an image.[18] That the noumenon is unknowable follows trivially from the fact that the categories are inapplicable to it, as there is no accompanying synthesis of intuition.

Kant emphasizes the peculiar status of the noumenon by distinguishing between the negative and the positive senses of the term. In the negative sense, the noumenon is a thing "insofar as it is not an object of our sensuous intuition." In the positive sense, it is "an object of a non-sensuous intuition . . . namely the intellectual, which however is not our own."[19] Kant then goes on to say:

> Since such a form of intuition, namely, the intellectual intuition, lies strictly beyond our powers of knowledge, so too the use of the categories may in no way extend beyond the bounds of the objects of experience. Indeed, there are *Verstandeswesen* that correspond to sensed entities; so too there may be *Verstandeswesen* to which our sensuous capacity of intuition has no relation. But our concepts of the understanding, as mere forms of thought for our sensuous intuition, in no way apply to them. Hence what is by us called "noumenon" must be understood as such only in the negative sense.[20]

The noumenon is therefore a limiting concept.[21] It expresses the limits of sensibility. Looked at from the opposite direction, the noumenon establishes the phenomenon as the "original" of scientific knowledge, of which the subjective appearance (the second sense of *Erscheinung*) is in effect an image. As Kant expresses this, it is "the subjective sequence of apprehensions of the objective sequence of

17. Ibid., B62, B69. See Gerold Prauss, *Erscheinung bei Kant* (Berlin: Walter de Gruyter, 1971), 15 n. 5.
18. *KrV* B306f. and, more succinctly, A249.
19. *KrV* B307.
20. Ibid., B308f.
21. Ibid., B310f.

appearances."[22] The subjective appearance occurs contingently "in that it is not valid through a relation to sensibility as such"—that is, through the constituting function of the transcendental ego—"but only through a particular positing or organization of this or that sense."[23] At the same time, however, as the accommodation of the noumenon to the transcendental ego, the phenomenon is not an original but what I have called a surrogate or image. In this case, the original (the noumenon) is a negative concept: It is absent, except as a *Gedankending* or limiting condition.

We are therefore face to face with the following peculiar situation. The ultimate level of "reality" is a concept or construction of the human intellect, produced as the ostensibly necessary consequence of the attempt to explain synthetic a priori propositions. Kant never proves that such propositions exist, nor could he. Instead, he assumes that there are such propositions, without which a genuine science of nature would be impossible, and then proceeds to invent concepts, positive and negative, which make such propositions possible. I suggest that the noumenal as well as the phenomenal dimension, that is to say, the world as a totality, is a Kantian production, but one of which we cannot say unambiguously that it is an original or an image.

As a production, Kant's world is an original, but as an original, it is an image of some unspecifiable paradigm, analogous to the paradigm consulted by the divine artificer in Plato's *Timaeus*. This is patently true of the phenomena, but it is indirectly true of the noumena as well, which are produced by the human intellect as the bound of sensibility. The positive function of the noumena for mankind is paradoxically to function negatively. They are present to thought as absent from experience and knowledge, which is to say that they function positively as mere "things of thought" or as opaque images of a still more inaccessible original.

I am about to turn from Kant's treatment of phenomena to his doctrine of Ideas and Ideals. In this doctrine, we find an entirely explicit residue of the Platonic problem of original and image. By way of introduction, let me note that in Kant's lexicon, a subjective appearance

22. Ibid., B238.
23. Ibid., B62. See Prauss, *Erscheinung bei Kant*, 18, and Bernard Rousset, *La Doctrine kantienne de l'objectivité* (Paris: J. Vrin, 1967), 305.

is not the same as either an illusion (*Schein*) or fantasy (*Phantasien*). *Illusion* refers to the interpretation of objective appearances as things in themselves.[24] In the *Critique of Judgment* (hereafter Third Critique), Kant refers to fantasies as "beautiful views of objects."[25]

In his discussion of illusion, Kant refers to the dialectical logic of illusion and to the transcendental illusion—to the attempt to derive knowledge of objects from logical rules and categories without sense perception, or to the attempt to apply categories beyond the sensuous limits of experience to objects in themselves that in fact transcend experience.[26]

As to fantasy, it is neither an illusion nor an objective appearance, but we may be permitted to say that it is regulated by objective appearance. I mean by this that in Kant, the poetic function of the imagination is still closely bound to the objects of scientific experience. The nonobjective imagination of late modernity is still alien to Kant's "classical" spirit. This is no doubt part of the reason why Kant saw no prospective dangers in his conception of the spontaneity of the intellect. The spontaneity of reason actualizes as Ideas and Ideals, which regulate but are not constitutive of the domain of experienced objects. The spontaneity of understanding actualizes as concepts or rules for thinking experienced objects. When spontaneity is equated with freedom, and thereby separated from objectivity, the result is a deepening of the problem of original and image. Pure spontaneity can produce nothing but originals, which is to say that originals are images of original chaos.

The preceding discussion of the restriction of both fantasy and imagination by objective appearance serves as a transition from phenomena to Ideas. Kant's phenomena are not, like those of Plato, images of Ideas. On the contrary, they serve as originals relative to the subjective appearances, which accordingly play a role analogous to that of the phenomena in the usual Platonic sense. The objective appearance or essence of empirical objects is a production, the result of a function of the understanding and not the content of an intellectual intuition. The Ideas and Ideals are also not intuited but are productions—in this case, of reason. As we are about to see, Kant

---

24. *KrV* B69–71. Cf. the discussion of dreams and outer objects at B519–21.
25. "Schönen Aussichten auf Gegenstände." Kant, *Kritik der Urteilskraft* (hereafter *KdU*, Hamburg: Felix Meiner Verlag, 1954), 86.
26. *KrV* B85f., B349ff.

varies in his definitions of the relation between the Ideal and the Idea, but it can be said in general that the relationship itself is one of rule to example. The rule, expressed with the same generality, is a concept of totality, and not a paradigm of inner-worldly objects. But the Kantian example is also not an object in this sense; in Kant's terminology, both rule and example are regulative rather than constitutive of experience.

In Kant's interpretation of Plato, "what is for us an Ideal was for Plato an Idea of the divine understanding."[27] Again: "Plato accepted an antecedent spiritual intuition by the godhood as the original source of pure concepts of understanding and fundamental principles."[28] I referred to this earlier as Kant's Neoplatonizing of Plato. In a sense it is also a Kantianizing of Plato, because for Kant, too, the Ideal and the concepts of understanding are produced. The fundamental difference with Plato, as Kant understands it, is not on this point, but rather that Kant replaces intellectual intuition with productive discursivity or "Aristotelian" conceptualizing.[29]

Kant distinguishes three kinds of Ideal and Idea: speculative (theoretical), practical (moral), and aesthetic. Speculative Ideas include all expressions of a totality of conditions or of a perfect being.[30] "They are thought entirely problematically, in order to ground regulative principles in reference to them (as heuristic fictions), to be used systematically by the understanding in the field of experience."[31] This is an important and neglected text, which must be taken together with the previously cited passage in which Kant refers to the regulative Idea of God or the ground of totality as a heuristic concept.[32] Before considering it further, let me first cite Kant's account of speculative Ideals.

The Idea is a "cosmical concept" of absolute totality in the synthesis of appearances. In the same passage, Kant distinguishes the Ideal of pure reason as that of the absolute totality in the synthesis of all possible things in general.[33] Elsewhere, Kant says that transcendental Ideals, as it seems, are still further removed than Ideas from objective

27. Ibid., B596.

28. Letter to Marcus Herz, 21 February 1772, in *Akademie Ausgabe* 10:131.

29. This point is insisted upon and documented with great skill by Claude Piché in *Das Ideal: Ein Problem der Kantischen Ideenlehre* (Bonn: Bouvier Verlag, 1984).

30. *KrV* B434.

31. Ibid., B799. Cf B672, where Kant speaks of the Idea as a *focus imaginarius*.

32. Ibid., B698–701.

33. Ibid., B434f.

reality because they are not mere rules for carrying a sequence to completion. Instead, they are the Ideas understood "not merely *in concreto*, but *in individuo*, that is, as an individual thing, determinable or indeed determined through the Idea."[34]

If we compare the passages just cited, the following point emerges. The aforementioned expression "heuristic concept" or "heuristic fiction" is applied to the transcendental (that is, to every) Idea. The cited expressions may remind us of the Platonic "noble lie."[35] I restrict myself to the following suggestion. The noble lie unites politics with nature in a way that is intended to veil over the produced or poetic status of the ostensible political paradigm (the "Idea" of the city, as it were). Kant's heuristic fictions, on the other hand, play a crucial role in the transformation of Newtonian nature into a product of pure reason, and more generally, in rendering mankind independent of both God and a divine nature.

The Kantian domain of the heuristic, the regulative, the "as if," differs in degree and in rhetorical presentation, but not in its essential function, from the Platonic domain of teleological myth. One may further say that in Plato, the regulative function is also present within the role assigned to Ideas. As a representative text, I cite the *Phaedo*. Socrates is in the process of explaining why he rejected physical for teleological causality. If one wishes to know the cause of something, he asserts, one must know what is best for it. This extends to human activity, which is caused by human intention, by a perception of what it is best to do.[36]

Socrates goes on to recommend the study of things (*ta onta*) by discursive reason (*en tois logois*). The first step of his procedure of study is as follows: "In each case I assume [*hypothemenos*] an explanation [*logos*] which I judge to be the strongest, and whatever seems to me to agree with this, I posit [*tithēmi*] as being true, whether with respect to causes or all of the other beings; whatever does not so agree, I regard as untrue."[37] The *logos* in question is of course the employment of Ideas as both causal and teleological explanatory principles of things. Putting to one side for the moment the question of whether this hypothesis is validated by an intellectual intuition, the point here is that Ideas play

34. Ibid., B596.
35. Plato, *Republic* 3:414b8ff.
36. Plato, *Phaedo* 97c6ff., 98e2–5.
37. Ibid., 100a3–7.

both what Kant calls regulative as well as constitutive roles for Plato. In other words, whether or not the Platonic Ideas are mythical rather than epistemological or ontological beings, there is a functional link between myths and Platonic Ideas. Both are "heuristic."

To return now to Kant's presentation of Ideas and Ideals, I want next to cite at greater length a previously noted passage in the First Critique:

> What is for us an Ideal, was for Plato an Idea of the divine understanding, an individual object in God's pure intuition, the most complete of each type of possible being and the ultimate ground of all images (*Nachbilder*) in appearance.
>
> Without our soaring so high, however, we must admit that human reason contains not only Ideas but also Ideals which indeed do not, like the Platonic [Ideas], have creative but rather practical force (as regulative principles).[38]

This text is contained in the general discussion of the Ideal of pure reason and gives the impression that all Ideals are practical. We know, however, from an earlier text, that this is not Kant's view. The practical force of Ideals is regulative, not constitutive. But this does not preclude the existence of a speculative Ideal, namely, the concept of the *ens realissimum* or of that which possesses all of reality, the thing in itself as completely determined, the basis "for the complete determination that necessarily belongs to all that exists."[39]

In the continuation, Kant says that reason, in achieving its purpose,

> namely, of representing to itself solely the necessary complete determination of things, does not presuppose the existence of such a being [*Wesen*] that corresponds to this Ideal, but only the Idea of that being, in order to derive the conditioned or restricted totality from an unconditioned totality of complete determination. The Ideal stands to the Idea as the *Urbild* (*prototypon*) of all things, which, taken together as imperfect copies (*ectypa*), derive from it the material of their possibility, and insofar as they approach it more or less, they are on each occasion infinitely far from attaining it.[40]

38. *KrV* B596f.
39. Ibid., B604.
40. Ibid., B605f.

This passage states, if I understand it correctly, that the original is the speculative Ideal of the completely determined thing in itself, whereas the copies are the various imperfect Ideas by which we attempt to think the totality of things. In a lengthy section of the First Critique, Kant goes on to refute the various arguments by which we attempt to prove the existence of the *ens realissimum* as God. His conclusion is that "the supreme being remains a mere Ideal, if a flawless one, for the merely speculative use of reason."[41] The existence of God can be neither proved nor disproved speculatively. More important for our immediate purpose, what one can call the theological and the epistemological or cosmical functions of the speculative Ideal combine to produce an original (*Urbild*) that can be thought only in radically imperfect copies. The domain of the transcendental is articulated by the Platonist problematic of original and image.

In the passage just analyzed, the Ideal is the original and the Idea is the copy. I want to show next that Kant fluctuates in identifying the distinction between original and copy in the case of practical Ideals and Ideas. Let us first look at the sequel to Kant's discussion of the Ideal in the opening section of book 2 of the First Critique.

Having just spoken of the practical force of Ideals in general, Kant goes on to distinguish between moral concepts resting upon something empirical (such as pleasure) and those which, by allowing reason to set limits to a lawless freedom, may, when considered solely with respect to their form, serve as examples of pure concepts of reason. "Virtue, and with it, human wisdom in its total purity, are Ideas. But the wise man (of the Stoics) is an Ideal, that is, a man who exists merely in thought, but who is fully congruent with the Ideal of wisdom. Just as the Idea gives the rule, so the Ideal serves in such a case as the original (*Urbilde*) for the complete determination of the copy."[42]

The Ideal of the wise man stands to the copies we make of it as does the Ideal of the *ens perfectissimum* or God to its copies. In both these cases, the copies are Ideas. The Ideal of the wise man and its copies belong to the practical domain. In the *Critique of Practical Reason* (hereafter Second Critique), Kant reverses the terminology of original and copy. He says that practical or moral Ideas have a greater definiteness than speculative Ideas; some examples of the former are freedom,

41. Ibid., B669.
42. Ibid., B597.

holiness, happiness, and personality. These Ideas "serve as originals [*Urbilder*] of practical perfection, as an indispensable guide of ethical comportment and at the same time as a measure of comparison."[43] In this passage, contrary to the text just cited from the First Critique, the Idea, not the Ideal, is the paradigm or original. One may note a similar fluctuation of terminology with respect to holiness, which is called both an Idea[44] and an Ideal.[45]

Fluctuation in terminology is not unusual in Kant; nevertheless, it does not preclude our drawing the inference that some problem underlies the distinction between Ideal and Idea. That problem is clearly the old Platonic problem of the original and the image. In Kant, the fluctuation renders it ambiguous whether the Ideal is the rule of which the Idea is the copy, or vice versa. I believe that this is connected to the incomplete success with which Kant replaces intellectual intuition with discursive or conceptual thinking. The point is especially clear in the case of practical Ideas, which are more definite than speculative Ideas; consider in particular the case of the wise or holy man, who seems to be no less an object of intellectual intuition than the Platonic Idea of justice.

In the Third Critique, Kant introduces the distinction between the aesthetic Ideal and Idea. Here, the Idea is the original (*Muster*), and the Ideal is the attempt to approximate to it. There is no determinate Idea of good taste; in order to demonstrate our aesthetic judgment, we must exercise it as our own capacity. Accordingly, each person must produce it from within himself in each act of judgment about the beautiful. The highest paradigm of taste is a "mere Idea" implied but not given definiteness in the act of judgment itself.[46]

The Idea is not a discursive rule, because we cannot decide in advance the domain of the beautiful. On the other hand, it is not an intuition; it must be general, whereas each aesthetic intuition is of this or that beautiful object. Given this indefiniteness, the Ideal cannot be a concrete exemplification of the Idea, as for example the Idea of God is of the *ens perfectissimum*. The Ideal is not something we possess but something we are striving to produce in ourselves. It is an Ideal of the

---

43. Kant, *Kritik der praktischen Vernunft* (hereafter *KpV*, Hamburg: Felix Meiner Verlag, 1952), 146f.
44. Ibid., notes to 11f. and 146f.
45. Ibid., 97.
46. *KdU* 72–77, par. 17.

imagination "because it rests upon exhibition, not upon concepts; the capacity of exhibition, however, is the imagination."[47]

Exhibition (*Darstellen*) seems to be perilously close to intuition, as is tacit in the attribution of the Ideal of beauty to the imagination. As the German word for imagination also makes explicit (*Einbildungskraft*), the concept of the image is implicit in the Ideal of beauty, as this or that manifestation of the Idea. The Ideal we are striving to express is nothing other than ourselves, that is, the Ideal of Man, the only being who contains within himself the purpose of his own existence.[48]

Kant not surprisingly goes on at the end of paragraph 17 in the Third Critique to relate the Ideal of beauty to morality, and so, in the earlier passage, to the Ideal of perfection. Despite the "disinterestedness" of aesthetic judgments, there is a connection between the perception of beauty and goodness. In fact, as Kant says later, "The beautiful is the symbol of the morally good."[49] To which we may add, a symbol is an image that is neither a photographic copy nor the exemplification of a rule. It is an image in a sense that includes, but is not equivalent to, a faculty of intuition. Otherwise expressed, the imagination, or the capacity of combining the manifold of intuition, must itself be unified by the concept of understanding in its usual operation. In the present case, however, there is no concept or rule but a symbol.

The upshot of this line of investigation is as follows. With some fluctuation in the role assigned to each, Idea and Ideal are related as original and image. *Image* must be understood not in the sense of a photographic copy or even of an approximate likeness, but in the sense of a concrete example of a rule, or, more vaguely, as a symbol. Furthermore, both original and image are produced by pure reason. As mere beings of thought, or heuristic fictions, their comprehensive status is unclear: From the highest level, that which lies beyond the functions of the transcendental ego, it is unknown whether these fictions are originals or images.

If they are genuine originals, then Kant has created the regulative concepts that supply unity and direction to the world of experience, which is also created by the understanding through the production of

---

47. Ibid., 73. I translate *Darstellen* as "exhibition" and reserve "presentation" for *Vorstellung*.
48. Ibid., 74.
49. Ibid., 213. For morality and sublimity, see 110f.

its own concepts. In this case, it is unclear why further worlds may not be created; that is, if the transcendental ego is a creation of Kant's philosophical ingenuity, it may be replaced by some other creation.

If the heuristic fictions are not originals in this sense, then they must be images of the nature of the noumenal world, or more properly, of the teleological nature of the noumenal world as a creation of a divine intelligence or as the Platonic order of eternity. In this case, the originals are absent; that is to say, they are entirely unknowable. Kant is thus free to play the role of a philosopher god, a more exalted role than that of a philosopher king.[50]

In the Kantian philosophy, possibility plays a higher or more fundamental role than actuality: Concepts of empirical objects and transcendental Ideas or Ideals are rules for the possibility of objects or of their totality. The two main cognitive functions of the transcendental ego, reason and understanding, are also logical possibilities, functions of thinking that must be actualized by the activity of thinking. Differently stated, the transcendental ego is a logical construction, not a fully actual absolute ego. To say that thinking is spontaneous is thus not to say that it is eternal or fully actual, but rather that it actualizes in accord with the logical rules embodied in the transcendental ego. And the same is true of the world of experience.

In Plato, on the contrary, actuality is higher than or prior to possibility. The Ideas are eternal and unchanging, always fully what they are—which is not, incidentally, the same as to say that they are fully present to the human intellect. The Platonic Idea is thus a fully actual paradigm of a family of particulars, not a logical rule or condition for the possibility of a totality. Correlatively, the Kantian phenomenon is the objective actualization of a logical possibility, whereas the Platonic phenomenon, in the canonical sense of the term, is an image or interpretation, and in this sense a possible manifestation, of an actual paradigm.

This opposition underlies the post-Kantian criticism, made popular by Nietzsche, that Plato empties the world of experience of substance or reality. One may argue on behalf of Platonism, however, that the objective appearance of the world depends upon the equivalence be-

---

50. Cf. Plato, *Philebus* 28c6: "The wise all agree, thereby exalting themselves, that *nous* is king for them of heaven and earth."

tween possibility and necessity, that is to say, upon the guarantee that the spontaneity of thinking always actualizes in obedience to the set of rules called by Kant the transcendental ego. Unfortunately, there is no such guarantee: Possibility cannot be equivalent to necessity. Such an equivalence leads to Eleaticism, not to modern philosophies of transcendental or even historical freedom.

To restate the point in the terms of my primary theme, the world requires for its stability a structural relation of original and image. If there are no images, Eleaticism results, or the annihilation of the world within a monadic Being. If there are no originals, the result is the infinite multiplication of Eleaticism: infinite worlds, or chaos. One thinks here inevitably of the contemporary metaphysicians of modal logic. Unfortunately, it seems that the relation between original and image is itself finally unintelligible, if by *intelligible* we mean logically or conceptually explicable. This is easily illustrated by a concise reflection on the doctrine of Platonic Ideas.

In Plato's mythical language, the Ideas are "recollected" from our perception of them in a previous or discarnate existence. As Leibniz somewhere observes, a recollection of an Idea is already an image and not the Idea itself. The same point can be expressed in nonmythical language. The Platonic Idea is a pure form. If the form of the image is the same as the Idea, then there is no formal or eidetic difference between the Idea and the image. If, however, there is such a formal difference, then the image must be an image of some other Idea. But of which? How can we identify an Idea that is other than its image?

There would then seem to be good reason to shift from intellectual intuition to a doctrine of discursive concepts. But a concept, whether defined as a predicate or as a rule, is either validated by an intellectual intuition of an eternal or transcendental original, or else it is a mere stipulation, a conventional and so historical linguistic entity. In the case of Plato, if the linguistic analysis of the later dialogues is not backed up by the perception of translinguistic forms, then Plato becomes a nominalist. Kant, as we have seen, intends to avoid this consequence by what I have called the equation of possibility with necessity, an incoherent or at least indefensible procedure.

Kant's doctrine of spontaneous production is a transcendental version of the thesis that we know only what we make. The derivation of knowledge from production, as we have just seen, gives priority to possibility rather than to actuality. This quarrel between Platonism and Antiplatonism continues to underlie contemporary philosophy, and therefore the mathematical and natural sciences as well. By a curious irony, the quarrel can be resolved in favor of Platonism only by recourse to a quasi-Kantian argument: One must hold that the logical condition for the possibility of the world is the primordial and unknowable structure of original and image.

In my opinion, there is in fact no resolution to this quarrel, and in this fundamental sense, there is no progress in philosophy, no quarrel between ancients and moderns but rather a quarrel within the domain of Platonism, or if you prefer, of Kantianism. Whereas I regard the argument just sketched as decisive, I make no claim to a proof of the aporetic nature of philosophy. The reader must decide this point for himself. I restrict myself here to providing evidence that the aporia is present in both Plato and Kant.

It is now time to turn more directly to Plato. What follows is hardly an exhaustive analysis but rather a sample of evidence demonstrating that the Platonic dialogues are characterized throughout by the problem of the original and image, even within the domain of the Ideas as taken separately from their generated appearances. Stated with maximum concision, the Ideas "appear" in two senses. First, they show themselves to the eye of the intellect. Second, they are themselves appearances (recollections) of some absent or inaccessible original. There is a third point: As already indicated, the ostensible shift from intuition to conceptual analysis is for the most part an illusion, but even if it genuinely occurs, it solves nothing.

According to the main line of modern scholarship, there are two important stages in Plato's doctrine of Ideas, based respectively upon intellectual intuition and linguistic analysis. The first stage is represented by such dialogues as the *Republic*, *Phaedrus*, and *Phaedo*. The second stage presumably takes on its purest form in the *Sophist* and is also prominent in the *Philebus*. I note first that the *Timaeus*, traditionally considered a late dialogue, also contains the original/image paradigm associated with intellectual intuition, and has for that reason been reclassified by influential scholars as a middle dialogue—as belonging to the first of the two periods just mentioned.

I shall make no judgment on the proposed reclassification of the *Timaeus* except to say that it seems to beg the question. If we can show that the original/image paradigm, or the emphasis upon intellectual vision, is also present in the *Sophist* and *Philebus*, then the primary justification for redating the *Timaeus* disappears. As I have undertaken to do this elsewhere at some length, I restrict myself here to citing representative texts.[51]

No one would deny that, even in the so-called earlier period of the Platonic dialogues, intellectual intuition or perception of pure form is linked with discursive analysis—with giving explanations. The problem is that these explanations seem to be either explicitly mythical, metaphorical, or hypothetical. In my opinion, this is the inevitable consequence of the disjunction between vision and speech. We have already noticed the passage in the *Phaedo* in which Socrates refers to the doctrine of Ideas as a hypothesis. In what is presumably a more authoritative discussion of dialectic, namely, in the *Republic*, it is not the Ideas, but their images, including sensible things and mathematical forms, that hold the status of hypotheses.[52] These hypotheses must be "discharged" in the process by which the soul rises to the domain of pure Ideas. Dialectic thus treats exclusively (in its pure stage) of "Ideas themselves proceeding through themselves to themselves, and terminating in Ideas."

It follows that Ideas are not in fact "recollected" from their images but must be seen exclusively by the intellect if we are to shift from myth to science. Unfortunately, Socrates does not explain how this is to be accomplished; indeed, his entire discussion with the youthful Glaucon is saturated with the metaphors of vision: the divided line, the sun as the offspring or (as Kant might say) symbol of the Idea of the good, and so on. One may suspect that the shift from metaphor to pure knowledge is a shift from discourse to silence. The genuine dialectician, on the contrary, would have to give speech to the silent vision of the demiurge in the *Timaeus*. But speech is historical or generated; it constructs "concepts" that are themselves rooted in the world of sense perception. Far from grasping the Ideas, our concepts stand between them and us.

The disjunction between vision and speech is well represented in the *Phaedrus*. As I have had occasion to note elsewhere,[53] the only discussion interrupting the silence of the soul in its ascent to the hyperuranian beings is a debate between the noble and base horse as to whether or not to have sexual intercourse with a beautiful youth.[54]

51. See Rosen, *Plato's "Sophist"*.
52. *Republic* 6:511a1ff.
53. In Rosen, *Hermeneutics as Politics* (New York: Oxford University Press, 1987), 77.
54. Plato, *Phaedrus* 254a3ff.

To regard the *Phaedrus* as a defense of the ontological superiority of speech to writing is thus to misunderstand the central passage of the dialogue, or else to mistake Eros for ontology.

In his myth of the soul, Socrates first speaks of the souls of the gods or the divine intelligence, to which is vouchsafed a temporary or temporal (*dia chronou*) vision of hyperuranian being (the Ideas).[55] He then turns to the best of the human souls:

> Such is the life of the gods. But as to the other souls, the one which best follows the god and is like him raises the head of the charioteer into the outer place [heaven] and is carried around by the revolution [of the cosmos], disturbed by the fuss of the horses and viewing with difficulty the beings [*ta onta*, the hyperuranian beings]. And another [presumably still of the best human type] sometimes rises and sometimes sinks. Thanks to the violence of the horses, it sees some things [pure *onta*] and others not.[56]

This passage brings Plato very close to Heidegger in one crucial respect: Noetic intuition, the thinking of the pure forms, is conditioned by time and is even perspectival. This is true for gods as well as for mortals. It does not follow that the Ideas are themselves perspectives or temporal creatures. What we are justified in concluding from this text is that a perspectival and temporally conditioned vision of the eternal is not a sufficient basis for an ontology.

Differently stated, our discarnate vision of the Ideas is neither an inference from generated instances nor a direct, full, and ontologically satisfactory view. It is rather a temporalized image. One may observe that there is no thematic reference to mathematics in the *Phaedrus*, whereas in the *Republic*, mathematics, although carefully distinguished from philosophical dialectic, is said to turn the soul in the direction of the Ideas.[57] The key point, however, is that mathematics is a dream about being because it does not know its own principles.[58] The dialectician is a warrior who must be able to answer every objection, which is possible if and only if he has a *logos* of the good.[59]

Mathematics is a hypothetical knowledge of what is always. Philosophy yearns for something more, for dialectic as described in the

55. Ibid., 247d1ff.
56. Ibid., 248a1–6. Words in square brackets are my own clarification of the text.
57. *Republic* 7:522c1ff., 527b5–9, and especially 531d8ff.
58. Ibid., 533b1–c5.
59. Ibid., 534b4–d1.

previous citation from the *Republic*, or for knowledge that dispenses entirely with images and so with hypotheses while proceeding by way of Ideas alone. As long as we are restricted to metaphorical discussions—or what one might dare to call advertisements—of pure dialectic, we are entitled to conclude that no genuine account of dialectic is possible.

I will come later to the discussion of dialectic in the *Sophist*, in which pure intuition is presumably jettisoned on behalf of conceptual analysis. I want for the moment to stay with the *Republic* and to argue that the famous Socratic distinction between the intelligible (*to noēton*) and the visible (*to horaton*) cannot be sustained.[60] In the first place, the intelligible is itself visible to the mind's eye. This is of course a metaphor, but it is an inescapable metaphor. As has often been observed, recourse to vision is necessary in order to express the notion of the full presence of the Idea to the intellect. Vision is the sense that discerns shapes most fully and precisely. If hearing or speaking intervenes between the Idea and the intellect, our immediate referent is a linguistic expression. But the expression is a concept, that is, either a spontaneous function of the understanding or a nominalist production.

Second, as we have seen with the assistance of the *Phaedrus*, vision is itself already detached from the original; a visual image interposes itself between the absent original and our temporally or (what comes to the same thing) linguistically bound intelligence. In the language of the *Phaedo*, the Idea is a hypothesis, assigned a regulative as well as a constitutive role; to that extent, it is a concept, or what would today be called a theoretical construction, designed to render experience scientifically intelligible, and in this sense is not a copy of reality but an image or symbol of order.

As a representative text, let us consider *Republic* 5:476e4ff. In this passage, which prepares the way for the distinction in book 6 between the intelligible and the visible, Socrates is discussing the tripartite distinction of knowledge, opinion, and ignorance. He who knows, knows something that is; that which is altogether (*to men pantelōs on*) is altogether knowable (*pantelōs gnōston*).

Socrates introduces the genus of beings called "powers" (*dynameis*), which lack all properties belonging to objects of visual sense per-

---

60. The distinction is drawn at 6:509d1ff., in connection with the "divided line," which is itself a visual image of intelligibility.

ception. This genus includes scientific knowledge. In distinguishing between the form (*eidos*) of sensory objects and the genus of powers, Socrates says that he must "look at" the relevant characteristics in both cases.[61] We should also note that Socrates refers to his knowledge of the distinction itself by means of the verb *phainomai*. The same verb recurs regularly to designate "how things look to one."[62] The same idiom is employed in the denial that opinion is more "lucid" than knowledge.[63] In the culminating defense of characteristic Ideas, Socrates condemns those who view many beautiful things but who cannot see the beautiful itself. He praises as knowers those who view each of the Ideas.[64]

It is unnecessary to multiply examples of the use of metaphors of vision in connection with scientific knowledge and perception of the Ideas. Perhaps the most famous single doctrine in the Platonic dialogues, the Idea of the Good, is introduced by means of an image ("an offspring . . . that is most like it") of the sun.[65] In this passage the two points concerning vision and imagery are both illustrated. The Ideas are on the one hand visible; they "present" themselves, and therefore the term *phainomena* may be applied to them in an honorific sense. But they do not present themselves directly or fully to the human intelligence. Vision of the Ideas is mediated, whether through recollection, hypothesis, or the exigencies of discourse, by images: by metaphor. Even if the Idea is held to present itself fully to the eye of the intellect, there is a disjunction between vision and *logos* or the discursive account of what we see.

This disjunction can only be filled by myths: tales told by the ancestors, who lived closer to the gods and were wiser than we.[66] If it is true that he who lacks a visible paradigm in the soul of that which is entirely true is like a blind man, then the very language of vision in which this truth is expressed provides an image of our blindness.[67]

The peculiar interplay between vision and discourse is dramatically evident in the *Sophist*, the dialogue most often cited to illustrate Plato's ostensible shift from the one to the other. In this dialogue, the Eleatic

61. Ibid., V, 477c8–d1.
62. Ibid., 477c6; cf. 478c13.
63. Ibid., 478c14.
64. Ibid., 479e1–2, e7–8.
65. Ibid., 6:506d6ff.
66. Plato, *Timaeus* 20d1ff., 40d6–e4.
67. *Republic* 6:487c7.

Stranger describes dialectic, the science of the free man, as division and collection in accordance with kinds. Theaetetus, his interlocutor, is first instructed to "look more clearly at what has been said about the being of the greatest kinds" and is then told that the practitioner of dialectic "has a distinct perception of one Idea through many."[68]

At this point, I turn directly to the passage in which the Eleatic Stranger raises the need to shift from vision to discourse. He tells Theaetetus that if they can see neither being nor nonbeing by whatever illumination is available, or if there is no light to be found, then they "must force the *logos* between both in as auspicious a manner as possible."[69] The Stranger refers to this same passage in the sequel to the *Sophist*. In the *Statesman*, he asks Young Socrates, "Just as in the case of the sophist we forced nonbeing to be since the *logos* had escaped us at that point, so now must we not force the greater and the less to be measured, not only with respect to each other, but with respect to the genesis of the measure?"[70]

The discussion in the *Sophist*, far from being exclusively visual or discursive, is conducted in twilight. The ostensible shift to linguistic or conceptual analysis is in fact rooted in direct or prophetic vision of the pure forms (except for sameness and otherness).[71] Discourse is subsequent to this prophetic vision: "Discourse comes to us from the weaving-together of the forms with one another."[72] Theaetetus cannot see prophetically how the forms combine;[73] as what we mean by sameness and otherness depends upon our decision concerning the laws of separation and combination, he does not see directly sameness and otherness.[74] This is part of the reason why we must shift from vision to the force of speech when it comes to being and nonbeing (which latter is explained by means of otherness).

The force in question consists in the substitution of discursive concepts—that is, theoretical or technical constructions—for original vision. This shift is necessary for the sake of epistemic or philosophical theory in the modern sense of explanation. But the shift from *theoria*

68. Plato, *Sophist* 249d6ff., 253d1–3.

69. Ibid., 251a1–4. The verb in question is *diōtheō*.

70. Plato, *Statesman* 284b7–c1. See my *Plato's "Symposium,"* 2d ed. (New Haven: Yale University Press, 1986), 339ff. The verb here is *prosanankazomai*.

71. *Sophist* 250c1–2.

72. Ibid., 259e5–6.

73. Ibid., 251d5–e3.

74. Ibid., 254e2–255a3.

to theory construction is not simply a shift from intellectual intuition to linguistic analysis. Our constructions are visual in two senses: They are based upon what we have prophetically seen, and they consist in images (today called *models*).

These considerations help us to understand why Socrates says in the *Philebus*, a late dialogue, that diaeresis (dialectic) is a gift of the gods, thrown down by a Prometheus from heaven to mankind "together with a most shining fire." It is also why he says that the hypothesis (*themenos*) that there is one Idea for each kind of individual is derived from a saying handed down by the ancients, who were our superiors and who lived closer to the gods than do we.[75]

To borrow an expression from Hegel, thinking is for Plato a mixture of force and understanding. There is no fundamental difference between the two periods of middle and late dialogues on this point. The most one could say is that in the late dialogues, Plato experiments with theoretical construction in the sense just defined, and to a much stronger degree than is evident in the middle dialogues. But this experiment is conducted in terms that establish my two contentions about vision. Whereas the Ideas are appearances in an honorific sense, they are so as the result of a hypothesis or thanks to the force of conceptual innovation. The *logos* is not simply eternal or (in a Kantian expression) transcendental. It fails us at crucial points, as the Eleatic Stranger says in the passage cited from the *Statesman*.

I should like to give one last illustration of the mixture of vision and discourse. In the *Sophist*, the Eleatic Stranger says, in the idiom to which we are accustomed, "It now appears to me that I see two forms of mimesis."[76] The forms are (1) *fantastikē:* the production of images that accommodate the proportions of the original to human perspective, and that are accordingly inaccurate but that produce an accurate appearance in the case of large works; and (2) *eikastikē:* the production of images that accurately reflect the original proportions, but that in the case of large works produce an inaccurate appearance.

As I pointed out previously, we cannot distinguish between accurate and inaccurate images unless we can see the original as independent of images. This independent vision is what Plato means by *noēsis* or intellection intuition. On the other hand, every attempt to state what we see, whether accurate or inaccurate, is the production of an

---

75. Plato, *Philebus* 16c5ff.
76. *Sophist* 235d1. The verbs are *phainomai* and *kathoran*.

image. The accurate image gives an inaccurate appearance; the accurate appearance is derived from an inaccurate image. I understand this to mean that, contrary to the celebration of mathematics as the paradigm of scientific knowledge, in the last analysis, as philosophers, we depend upon fantasms or metaphors: upon myths. But this is also true of mathematics, which, for all its accuracy, cannot "discharge its hypotheses" or explain its principles.

In discussions of being and appearance, the term *phainomena* normally has a pejorative sense: for example, "phenomena, not however beings in truth."[77] Yet the Platonic spokesmen regularly apply terms that are etymologically cognate to *phainomena* in order to praise the lucidity of the Ideas. I have been arguing that the Ideas appear in a corresponding double sense. To prophetic vision, they are fully present; to the vision mediated by discursive intelligence, they are present "through a glass darkly," in images, and so their presence is a kind of absence. The problem of original and image is thus not merely that of the relation between Ideas and phenomena. At a deeper level, it is the problem of the nature of the Ideas themselves, that is, of our knowledge of the Ideas.

This is the same problem that we found previously in Kant. The fact that the problem is articulated in technical terminology differing from Plato's is a normal consequence of the productive nature of *technē*. What one may call the ontological difference between Plato and Kant has to do with the hypothetical or mythical location of the absent original. Whereas we cannot ourselves arrive at this location, we are in each case able to say something decisive about what blocks our path. For Kant, the transcendental ego stands between us and the noumena (and this is not to deny the salutary consequences derived by Kant from this ontological obstacle). In so doing, it produces spontaneous hypotheses that point us toward the promised land but do not allow us to enter it.

Plato's discussion of what stands between us and the original is in my opinion even more complex than Kant's. It would be widely held by modern scholars that Kant's teaching is superior to Plato's on at least one point: Kant replaces myth with technical analysis. In my opinion, it is only partially true that such a replacement occurs. But to the extent that it does, the results are not necessarily superior, and certainly not to the extent that an inaccurate image provides human

---

77. *Phainomena, ou mentoi onta ge pou te alētheia. Republic* 10:596e4.

vision with an accurate appearance of large works, such as speech about the whole. I shall therefore leave it at this: In place of the transcendental ego, a technical artifact, Plato employs poetry as a fantasm of the disjunction between vision and *logos*.

What are popularly known as Platonism and Antiplatonism may thus be found in both Plato and Kant. The technical differences between the two thinkers arise from different attempts to solve the same problem. But there is no solution to this problem, because each formulation of the solution is necessarily a restatement of the problem. Language is a human production, and in that sense an original; as a statement of the structure of eternity, however, it is also an image. This holds true of formal or artificial as well as of natural languages. It explains, if I am not entirely mistaken, why contemporary philosophers of science believe simultaneously that scientific theories (models) are not direct representations of physical reality, and that science is knowledge of physical reality.

CHAPTER FOUR

Freedom and Spontaneity in Fichte

The quarrel between the ancients and the moderns is especially evident with respect to the pivotal concept of freedom. Aristotle formulates the classical political view when he says that whatever the law does not explicitly permit is forbidden. The history of the modern epoch portrays the gradual evolution toward the converse of this view: whatever the law does not explicitly forbid is permitted.

This is not the place to decide the delicate question concerning the relation between theory and practice. Suffice it to say that classical conservatism, of which Aristotle is the preeminent example, does not require a metaphysical foundation to justify its conception of freedom as ruling and being ruled and hence as bound by the law. The modern situation seems to be quite different. Evidently a justification of some sort is required in order to reverse the classical perspective and so to define the state in terms of the individual person.

It would no longer be persuasive to argue that the classical situation is the natural one, in the Aristotelian sense of *best*. And yet, because modern individualism depends upon revolutionary speeches as well as deeds, and the slogan "man makes himself" would be widely acceptable at least to late modern political thinkers, there must be some plausibility to the thesis that the modern conception of freedom is artificial. The term *artificial* is not necessarily pejorative; on the other hand, it is not self-evidently laudatory. Let me say cautiously that it defines a problem.

In the twentieth century, we speak rather easily of "a theory of the individual person" or of *individualism*. Even the advanced thinkers of deconstruction retain this slightly old-fashioned idiom in their preference for difference over identity. The advanced thinker of the early nineteenth century spoke of the identity of identity and difference, thereby implying the retention of the classical notion of limitation

This essay first appeared, in somewhat different form, in the *Philosophical Forum*, Volume XIX, Numbers 2–3, Winter-Spring 1988.

upon freedom, a limitation of law and order, or of intelligible structure, necessary to preserve freedom from chaos.

To say this in another way, as late as Hegel, we see the recognized
need to ground political freedom in a rational account of the whole.
Such a view is not so far removed from Aristotle as might at first
seem to be the case. The Aristotelian distinction between theory and
practice (to say nothing here of production), or the apparent independence of the *Nicomachean Ethics* and the *Politics* from the *Metaphysics*,
does not cancel the fact that Aristotle's political doctrine is based upon
a conception of human nature, and hence of nature. It is clearly part
of Aristotle's doctrine that political phenomena are visible independently of physical, logical, or metaphysical phenomena, for political
purposes. This is not the same as to say that they are independent
for philosophical purposes, or that the philosopher, in order to understand the whole, does not have to think through the relation between
divine and human nature.

It is evident, however, that after Hegel the impetus to justify political freedom theoretically is gradually replaced by an obsession with
freedom as an ontological category. There seems to be something
about both branches of the main tradition of modern philosophy,
British empiricism and German Idealism, that renders unstable the
comprehensive modern tendency to unify theory and practice, or still
more sharply, to transform both theory and practice into production.
In the case of British empiricism, we may say merely that the disappearance of the concept of substance left a universe of discontinuous
particulars: not a fruitful basis for the grounding of political freedom
in a theory of the whole, but quite suitable for the dissemination of
the notion that the freedom of the individual person is a self-evident
truth.

In German philosophy from Kant to Hegel, one sees a steady movement toward the thesis that (in Hegel's words) substance is subject.
Substance is not dissolved but brought to life and endowed with self-
consciousness. One can say that the success with which freedom is
given a theoretical grounding is a function of the success of the unification of substance and subject. By *success* I mean the degree to which
that unification is rendered accessible to conceptual description. To
anticipate a later point, there are various ways in which to justify the
primacy of freedom, not all of them theoretical in the proper or full
sense of the term.

In this chapter, I shall be primarily (but not exclusively) concerned with Fichte, whose failure on my reading to unify substance and subject (not his terms) is a peculiarly illuminating and influential one. Fichte will be for us the paradigm of a theory, the failure of which licenses the abandonment of theory or rational justification of the primacy of freedom. As such, he will be paradigmatic for the subsequent post-Hegelian development of an irrational or at least nonrational ontology of freedom. It is my contention that we have much to learn about the incoherent status of philosophical theory in our own century from a study of Fichte's failure. To say this is not to advocate a return to the past but to indicate a wish to contribute to a more reasonable future.

I start once more with the difference between the ancients and the moderns and specifically with a contrast between Plato and Fichte. In the *Sophist*, Plato assigns to the Eleatic Stranger the paradigmatic version of the classical conception of philosophical freedom. Speaking of the knowledge of the combination and separation of pure forms, which Theaetetus agrees must be a science and perhaps the greatest of all sciences, the Eleatic Stranger asks his young companion: "What shall we call it, Theaetetus? Or by Zeus! Have we stumbled unwittingly upon the science of free men and, although we were looking for the sophist, happened first to have found the philosopher?" (253c6–10).

The science in question is called dialectic (253d1–4). Just as political freedom is possible only by obedience to the laws of the polis, so the freedom of the highest human individual is obedience to the "laws" of the combination and separation of the elements within the structure of intelligibility. The philosopher does not make the formal units of this structure or see them by any peculiar cognitive gift that distinguishes him from the nonphilosopher.[1] What distinguishes the two human types is the science or method of dialectic, namely, the determination of the properties and relations of pure forms.

To the extent that dialectic requires conceptual constructions and

1. In the *Sophist*, the Stranger introduces the forms immediately, as directly accessible to us. In the *Republic* (5:476b4ff.), Socrates states that the nonphilosophers are unable to see "beauty itself" and the other Ideas. This inability is enough to show that there is no single, self-consistent, and technically well-articulated theory of Ideas in the Platonic dialogues. For further discussion, see my *Plato's "Sophist"* (New Haven: Yale University Press, 1983).

so discursive presentation in a historical language, it is at least partly artifactual.[2] We need not argue the point here in detail; suffice it to say that the classical dialectic, including the Platonic variety, is at least in part a *making*. Whether the intended independence of the pure forms themselves from the productive activity of cognition holds or not is a question for a different investigation.

The key point for us is that, in the Platonic paradigm of ancient philosophy, beings are antecedent to, as the necessary condition for, freedom. The modern situation, as exemplified by Fichte, is quite the reverse. In the *Zweite Einleitung in die Wissenschaftslehre*, section 7, we read: "Let me on this occasion say it once with complete clarity: the essence of transcendental Idealism in general, and its exposition in the *Wissenschaftslehre* in particular, lies in this, that the concept of Being is not regarded as a *primary* and *original* concept, but merely as a *derived* concept, and indeed derived through opposition of activity, hence thought only as a *negative* concept."[3]

This citation lays the foundation for the key point in my analysis of the modern conception of freedom. Freedom is a negative concept in the sense of a revolution against restriction. As such, it provides no basis for a positive assessment of any product of freedom. These products become the "projects" of what is finally indistinguishable from chaos. In Fichte, of course, this subsequent result is concealed behind the terminology of transcendental or absolute activity. "In general, what is the content of the *Wissenschaftslehre* in two words? This: the *Vernunft* is absolutely independent; it is only for itself. . . ."[4] More generally, "the Ego is originally only an acting" and "every Being signifies a restriction of free activity."[5]

For Fichte, freedom is antecedent to, as the necessary condition for, Being. This is the reverse of Platonism. Like all modern philosophers, Fichte replaces the Platonic doctrine of Eros with a doctrine of passion or desire (in Fichte's terminology, *Streben*). The Platonic Eros is

---

2. The logician's term *natural language* is thus highly misleading. In contrast to a formal calculus, a historical language is natural in the sense that it grows up in use. But it remains an artifact of history, a particular determination of a natural faculty that incorporates technical productions of a given historical people, which productions mediate our sensory and cognitive grasp of beings or things, and hence of our experience.

3. Fichte, *Erste und Zweite Einleitung in die Wissenschaftslehre* (1797; Hamburg: Felix Meiner Verlag, 1954), 85.

4. Ibid., 60.

5. Ibid., 81–82.

directed by the Ideas. Modern desire, and in particular the Fichtean striving, is infinite. (Note that even Heidegger's doctrine of the radical finitude of *Dasein* depends upon an act of limiting resolution: here too, Being is a product of the restriction of freedom.) Not only is Being a limitation of freedom, but the path back to freedom for the thinking being is by a *via negationis* of the determinations of Being.

In a loose sense, the modern philosopher desires self-knowledge, not of himself as empirical and finite self-consciousness, but as what Hegel calls the identity-within-difference of absolute constructive activity and the intelligible structure of construction. That this sense is too loose is apparent from its historical consequence: dissolution of the Absolute into the discontinuous continuum or self-contradiction of historical individualism. That the dissolution was inevitable is suggested by the two major revisions of Kantian dualism by Fichte and Hegel.

In Kant, there is no absolute ego. The transcendental ego possesses neither self-consciousness nor life but is a set of logical rules. In Fichte, the transcendental ego is brought to life as a kind of *deus absconditus*. In Hegel, it is the historical individual who, precisely as free, complete, or reunited with God through the mediation of the concept, disappears. This disappearance is in effect the criticism leveled against Hegel by Schelling and Kierkegaard. It cannot be countered by the brandishing of a logical construction.

But this remark by the way. I asserted that the Fichtean thesis is the reverse of Platonism. Fichte represents the characteristic axiom of the modern epoch: freedom is higher than Being. The peculiarly modern term *ontology* is thus misleading, because its first principle is not Being but freedom. Needless to say, there cannot be a *logos* of freedom, a strictly *negative* concept, whereas a *logos* about Being, which is a restrictive derivative of freedom, becomes a *mythos* or *nomos*, a conventional account of contingency.

Why do modern thinkers value freedom above Being? I do not ask here for a "ground" [*Grund*] of freedom, which, if it were available, would transform freedom into bondage. But one cannot simply counter with the defense that, if Being were prior to freedom, the same disastrous result would follow. The classical position, succinctly stated, is this: there is a discontinuity—between Being in the cosmic or divine sense and in the sense of human nature—that leaves room for freedom, but at the same time a freedom that is regulated, or preserved from chaos, by its two boundaries.

In attempting to formulate the modern position, let me borrow an Aristotelian tripartition for my own purposes. One may give a theoretical, practical, or productive account of the value of freedom. The productive account is that freedom enables us to do as we like, not simply in the sense of satisfying random desires, but in the deeper sense of reconstituting our environment in our own image and thereby becoming masters and possessors of nature. Shortly stated, it enables us to become gods.

The practical account is that freedom, as Kant puts it, is the *ratio essendi* of the moral laws. This is not a theoretical account, because the fact of freedom rests upon the immediate evidence of the moral laws, not upon their ability to be deduced from a higher principle. The moral laws are facts of the conscience or of a rational person's self-respect.[6] Clearly there can be no connection between morality and the exercise of theoretical reason in Kant. The operative sense of rationality is that of obedience in the moral context to rules that can be made universal. An adequate study of the Kantian moral theory would show, I believe, that the paradigm of mathematics underlies Kant's conception of practical reason. For our purposes, the main point is that the ultimate content of rationality is spontaneous self-legislation. One is moral by fulfilling a formal criterion, and this fulfillment is possible because we are free.

Needless to say, the peculiar Kantian doctrine of rationality as capable of being made universal is not necessary to the practical justification of freedom as the highest principle. If anything, it is a hindrance, because freedom is constrained to express itself in lawlike activity. Kant's version of the practical argument, although it is intended to stand apart from theoretical considerations, is marked by an inner tendency to collapse into the characteristic modern theoretical justification of freedom on the principle that we know only what we make.

And indeed, the classical statement of the theoretical defense of freedom as transcendental spontaneity is also to be found in Kant. The world (whether as the object of science or the environment of action) is for Kant not a project but a production of the transcendental ego. In other words, the objects of knowledge, or beings, must conform to conditions set by the categorial and sensory apparatus of the

6. Kant, *Kritik der praktischen Vernunft* (Hamburg: Felix Meiner Verlag, 1952), 4, 33–34, 86–87, 92, 142, 149.

knower in the only relevant case known to us: ourselves. A being, in the sense of an object of theory, must exist *for us*, that is, in accord with conditions codified under the title *transcendental ego*.[7] The pivot of the following pages is to see how a transcendental production becomes a free project.

It is striking to note that, in Kant, there is no productive justification of freedom, as there is in Descartes. This is so because the Cartesian method is essentially one of the replacement of essences or beings as they are in themselves by mathematical constructions that permit us to manipulate our physical environment regardless of whether we understand it as it is in itself or not. The sense of the expression *in itself* is translated to the method, hence, to mathematics (specifically if not exclusively in the form of mathematical physics). But mathematics is in effect a human invention, not the expression of a natural or transcendental order.

Correlatively, there is no distinctively moral justification of freedom in Descartes. In the French Enlightenment generally, it is taken for granted that moral and political problems will tend to disappear as our scientific and theoretical knowledge grows. For this reason, there is no restriction placed upon technology in this branch of the modern tradition. Politics and morals require "provisional" attention, in Descartes's expression. The following passage from d'Alembert may be taken as paradigmatic: "Of the four great objects which we have just presented to our readers, and which constitute the important matter of the *Encyclopédie*, there is none that is able to enlighten us equally, and which as a consequence is more worthy to be transmitted to our descendants, than the tableau of our real knowledge; this is the history of the human spirit; the rest is nothing but romance or satire."[8]

By "real knowledge," d'Alembert means the mathematical and empirical sciences and their technological applications. Kant's view is quite different. As is already explicit in the *First Critique*, answers to questions about the origin of the world and human freedom would be worth more than all of mathematics, which "cannot give satisfaction with respect to the highest and most important ends of mankind" (B492). In general, Kant uses the term *satisfaction* (*Befriedigung*), so im-

7. This point is introduced into the *Kritik der reinen Vernunft* at Bxvi.
8. *Essai sur les élémens de philosophie*, in *Oeuvres de d'Alembert*, vol. 1, pt. 1 (Geneva: Slatkine Reprints, 1967), 125.

portant in Hegel, not in conjunction with the productive desire to master nature, but in conjunction with practical or moral and theoretical desires.[9]

One must of course distinguish carefully the doctrines of the major thinkers in the series of German philosophers from Kant to Hegel. Nevertheless, it is fair to say that all of them pay more attention to morality, if not to politics, than do their French predecessors or their nineteenth- and twentieth-century successors (of all nationalities) in the modern celebration of freedom. Mathematics on the one hand and historicity on the other, despite their apparent incompatibility, seem to function alike in turning our attention away from simple decency toward ontology.

In this context, Fichte is of special interest, because he attempts to radicalize the conception of human freedom on the basis of an interpretation of Kantian spontaneity. Despite the extreme difficulty of his terminology, Fichte is in the crucial sense a much simpler and more straightforward thinker than Kant. Fichte removes a fundamental ambiguity in Kant by making the transcendental machinery of world-construction a straightforward consequence of the spontaneous activity of the Absolute. This transformation holds good throughout the various shifts in Fichte's development, of which the most important is probably that marked by the *Wissenschaftslehre* of 1804.

The continuity in Fichte's thought is expressed as follows. Whether Fichte speaks of the activity of an absolute ego or of the light radiating from a hidden god, it remains true that the origin (*Urgrund*) of world-constitution is intellectually or discursively inaccessible. For this reason there cannot be a Fichtean ontology: What the early Heidegger calls the hiddenness (*Verborgenheit*) of Being is in Fichte permanent, although of course it is not Being that is for Fichte concealed or inaccessible. As a result, freedom is absolute, which is to say that it is effectively an ungrounded first principle. In Fichte, there is no transcendental restriction on spontaneity.

The complex career of freedom in the modern epoch can be summarized as follows. From Descartes to Hegel, freedom assumes ever more explicitly the status of first principle. Nevertheless, freedom is not justified for itself alone, but for what it makes possible: its

---

9. E.g., Kant, *Kritik der reinen Vernunft* B701, B786ff., B884, and the final sentence of the work.

theoretical, practical, or productive consequences. After Hegel, freedom evolves into a self-justifying principle; accordingly, the previous hierarchical character of the consequences of freedom dissolves. One consequence is as spontaneous as the next, hence no better and no worse. Everything is allowed; freedom and nihilism coincide. This coincidence is the last result of the replacement of Eros by desire.

What appears spontaneously may disappear spontaneously. The notion of necessity thus becomes a pseudonym for contingency. The claim that morality depends upon freedom alone, or upon radical (absolute) freedom, in fact makes morality arbitrary. Kant was clearly aware of this problem; hence his insistence that freedom must manifest itself in a regular, law-abiding fashion. For Kant, freedom is the spontaneous order produced by the necessary regulations of the transcendental ego. It is therefore grounded neither in the decrees of God nor in the eternal or independent structure of nature.[10]

To this, I must object that a spontaneous order is regulated by the transcendental ego if and only if the transcendental ego is itself not spontaneous, that is, if the transcendental ego is self-grounding. In the first place, it is not evident how this self-grounding could be maintained. What Kant calls the necessary conditions for thinking a world of the sort in which we live, given that we are creatures of the sort that we are, are far too contingent to be entirely self-certifying. There could be some other way of analyzing the conditions upon which our conception of the present world depends. To summarize a long question, it is in no way evident that Kant's transcendental ego is independent of the actual state of knowledge about perception and thinking in his own time. Second, Kant himself never succeeds in extracting his doctrine of the transcendental ego from a web of hypotheses that we are apparently free to reject.

It is important to notice that the freedom to accept or to reject Kant's critical philosophy is not the same as the spontaneity of *Vernunft* within the critical philosophy. Neither is it the same as the moral freedom whose possibility Kant offers as a temptation to accept his teaching. Whereas Kant's comprehensive hypothesis (traditionally summarized as "the Copernican revolution," a phrase not used by Kant himself) is not spontaneous in the sense of being completely arbitrary, as it addresses genuine dilemmas to which resolutions are

10. I discuss this point at some length in chap. 1 of my *Hermeneutics as Politics* (New York: Oxford University Press, 1987).

eminently desirable, it is nevertheless a theoretical construction, very much like those of modern physics. And theoretical constructions are temporary palliatives, not a priori foundations.

Fichte, to repeat, simplifies this complex situation in one bold stroke: The pure ego poses itself absolutely by an absolutely free act. However, another Kantian complication is retained in the Fichtean doctrine: The aforementioned act is also necessary because it acts in a necessary manner. This simultaneity of free act and necessary manner of enactment holds good at every level of world-constitution, and so too in the process by which the ego reverses or (dare we say) deconstructs world-constitution in order to arrive at the Absolute. As Martial Gueroult puts the point, the ego is obliged to act freely. This free activity is thus, for it, necessity. The progress of human liberty is founded on the constitutive necessities of the human spirit.[11]

We see here the transition from Kant to Hegel: Logic is transformed into dialectic and the concept is spiritualized. For us, the more fundamental point is that Fichte makes explicit the problematic relation between freedom and necessity within spontaneity. This problem is easy to state. If freedom cannot fail in its task—if the stages by which freedom unfolds in the development of the ego are necessary—how is the ego free?

As Gueroult points out, Fichte distinguishes between the absolute and the individual ego. Each individual ego is free to choose between his private affirmation and interaction with other individual persons in society. The second choice brings the individual ego into "the concert of the artisans of the world of freedom," who work for the community of consciousness, the realization of absolute universal spontaneity, or the coming of the kingdom of God. By choosing private affirmation, the ego falls back into nature and its necessity. In this case some other ego will act in accord with the progress toward absolute freedom. The influences of my actions on others are predetermined, but it is not predetermined that I will perform those acts.[12]

The reader will recognize in this summary an anticipation of Hegel's phenomenology and philosophy of history. He will also perceive the shortcomings of Fichte's dialectic. What does it mean to say that the absolute ego acts freely? Fichte does not intend to grant to the Abso-

---

11. Martial Gueroult, "La *Wissenschaftslehre* comme système nécessaire de la liberté," in *Etudes sur Fichte* (New York: Olms Verlag/Hildesheim, 1974), 1–16.
12. Ibid., 11–13.

lute the possibility of not existing or of existing in some form other than that of the ego. Instead, he grants to the potential philosopher the freedom to return from his individuality to the pure or absolute ego by an act of intellectual intuition and thereby to construct (by a kind of productive version of Platonic recollection) the concept of the ego which, as the Absolute, is fully developed within eternity.[13]

Nevertheless, Fichte holds regularly that such activity, that is, the activity of the absolute ego and hence of the transitions from one stage of consciousness to the next, is completely spontaneous.[14] To take what many regard as Fichte's pivotal text, the *Wissenschaftslehre* of 1804, Fichte refers to the activity of the Absolute as a *"projectio per hiatum"* (218), a creation *ex nihilo*, which we can study in its effects but not in itself (that is, not as absolute self-construction, the process described by Hegel in the *Wissenschaft der Logik*). Our *Vernunft* is the *Urerscheinung* of inaccessible light, which is inaccessible rationally or as this or that visible thing (245, 257–61).

Spontaneity is, so to speak, absolutized, but with the net result that vision of the Absolute is equivalent to the self-negation of vision (296). Absolute activity is the activity of God (223) and is effectively spontaneous because it is not conceptually explicable, and not even intuitable, except as pure constructive activity (250–51). As present in man in the form of *Vernunft*, the Absolute externalizes itself but is hidden within itself qua externalization: "Thus reason points itself out as freely externalizing itself; freedom appears, is in fact the law and inner essence" (307). Freedom is the law of spontaneity.

I repeat: freedom appears as law: This is Kant's point about spontaneity, which must manifest itself in a lawlike way or else be indistinguishable from chaos. For my purposes, the further question of how the absolute ego can be both absolute and restricted by an entirely external negation is not central. Instead, I must emphasize the obscure

13. *Zweite Einleitung*, 43–46; *Grundlegung der gesamten Wissenschaftslehre* (Hamburg: Felix Meiner Verlag, 1961), 67ff., 77f.; *Die Wissenschaftslehre. Vorgetragen im Jahre 1804*, in *Fichtes Werke* (Berlin, Walter de Gruyter: 1971), 10:90–93: the essence of philosophy is "Alles Mannigfaltige . . . zurückzuführen auf absolute Einheit. . . ." And "das blosse Auffassen des Mannigfaltigen als solchen, an seinem Faktischen ist Historie." *Darstellung des Wissenschaftslehre* (1801), in *Fichtes Werke* (Berlin: Walter de Gruyter, 1971), 2:12: the intuition of the constituting knowledge of our rational nature yields a "Verklären dessen, was da ewig war, und ewig *wir selbst* war."

14. *Wissenschaftslehre* (1794), [hereafter WL], 80; *Wissenschaftslehre nova methodo. Kollegnachschrift K. C. F. Krause* (1798–99; Hamburg: Felix Meiner Verlag, 1982), 98, 169.

consequence that what appears as freedom is in fact necessity (as in Spinoza). This is true at the empirical level, because the structure of the historical person is absolute and predetermined. And it is true at the absolute level, since to be absolute means both to be spontaneous and also to act in an eternal and necessary way.

As Fichte says in the *Wissenschaftslehre nova methodo*, "Freedom allows itself to be described only *negatively* through: not to be defined" (213). Freedom, as we saw previously, is a negative concept. Its ground is inaccessible; hence it is effectively ungrounded. And therefore it cannot finally be distinguished from a primordial chaos in the manner of Nietzsche. Fichte's necessary stages of the enactment of freedom are intrinsically unable to resist being converted into historical perspectives.

However one looks at the matter, German philosophy seems to have been unsuccessful in its attempt to reconcile a structured freedom with infinite striving (Fichte's *Streben*), the Idealist version of the infinite desire of British empiricism. At this point, a brief contrast with Locke is instructive. For Locke, human life is perpetual dissatisfaction.[15] It is the eternal striving for pleasure, or the alienation of man from himself, thanks to the very appetites that drive him to work or (whether in an empirical or transcendental sense) to produce the intelligible world.

Fichtean striving is ostensibly structured by the Absolute. In Locke, there is no Absolute, not even an effective sense of substance. A cynic might say that Locke is free of the hypocritical hypotheses of German critical and Idealist philosophy. However one evaluates it, there can be no doubt that the central difficulty of modern philosophy is much plainer in Locke than in Kant and his immediate successors.

For Locke, thinking is reflection; in the Idealist interpretation, it is the separation of consciousness into the subject-object relation so that the ego projects itself into the world as concealed by the determinations of the finite product of its activity. In Locke's own account, the situation is more straightforward than in Idealism, but not radically different. Thinking consists of ideas, sensations, images, or in other words of the product of consciousness, not of the ego as conscious of itself as substance. Thus personal identity rests in the last instance upon agreement, that is, upon my accepting my memory of the past

---

15. Locke, *An Essay Concerning Human Understanding*, ed. A. C. Fraser (1891; reprint, New York: Dover Publications, 1959), 2:162, 304.

as *my* past.[16] I am conscious, Locke says, by perceiving that I perceive; but in the act of perception, *what* I perceive is this or that sensation, idea, and so on.[17]

For the Idealist, the separation or alienation of reflection is ostensibly overcome by intellectual intuition. In this case, the finite ego effectively disappears. Or else, from a practical standpoint, the labors of reflection are rendered obedient to the categorical imperative, the command to strive for the infinite or to understand human life as an expression of the absolute spontaneity of the activity that actualizes in the opposition of subject and object.[18]

In this case, the Absolute becomes a project or hypothesis that can never be fulfilled; we are left with finite empirical activity that motivates itself or exhibits a historical spontaneity to which a salutary but finally empty interpretation is given. The Absolute becomes the ideal completion of history, accessible only in a dream. As such, it is easily jettisoned by those hardheaded thinkers who seek to awaken the human race to the realities of scientific mastery of nature. The Absolute deteriorates first into the (Hegelian) end of history, then into the ideal of scientific progress, and finally into mere flux: mere *differance*.

Locke distinguishes between wit, which collects ideas quickly and variously for pleasure ("to make up pleasant pictures and agreeable visions in the fancy"), and judgment, which separates ideas "wherein can be found the least difference, thereby to avoid being misled by similitude."[19] He thereby in effect dissolves Platonic dialectic, which includes both division and collection; and the Kantian combination of synthesis and analysis.

Similarly, Locke replaces the Platonic Eros with uneasiness: "The chief, if not only, spur to human industry and action is *uneasiness*."[20] Uneasiness is inseparable from desire. It has no ultimate goal but only its immediate dissatisfaction with whatever is at hand. Eros provides significance to this world (contrary to Nietzsche's critique of Platonism) by directing us toward a higher world. Uneasiness robs

16. The first point follows directly from Locke's repeated assertion that thinking is the activity, not the essence, of the soul or mind. Locke, *Essay*, 1:128, 183, 301. For personal identity, see 1:460.

17. Ibid., 1:448ff.

18. *WL* (1794), 214ff., 226.

19. Locke, *Essay*, 1:203.

20. Ibid., 304.

this world of its significance but does not supply another source, higher or lower, of value. In this respect, uneasiness is a prototype of Nietzsche's will to power, which has received excessive and misplaced praise as the engine of creativity but which is in fact rooted in chaos.

Separation and uneasiness: these are the essential attributes of British empiricism. Like Kant before him, Fichte attempts to overcome their disastrous consequences. But he is unable to surmount the Kantian dualism that makes synthesis and morality literally unintelligible and so preserves them at the level of arbitrary hypothesis. The moral transformation of uneasiness is on the one hand determined by "absolute" necessity and so cannot be moral. On the other hand, its fulfillment remains the object of a command, the categorical imperative. The fulfillment of this command lies always just on the other side of historical striving, which can find no ease in this world. As to judgment or conceptual thinking, it is for Fichte separation, exactly as for Locke: "I am originally neither the reflecting nor the reflected, and neither is defined by the other, but I am *both in their unification*, which unification I cannot indeed think, precisely because in thinking, I separate the reflected and the reflecting."[21]

The Fichtean distinction between the activity of the ego and the observation by the philosopher of this activity, or between infinite and finite activity (which can be unified only in the conceptually vacuous intellectual intuition), amounts to this.[22] Philosophical activity begins from the spontaneous constitution of the ego on the two levels of the Absolute and the finite. At the finite level this spontaneity is the free choice of the thinker, who rises to the self-constituting level of conscious activity through an intuition of the essential unity of the structure of his own self-consciousness with the categorial or lawlike structure of the absolute ego.

At this point, the thinker must proceed to the task of reconstituting the unity of the two egos in conceptual terms by analysis (separation). This task can never be completed, because analysis separates the finite ego from the Absolute. There is thus a subterranean connection between Fichte and twentieth-century analytic philosophy that is already implicit in our comparison of Fichte and Locke. In Kant, with

21. *Zweite Einleitung*, 76.
22. Ibid., 40. Cf. the distinction between *Ansicht* and *Einsicht* in WL (1804), 191, and *WL nova methodo*, 9f.

whom historically informed analytical philosophers normally associate themselves, the transcendental structure or context of analysis is synthetic and is known with certainty. In Fichte, the categorial structure of analysis, as accessible to reason, is itself a consequence of analysis. Knowledge of this categorial structure is a product of absolute spontaneity, which is not accessible to reason but only to intellectual intuition.

In sum: For Fichte, absolute constitution is spontaneous or free, whereas rational analysis is necessary. Philosophy is thus the necessary articulation of spontaneity. If I am free, I know nothing—strictly speaking, not even myself. If I have mastered Fichte's *Wissenschaftslehre* and hence know the categorial structure of the world as a product of the spontaneity of the absolute ego, I am, as this finite knower, not free. But this is to say that I do not know the one thing needful.

Nor can I know it, because the ostensible necessity of the categorial structure itself is guaranteed by the unknowable absoluteness of the originary, all-constituting Absolute. In order to account for self-consciousness, man must lose self-consciousness. As self-conscious, man remains in the domain not of *Wissen* but of *Glauben* which, exactly as in Kant, is rooted in "the exhibition of the moral law within us." [23] (Fichte is referring here to the justification of the possibility of intellectual intuition.)

In Kant's official system, freedom is practical, not theoretical. In Fichte, freedom is transcendental or ontologically grounding but in a way that combines production with practice. This follows from Fichte's conception of the ground as pure activity. Whether this ground is the immediate act of self-position or the production of the world by a hidden god, it is in itself inaccessible to conceptual thinking.[24] As a result, we cannot know the ground as a limitation upon the freedom it establishes.

The world and the finite ego are a free production of spontaneity in two senses. First, the *Urgrund* is spontaneous because subject to no determinations of any kind. Second, the world-process that emerges from an indeterminate ground has no conceptually determinable origin. From a rationalist standpoint (and on this score, Hegel is a rationalist), this double spontaneity is a defect precisely because it makes conceptual knowledge of the first and last things impossible. Freedom

---

23. *Zweite Einleitung*, 52.
24. See W. Janke, *Fichte* (Berlin: Walter de Gruyter, 1970), x–xi.

becomes a matter of faith. When faith is lost, the elaborate articulation of the necessary structure of creation is reduced to contingency upon man's will.

In the Fichtean formulation, the inaccessibility of productive activity leaves the product free, whereas the simultaneity of the two allows the product to stand surrogate for the activity with respect to cognitive analysis. I will call the relation between production and product an identity-within-difference. Hegel insists upon a conceptual description of that grounding activity. However, he purchases it at the price of freedom, which is now indistinguishable from the necessity of the concept.

Fichte retains freedom. I would go farther and say that he introduces the notion of *ontological freedom* (the ungrounded ground). However, he purchases it at the price of rationality. Fichte is thus paradigmatic for the nineteenth- and twentieth-century doctrines of freedom as pure spontaneous activity, and so for the overcoming of traditional rationalism.[25] This overcoming is implicit in Positivism, which starts with the given or phenomenal. It is explicit in the contemporary rejection of the given as a myth or theoretical construction and so not as the product of rationality but rather of history, hence of chance, or of how things happen to appear to an antecedent generation. I will call this historical phenomenalism.

There is another way to state Fichte's importance for twentieth-century philosophy. Whereas Kant replaces classical substance, nature, and form by the transcendental or by logical possibility, Fichte makes activity central. Kant's ego, for example, "appears . . . only as determined," whereas the ego is for Fichte apparent "as determining."[26] Intellectual intuition, *Vernunft*, the self-positing of the ego: All are activity.[27] "Only activity is absolute."[28]

Conversely, "every Being signifies a limitation of free activity."[29] In the terminology of the later doctrine (1804), there is only one absolute

---

25. "Soll das absolut Unbegreifliche, als allein für sich bestehend, einleuchten, so muss der Begriff vernichtet, und damit er vernichtet werden könne, gesetzt werden; denn nur an der Vernichtung des Begriffes leuchtet das Unbegreifliches ein." *WL* (1804), 117ff.

26. *WL nova methodo*, 41.

27. Ibid., 47, 98; *Zweite Einleitung*, 102: Intuition is "das in such zurückgehenden Handeln."

28. *WL nova methodo*, 61.

29. *Zweite Einleitung*, 82. At a deeper level, of course, *Sein* is intrinsically (for the philosopher) a *Handlung* (85).

principle; the manifold "is to be derived purely from the reciprocal activity of the light with itself."[30] At the human level, "there is within me a drive to absolute, independent self-activity."[31] In the 1794 *Wissenschaftslehre*, this activity is called "infinite striving," the activity of the absolute ego.[32] In sum: not only human being, but Being and, in the ultimate sense, the Absolute, are all activity: process, not fixed structure.

It would not be going far enough to say that for Fichte, man makes himself. This at least implies a limit to or completion of the process. In Fichte there is no limit to activity; even an intuition of the identity-within-difference of the producer and the product is an intuition of pure activity rather than of a finished structure. In Kant, there is infinite progress in the phenomenal sciences, but the transcendental structure of man and world is always (a priori) complete. In Fichte, this last completeness is itself phenomenal. Completeness is conceptual or empirical vacuousness.

For all practical purposes, life for the Fichtean Idealist is the same as for the Lockean empiricist: infinite striving, infinite activity toward an infinitely distant goal, hence one that will soon be shifted from the absolute to the historical level and finally abolished altogether, like substance before it. In this way the attempt to inject moral stability into human practice results finally in the emptying of significance from practice. Pure activity, in the absence of the Absolute, is pure vacuousness. Activity deteriorates into chaos (the dissolution of identity into difference, as initiated by Nietzsche).

The ontological primacy of activity is a direct consequence of the attempt to overcome dualism by the aforementioned identity of substance and subject. This identification has a long history, stretching back to Christian Neoplatonism.[33] The underlying motivation may perhaps be formulated as follows: life cannot be derived conceptually from what is not alive. The problem is then how to unify the living and the nonliving without reducing the one to the other. This is the philosophical version of the theological attempt to conceive of God as

---

30. *WL* (1804), 119.

31. Fichte, *Die Bestimmung des Menschen* (1800; reprint, Hamburg: Felix Meiner Verlag, 1962), 85.

32. *WL* (1794), 179, 188. Note that this cannot be known in itself, but only via reflection, that is, via the objects that limit it (187).

33. Still worth reading on this topic: Gerhard Huber, *Das Sein und das Absolute* (Basel: Verlag für Recht und Gesellschaft AG, 1955).

accessible to human intelligence but without assimilating Him to the world. *Activity* seems to be a middle term between God or the Absolute, the principle of life, and Being, or the products of the divine activity.

Fichte's doctrine of intellectual intuition is the ostensible explanation of how we grasp pure activity, the point of union between agent and product. Because pure activity is said to be completely spontaneous, this intuition unifies the finite ego with the ungrounded constitution-process of the world but not with the Absolute as ground of that process.[34] There is no first principle of a deduction of the structure of activity. This structure is deduced from spontaneity. The deduction is thus an optical illusion or, if you prefer, a hypothesis.

Whether or not we regard the doctrine of intellectual intuition as plausible, there can be no doubt of its recalcitrance to discursive analysis or description. This is obvious enough from Fichte's continuous attempts to explain himself. And how could it be otherwise, because intuition unites, whereas description analyzes or separates (unless, of course, one reverts to Platonic myth and gives up the notion of philosophy of *Wissenschaft*).

The fact is that in pure intuition there is no structure to describe or to explain. There can accordingly be no correct or coherent analysis of the structure of self-consciousness, a topic on which much ink has been spilled by Fichte specialists, to say nothing of contemporary analytical philosophers. There is nothing but the act of unification with the Absolute.[35] So-called analyses of activity are in fact analyses of the products of activity. What is required is not logical analysis but experience.

Freedom and self-consciousness unite in spontaneity. When all is said and done, the primacy of spontaneity disconnects absolute activity from a principle of intelligibility. Not only is there no deduction of the categories from a single principle; there is no formulatable principle. What we seem to learn from Fichte is that the concept of radical or ontological freedom is a pseudoconcept. Surely there is an important lesson here for those who talk endlessly of liberating human thought from the reifying limitations of Platonism.

34. *WL* (1794), 80.
35. *WL* (1794), 214f.

CHAPTER FIVE

Sōphrosynē *and* Selbstbewusstsein

The importance of Greek thought for the Hegelian science of wisdom has long been acknowledged. Nevertheless, if one considers the extraordinary increase in Hegel scholarship during the past two decades, it is somewhat surprising how few technical studies have been devoted to the connection between Hegel and the Greeks.[1] The relative lack of attention to the details of this connection is in my opinion the most important reason for a certain imbalance in favor of Hegel's religious thought that one may notice in the recent literature. This is especially true in the case of the crucial theme of self-consciousness.[2] It is not so difficult to establish the classical antecedents of Hegel's analyses in the domains of logic, ontology, and epistemology. The case of self-consciousness is at first glance quite different. One might be tempted to say that the general problem of subjectivity is modern rather than ancient, Christian rather than pagan. Whereas Hegel's teaching depends upon the assimilation of Aristotelian noetics, it could seem that Hegel reads Aristotle from the outset in the perspective of Christian Neoplatonism. Does not Hegel violate the pagan

This essay first appeared in the *Review of Metaphysics*, June 1973.

1. Of the older studies, I mention only W. Purpus, *Zur Dialektik des Bewusstseins* (Berlin: Trowitsch & Sohn, 1908). One of the best technical analyses of Hegel's logic, P. Rohs, *Form und Grund*, in *Hegel-Studien*, vol. 6 (Bonn: H. Bouvier, 1969), emphasizes the Greek elements in Hegel's thought. Cf. also H. G. Gadamer, *Hegels Dialektik* (Tübingen: Mohr-Siebeck, 1971). F. Kümmel, *Platon und Hegel* (Tübingen: Max Niemeyer, 1968), is disappointing but useful and a step in the right direction. A. Kojève's posthumous *Essai d'une histoire raisonnée de la philosophie païenne* (Paris: Gallimard, 1968–73) is in many ways the most extraordinary contribution to the subject but, like his lectures on the *Phänomenologie*, must be used with great caution. A good article: R. Wiehl, "Platos Ontologie in Hegels Logik des Seins" in *Hegel-Studien*, vol. 3 (1965). Although primarily concerned with the Neoplatonist period and after, G. Huber's *Das Sein und das Absolute* (Basel: Verlag für Recht und Gesellschaft AG, 1955) should certainly be mentioned. Heidegger's essays on Hegel are also required reading for the serious student.

2. For a more general discussion, see my article, "Self-Consciousness and Self-Knowledge in Plato and Hegel," *Hegel-Studien* (Bonn: Bouvier Verlag, 1974) 9:109–29.

teaching by importing the dimension of self-consciousness into the *noēsis tēs noēseōs?*

If I am not mistaken, these doubts, although obviously not al-together unjustified, are given illicit support for two reasons. The first has to do with our failure to distinguish clearly between self-consciousness and self-knowledge as a fundamental dualism in the Platonic dialogues. Once we immerse ourselves in the details of the Platonic account, it will become evident that the situation in Plato is essentially the same as that to be found in Fichte, who is the most important of Hegel's predecessors on this issue (and all the more be-cause Hegel fails to distinguish carefully between Kant and Fichte),[3] and who provides Hegel with the conditions for his own account of self-consciousness. In the language of Fichte and Hegel, the Pla-tonic doctrine of discursive thinking (*dianoia*) is fundamentally that of *reflection*, or (stated with maximum brevity) the process by which mind, soul, or spirit separates itself from itself through the objectify-ing activity of cognition. Fichte attempts to overcome this separation by recourse to intellectual intuition. Plato's *intuition* (*noēsis*) is not ade-quate to this task because it consists in the apprehension of determi-nate form and is thus the very principle of objectivity. Instead, Plato turns to poetic notions such as Eros, recollection, and divine mad-ness. More generally, he gives a mythical account of the phenomenon of self-consciousness but never a logical or scientific explanation. The Platonic dialogues are then the source of the problem of reflection, or in Hegel's terminology, of the alienation of Spirit. This in itself guar-antees the importance of Plato for the study of Hegel. But it can also be shown that Plato's own efforts to overcome the "alienation of sub-ject and object" are in certain important respects anticipations of the Hegelian solution. One must be careful not to minimize the difference between Plato and Hegel. Nevertheless, the difference is dialectical in the Hegelian sense. What is for Plato an aporia provides Hegel with the ingredients essential for the transformation of Christian subjec-tivity into Absolute Spirit.

The second obstacle to an adequate understanding of Hegel's rela-tion to Plato is his explicit discussion of the Platonic teaching. This discussion is neither precise nor self-consistent.[4] Even when Hegel

3. This point has been frequently discussed by recent authors. I mention in passing the work of H. Girndt, D. Henrich, I. Görland, W. Janke, and L. Siep *inter alia*.
4. The most important example concerns the Platonic Ideas. Hegel tends to interpret

praises Plato, he is careful to emphasize his limitations, especially in the case of subjectivity.[5] If we restrict ourselves to Hegel's explicit references to Plato, there is little reason to claim a detailed influence of Plato upon Hegel in the case of subjectivity or self-consciousness. In my opinion, however, it would be a serious mistake to restrict ourselves in this manner. Plato is not the only thinker whom Hegel assimilates without detailed acknowledgment. The moment we remember the identity claimed by Hegel between the history of philosophy and the logical development of the concept of the Idea, we are forced to recognize the presence of all of Hegel's world-historical predecessors in the science of wisdom.[6] It then becomes a task for genetic as well as conceptual analysis to recover the contributions made by his predecessors to Hegel's teaching. For non-Hegelian as well as Hegelian reasons, we would be naive to restrict ourselves in this study to Hegel's remarks in his persona as professorial lecturer on the history of philosophy.

With these preliminary considerations in mind, let us turn to the Platonic evidence. I shall be concerned fundamentally (but not exclusively) with two related themes. (1) The Platonic distinction between self-consciousness and self-knowledge leads toward an effort to locate self-knowledge in conjunction with *sōphrosynē,* usually translated as *temperance* or *moderation.* This translation is far from adequate; we should bear in mind the connection between *sōphrosynē* and *phronēsis* or *shrewdness, practical intelligence.* There is a conflict in Plato between theoretical or epistemic and practical wisdom that is the prototype of the separation between theory and practice discerned by Hegel in Kant and Fichte. The greatest part of my essay will be concerned with

---

the Ideas in a Neoplatonist manner. Cf. *Wissenschaft der Logik* (Leipzig: Felix Meiner Verlag, 1951) 1:31; *Vorlesungen über die Geschichte der Philosophie,* in *Sämtliche Werke,* ed. H. Glockner (Stuttgart: F. Frommanns Verlag, 1959), 18:199, 218 (*Sämtliche Werke* is hereafter cited as *SW*). According to Hegel, the Ideas, although outside the world of actuality, are accessible within the thinking of God. Hence they are not a *Jenseits,* but true determinate universals produced by thought. However, even if the Ideas do not constitute a *Jenseits* in the full sense, they remain potentialities or thoughts of a God who is himself a *Jenseits,* since the Hegelian reconciliation has not yet been reached. Cf. the essay by H. G. Gadamer, "Hegel und die antike Dialektik," in *Hegels Dialektik.*

5. Cf. *Vorlesungen über die Geschichte der Philosophie, SW* 18:269ff., and *Enzyklopädie der philosophischen Wissenschaften,* ed. Nicolin and Pöggeler (1830; Hamburg: Felix Meiner Verlag, 1969), par. 552, pp. 436ff.

6. *Einleitung in die Geschichte der Philosophie,* ed. Hoffmeister and Nicolin (Hamburg: Felix Meiner Verlag, 1959), 34 (from the Berlin lectures of 1820).

this theme, and evidence will be drawn primarily from the *Republic* and *Charmides*. (2) The Platonic doctrine of Eros anticipates in important ways at least that aspect of Hegel's Absolute Spirit which we may call *negative work* or *negative excitation*.[7] However, Plato lacked a logical analysis of negation adequate to the task of uniting *sōphrosynē* and Eros in a self-conscious *Geist*. His teaching therefore remains at the level of reflection or alienation.

In early Greek literature, words or phrases expressing the idea of consciousness are extremely rare.[8] It is worth noting that consciousness or self-reflection is associated with guilt or something like conscience at least as early as Euripides.[9] Similarly, we find in Homer an initial reference to *dialegesthai* the ancestor of *dialectic*, in the sense of debating with oneself about the need to come to a decision because of consciousness of a moral dilemma.[10] These two points are

7. For a convenient summary of Hegel's doctrine of *Selbstbewusstsein*, cf. *Enzyklopädie*, par. 424ff. Hegel explains the origin of self-consciousness phenomenologically in terms of the initial encounter between two non-self-conscious (i.e., merely conscious) individuals who recognize each other, and so themselves, in the contradiction of their desire for a common object. The first step in this process is the negation of consciousness (the ego is negated or limited by the independence or externality of the other). The second step, marked by the submission of the other, or the assimilation of objectified, externalized desire, is the "negation of the negation." According to Hegel's logic, the negation of the negation preserves rather than cancels the element initially negated. The other (the slave) is preserved within the consciousness of the ego (the master); the dialectic of master-slave thus defines the intersubjective structure of self-consciousness. The master-slave dialectic fulfills itself or is *aufgehoben* within the rational state: hence the overcoming of alienation and the previous separation between theory and practice. Impulse and desire are thus the human forms of the logical excitation of negativity, the engine that drives the development of *Geist* toward wisdom or absolute self-knowledge. Hegel's "negative work" achieves its goal as the Platonic Eros cannot. Cf. *Phänomenologie des Geistes* (Hamburg: Felix Meiner Verlag, 1952), 20, 141ff., 217ff., 378; *Wissenschaft der Logik*, 1:35ff.; 2:472–73, 499. The definitive discussion of negative excitation as a logical process is to be found in the *Logik*, vol. 2, part 1. This discussion is the core of Hegel's analysis of reflection.
8. Cf. H. R. Schwyzer, " 'Bewusst' und 'unbewusst' bei Plotin," in *Les Sources de Plotin*, Hardt Foundation (Geneva: Vandoeuvres, 1960), 5:350ff.
9. Ibid., p. 350. The reference is to *synesis* in *Orestes* 396. Needless to say, the conscience in question is not Christian, but more a "talking with oneself."
10. *Iliad* A, 407: *alla tiē moi tauta philos dieleksato thumos?* Odysseus is debating which is the greater evil: to flee like a coward or to be caught alone in a battle with a crowd. Cited in L. Sichirollo, *Διαλέγεσθαι—Dialektik* (Hildesheim: G. Olms, 1966), 25.

of special interest because the first philosophical discussion of what looks like the problem of self-consciousness, in the Platonic dialogue *Charmides,* arises in conjunction with the nature of *sōphrosynē* as the connection between virtue and knowledge. In fact, Socrates' discussion has to do explicitly with self-knowledge and implicitly with the difference between self-consciousness and self-knowledge. This difference becomes visible within an ethical or political context. According to Hegel, the struggle for recognition between two egos makes self-consciousness manifest.[11] This struggle is not initially political but expresses the intentionality of spirit as desire. We see here Hegel's assimilation of doctrines associated with Descartes and Hobbes. The passions of the soul reveal themselves in a prepolitical state of nature but in such a way as to establish intersubjectivity and thereby to raise man from selfish desire to the level of ethical and political experience. Hegel's account, needless to say, should not be taken in a merely chronological sense, any more than the Hobbesian doctrine of the state of nature should be taken that way. There is an important similarity between the Hegelian and the Platonic teaching here. The origin of self-consciousness is for Hegel not presented within a political context. The same is true for Plato in the sense that we choose or receive from the gods, prior to incarnation or entrance into political life, the kind of life we will subsequently live.[12] In the language of myth, this choice or reception would be impossible if we were not already self-conscious. However, the mythical language also suggests that no logical explanation of self-consciousness is possible. In Plato, mythical or religious language is already political or closely connected with political experience: Man first becomes a problem to himself within the polis. The origin or *archē* of the problem is transpolitical, but the horizon of its visibility and the discourse in which it may be articulated are political.[13]

The Platonic separation of self-consciousness as a phenomenon from its *archē* constitutes in Hegelian terminology the alienation of

11. See note 7.

12. See *Republic* 10:617e4–5. In the myth of Er, the prophet says that responsibility for choosing a new life is the chooser's: *theos anaitios. Phaedrus* 248e5–49a5.

13. According to Socrates, the soul cannot see itself directly but only as reflected in another soul. See *Alcibiades* 1:132c–33b11. This dialogue contains the Socratic version of the master-slave dialectic. In order to gratify our fundamentally tyrannical desire (represented by young Alcibiades), we must see or know ourselves. But this takes place only within a political context.

man.[14] At the same time, Plato attempts to overcome, or at least to mitigate, the negative consequences of this alienation by recourse to *sōphrosynē*. Self-knowledge in the strict sense of *epistēmē* is impossible. But the attempt to develop a conception of self-knowledge in the sense of practical intelligence perpetuates the separation between theory and practice and leads to a radical ambiguity with respect to the unity of man. It will be convenient to begin my analysis of the Platonic situation with a brief inspection of passages from the *Republic*. I note first the obvious connection between the *Republic* and the *Charmides*. In the *Charmides*, Socrates critizes a definition of *sōphrosynē* (which in this dialogue may be translated as *temperance*, with the previous qualifications in mind), which is his own definition of justice in the *Republic*: "minding one's own business."[15] The contradiction points to the following central issue. The just city is possible only by an injustice to philosophers (to say nothing here of the nonphilosophers over the age of ten); they must turn away from their own business to attend to the business of the nonphilosophers. In addition to the ambiguity concerning the difference between justice and temperance, there is evidently a difference between philosophical and nonphilosophical justice or virtue. The self-consciousness of the philosophers, even though it arises in a political context, is at odds with political existence.

It is impossible to mind one's own business unless one knows what is one's own: One must possess self-knowledge. The only truly just

14. See *Republic* 6:519a1–b5. The difference between the vision of shrewd but evil men and that of the virtuous philosophers is described in terms of a turning around of the soul's vision toward true beings. This turn is inward in the sense of noetic intuition of Ideas. It is obviously related to the turning around of the released prisoner in the cave at 515c7. Only those can turn around who are capable of turning or looking inward. Again, self-consciousness is connected with virtue and arises in a political context.

15. *Republic* 4:433a3–7; *Charmides* 161b6. M. Foster, *The Political Philosophies of Plato and Hegel* (Oxford: Clarendon Press, 1935; reprinted 1968) covers some of the same ground as I do in my analysis of the *Republic*. I note here only my major disagreements with Foster: (1) Foster fails to distinguish between philosophical and demotic virtue and so does not appreciate the full richness of *sōphrosynē* or Plato's recognition of the shortcomings of his *technē* model of knowledge. He is wrong to say that Plato was unable to "think or speak" of "the activity of realizing form as anything other than itself a form." He therefore misses the full force of the dialectical relation between Plato and Hegel. (2) He traces problems arising from Plato's analysis of soul to a failure to distinguish between the economic and the political, instead of connecting them to his analysis of *episteme* as *technē*.

man is therefore the wise man. This is why Socrates says that wisdom alone is a virtue of the soul; the others are akin to the body (6:518d9).[16] Despite all efforts by Socrates to minimize the body in the just city, the philosopher can be king only by turning his attention to the body. What counts as justice for others is necessarily an injustice to himself.[17] If we regard the term *injustice* in this context as too strong, it is beyond dispute that, in submitting to the necessity of ruling, the philosopher is alienated from his natural desire; the result is again a contradiction between philosophy and political existence. The same point is implicit in an earlier reference by Socrates to "temperance, justice, and all of demotic virtue," of which the philosopher is the demiurge or maker.[18] These two passages, which occur in the context of the central discussion of philosophy, conflict with the earlier analysis of the forms of the soul, which is itself based upon the analogy between soul and city.

The incompatibility of philosophy or wisdom, the perfection of the soul, and demotic justice necessarily casts doubt upon the validity of the analogy between the soul and the city.[19] In fact, Socrates refers to an analogy between the city and man, which he expresses as hypothetical (2:368d7: *ei ta auta onta tunchanei*. It is drawn in order to overcome the difficulty of seeing justice in the soul (1:352d2–54a9; 2:368c8ff.). But comprehension of the analogy itself turns upon knowledge of philosophy, the perfection of the soul. As it would seem, in order to see the soul, we need the city. But in order to see the city, we must see the transpolitical perfection of the soul. And, as the *Republic* also makes explicit, the nature of the requisite philosophical vision is itself hypothetical or inaccessible within the context of the political discussion that shows its necessity.[20] All of *epistēmē* and not

16. Numbers in the text will identify passages from the *Republic* until otherwise indicated.

17. Cf. 4:419a1–420d5; 6:489b6ff. It is not natural for philosophers to seek to rule (6:496d6ff.; 7:517c8). Those who have escaped from the cave into the sunlight "do not desire to do the human things" (7:519c1ff. and esp. 7:519d8ff.). Only in this context can we evaluate Socrates' claim at 7:520a6ff. that no injustice is being done to the philosophers.

18. 6:500d7. Cf. 4:443d7: in addition to courage, the demotic virtues may include other kinds.

19. At 2:368c8ff., Socrates says that the city is an *anēr* writ large. Since this word might be translated as *citizen*, Socrates' terms already suggest a circularity of reasoning.

20. There are numerous references by Socrates to the tentative or incomplete character of the present treatment of philosophy. E.g., 6:506e1, 509c7–10; 7:517b6. Cf. references

merely self-knowledge, requires knowledge of the *archē*. Knowledge in the highest or comprehensive sense is dialectic, but this comprehensive science depends upon knowledge of the good. Unfortunately, the good is evidently not accessible to scientific knowledge. Science or dialectic proceeds by grasping the *ousia* of each thing and giving a *logos* of it (7:533c3ff., 534b3ff.). But the good is beyond the grasp of *logos* because it is beyond *ousia*.[21] The soul divines the good, but cannot grasp what it is (6:505e1ff. Cf. 506a6).

The conclusion that seems to emerge from the central section of the *Republic* is that there is no discursive science at all. We may correct this apparently disastrous inference from other passages in the *Republic* itself. Science is always a determinate kind of knowledge about a determinate kind of thing. There is no science altogether, no discursive knowledge of the whole, but only science of this and science of that (4:438e2ff.; 5:477d7, 478a6). This has the following consequence. The unity of virtue depends upon its identity as scientific knowledge or wisdom. Wisdom qua science is in turn possible only if there is a *logos* of the soul, the arena within which the whole (or the good) becomes visible to man. The soul renders the whole accessible because it is itself a mirror (or mirror-image) of the whole (10:596c4ff.). But every *logos* about the soul must be of this or that psychic property: In the language of Fichte and Hegel, discursive or reflective analysis objectifies the soul. Its results separate us from the unity or intrinsic being of what we seek.[22] In the absence of a Hegelian logic of Spirit as process, that is, as the *energeia* that poses forms but is not itself a form, there is no wisdom because no self-knowledge. Therefore, the thesis of the unity of the virtues is, if not contradicted or canceled outright, transformed into a *Sollen* in the sense that Fichte assimilates the Kantian categorical imperative into the doctrine of infinite striving.[23] The virtues ought to be unitary, but in fact there is a separation between wisdom and the demotic virtues of justice, temperance, and

---

to prophecy at 6:505e1–506a5 and 7:523a8. At 7:536c1, Socrates calls the discussion a game.

21. 6:509b6ff. Cf. 7:532a1ff. Dialectic gives a *logos* of what each thing is, but *noēsei labei* what the good is itself. Socrates does not rule out "seeing" the good, but explaining it; hence he sometimes calls it "the good," sometimes "the Idea of the good."

22. Similarly, in the *Sophist*, the attempt to give a *logos* about *being itself* produces assertions about self-identical formal properties other than being.

23. Cf. Fichte's *Grundlage der gesamten Wissenschaftslehre* (1794; Hamburg: Felix Meiner Verlag, 1961), 178f., 187ff., 204ff.

courage. The factual separation of the virtues is the political manifestation of the permanent historical alienation of the philosopher from the community.

There is, then, an intimate connection between the identity-within-difference of the four cardinal virtues and the analogy between the soul and the whole. It seems that this analogy is a noble lie designed to mitigate the destructive consequences of the inaccessibility to *logos* of the soul as image of the whole. But this in passing; we must turn next to further details concerning the wholeness of the soul. The unity of the soul depends upon the unity of theory and practice or of the four cardinal virtues. But the unity of theory and practice is, as we have seen, a *Sollen*: It rests upon an indemonstrable hypothesis or discursively inaccessible vision of the unity of the good. Differently stated, the distinctness of the Ideas from each other, as well as their determinate natures, makes impossible a dianoetically accessible Idea of the whole. Instead, we must have recourse to language, a partially human invention, to imitate or make wholeness by capturing the ontological relations of the Ideas. In Aristotelian terminology, there is no *summum genus*. Stated succinctly, the whole is a human hypothesis or interpretation of what ought to be. If the soul mirrors the whole, then it too must be a hypothesis. There is no Idea of the soul except perhaps in the metaphorical sense in which Aristotle calls the Platonic intellect a *topos eidōn*. The soul has many Ideas (4:443d7; Cf. 3:402b9ff.; 4:433a3, 437d3, 443d7, 445c1ff.; 10:596c4ff.). Socrates does say, to be sure, that the soul is a "one come to be from many" (4:443e1). But this does not alter the inaccessibility of its unity to discourse.[24] We have a practical assurance of the soul as a harmony but no theoretically valid demonstration. For reasons such as these, Socrates and Glaucon each refer to their discussion of the soul as a "speculation" *skemma*: 4:435c4, 445a6).

According to Socrates, it is very hard to give a *logos* concerning

---

24. According to the "likely myth" of the *Timaeus*, soul is made from the fundamental constituents of the whole: being, same, other; in this cosmogonical sense, it has "one Idea" (29c4ff.; 35a1ff.). This is merely to say that the soul is as problematic as the whole. More specifically, it does not account for the principle of subjectivity or self-consciousness that is the essence of psychic unity. In the *Phaedrus*, we are given an ambiguous demonstration of soul as the eternal principle of self-moving motion, but according to Socrates there is no *logos* accessible to mortals about what kind the form of the soul may be. We cannot explain the divine but must imagine it (243a3–6, 245c1–46a2, 246c6–d1).

whether the soul acts as a whole in performing each function, or whether there is a separate form for each specific function (4:436a8–b3). He decides in favor of the second alternative, having recourse to the principle of contradiction in so doing (4:436b5ff., 439d1ff.). The thesis, "one form, one activity," which is the principle underlying the class structure of the just city, is intimately connected to the denial of a comprehensive science, or to the assertion that each science is concerned with a distinct species (4:438e2ff.). The diversity of the sciences raises a doubt as to the possibility of a philosophical science competent to rule the entire city, and hence as to the possibility of the just city itself. More specifically, given the invisibility of the soul qua unity, the accuracy of our division or definition of its parts becomes questionable. The burden of Socrates' analysis supports the conclusion that each part of the soul (intelligence, spiritedness, and desire), and so each class in the city, has its characteristic virtue, and presumably *only* that virtue (as its intrinsic perfection), if it is to mind its own business (3:369e2–370b2, 395b3–4; 4:433a7, 439d1ff.). One might almost infer that the only available principle of the unity of the whole, the principle of contradiction, serves decisively to divide the whole into parts or to render it permanently inaccessible. This would be the Hegelian conclusion. In any case, Socrates proceeds to assign the cardinal virtues to parts of the soul.

Wisdom is assigned to the rulers as the virtue of intelligence. Nevertheless, because it is the same as philosophical justice, it belongs to the whole city (4:428a11ff., 428d1). Second, courage is the virtue of spiritedness, or the class of soldiers (4:441d1–3, 442b11). Because courage and spiritedness are closely associated with wisdom and intelligence, we can see why Socrates identified temperance and justice as demotic virtues. Allowing for the association between courage and intelligence, temperance and justice apparently pertain to the body, or to the appetitive part of the soul, and thus to the workers. But this would give two virtues to one part or class and divide the city into two camps, characterized by different kinds of justice (as Aristotle points out in the *Politics* 2:1264a26, b29f.). Socrates says initially that the city is just when each part does its work or minds its own business. No mention is made here of temperance; we are told that there are three forms in the city and the soul: wisdom, courage, and justice (4:441c4ff.). Some lines later, Socrates restates his conclusion by defining wisdom, courage, and temperance. Now justice is the odd man out. Temperance is said to mark the individual, and so the city, when there is friendship and harmony among the parts or functions, when all submit peacefully to the rule of the rational element (4:442c10–d1). In short, temperance is evidently indistinguishable from justice, to say nothing of wisdom. Intelligence and spiritedness must be able to exercise their own functions without being temperate or just. On the other hand, justice and/or temperance mark the *whole* city, allowing and preserving the presence of the other virtues (4:433b7ff.).

Intelligence and spiritedness, by doing their own work, are just. But precisely by doing their own work, they are not just, but wise and brave. This is a generalized example of the internal vacillations and contradictions in Socrates' analysis of the parts of the soul. I will simply restate the dilemma in terms of temperance. If temperance is restricted to bodily desire, then it cannot be a harmony or friendship of ruler and ruled. If it characterizes the whole, then it becomes indistinguishable from justice and perhaps wisdom.[25] In conclusion: Socrates defines the virtues as both one and diverse. They ought to be one, but this is impossible because of the inaccessibility of wisdom and the undefinability of the soul. The impossibility of self-knowledge leads to the separation of the philosopher from himself and thereby from the community of nonphilosophers, because the only genuine virtue is the pursuit or love (but not the possession) of wisdom. Until wisdom is publicly accessible within the laws and customs of the city, the self-consciousness of the philosopher must be the *unhappy consciousness*.[26] The philosopher's political responsibility takes him away from the pursuit of knowledge, especially self-knowledge, and so from happiness. The only sense in which Socrates can define the unity of virtue is by identifying it with philosophy; and this, to repeat, separates the philosopher from the nonphilosopher, who is marked by demotic virtue. To assert the unity of virtue is therefore to divide virtue in half. This is no doubt why Aristotle was led to distinguish between theoretical and practical virtue. Such a distinction, however, makes explicit the inaccessibility of psychic unity to discourse. The invisible

25. See 4:441e7. Intelligence and spiritedness must be made harmonious by music and gymnastic and then set the task of restricting the desires, which are "by nature most insatiable." See also 4:439e1ff. The part of the soul that forbids gratification of impulses or desires is logistic; the part forbidden is appetitive (and includes Eros).

26. Note that the enterprise of launching a just city is regularly characterized as a hope, dream, or wish (2:369a6; 4:443b7; 5:499c2–5). Cf. Hegel's discussion of the dream-wisdom of the Stoic in *Phänomenologie*, 158ff. Cf. 190: "was nur sein *soll*, ohne zu sein, hat keine Wahrheit."

soul is an ancestor of the invisible substance of modern philosophy. This is the fundamental aporia Hegel seeks to overcome in book 2 of the *Logik* by demonstrating the identity-within-difference of essence and its appearances. If this is not successful, then human nature must remain, in Socrates' striking words, cut up into little bits (3:395b3–4). The whole is dissolved by our efforts to grasp it.

If justice is minding one's own business and knowledge is *epistēmē*, then justice is impossible. Given the thesis of the unity of virtue, the same may be said of temperance and courage. The preservation of virtue clearly depends upon our establishing a sense of *knowing* other than *epistēmē* that will enable us to know ourselves. The special importance of *sōphrosynē* in the sense of temperance was evident from the *Republic* where, the unity of the virtues to one side, it seemed to be indistinguishable from justice. In the *Charmides*, we see the importance for self-knowledge of *sōphrosynē* in a sense of the term closer to *practical intelligence* than to temperance of appetite. Perhaps the word *prudence* encompasses the indicated senses of the Greek term. The prudent man knows what to do, and he is sober rather than mad. We should bear in mind, however, that prudence, as the opposite of madness, is in conflict with Eros, and so with the divine madness that gives us philosophy.[27] There is something radically unsatisfactory about having recourse to prudence. I shall return to this in the next section. Meanwhile, let us turn to the *Charmides* by considering two objections to the thesis of the *Republic* that justice, in the city or man, depends upon the rule of philosophy.

First, justice qua minding one's own business seems to rest upon injustice, or prudence upon hybris. This is easily seen by comparing the three definitions of prudence (*sōphrosynē*) offered by Charmides with the situation in the *Republic*. Charmides' definitions are being quiet, being modest, and minding one's own business.[28] As Socrates argues the case, it is evident that the man of intelligence is quick rather than slow, hence noisy rather than quiet. By giving advice, he calls attention to himself; in assisting his fellows or minding their business,

27. Cf. Xenophon, *Memorabilia*, 3.9. 4–7.

28. *Charmides* 159b, 160e, 161b6: *ta heautou prattein*. Numbers in the text will refer to the *Charmides* unless otherwise indicated.

he is hybristic as well as just or prudent.[29] Charmides thus presents us with a satire on the Socratic doctrine of virtue, which provides us with an instance of what Hegel calls "the inverted world." The separation between essence and appearance makes virtue vice and vice virtue.[30]

Second, as we have now seen at length, if wisdom is defined as *epistēmē* then it is impossible. As Socrates says in the *Charmides*, there is neither knowledge of knowledge nor knowledge of ignorance (166e6–7). He seems to exclude the possibility of what is today called metaphilosophy, epistemology, or critique of critique. In a more cautious passage, Socrates says he is too ignorant to *know* whether such a knowledge is possible. Instead, he has a prophetic awareness that *sōphrosynē* or virtue is beneficial, that is, good for man (169a–b, esp. a7ff.). Even this awareness seems to be excluded by the rigorous denial of knowledge *in any way whatsoever* (175b6ff. and esp. c4–6). Nevertheless, Socrates does not reject his prophetic sense, which seems to be compatible with knowledge (nonepistemic) of ignorance.[31] The reliance upon prophecy is also connected with the ironic reference to a "charm" for curing headaches (psychic illness) in those who are not, or do not know whether they are, virtuous (155e5ff.). Prophecies and charms are substitutes for *epistēmē* (Cf. *Timaeus* 71e2, 86b2; also 69d4, 86d3). Differently stated, they provide us with the horizon for a nonepistemic interpretation of *sōphrosynē*.

The initial connection between quietness and prudence raises the distinction between inner and outer that is critical to the phenomenon of self-consciousness. Self-consciousness is not discussed, or rather it is taken for granted, whether in the trivial sense that Charmides is conscious of his headache, or in the deeper Socratic injunction to "pay attention and look into yourself" in order to see what *sōphrosynē* is.[32]

29. 175d3–5. Socrates makes the dubious assumption that *quick* and *silent* are opposites, whereas *silent* and *slow* are correlatives. Charmides is too quiet to challenge this assumption. We should bear in mind his later political activities: quietness conceals quickness and is useful for political conspirators.

30. *Phänomenologie*, 122ff.

31. This prophetic knowledge is connected to the Socratic daimonion and to Eros, the sole *technē* claimed by Socrates in the dialogues. I shall return to this point.

32. *Charmides* 160d6. The point is not affected by the divergent manuscript readings. One cannot look at oneself in the context without being conscious of oneself, and so (following Burnet) looking into oneself. The entire dialogue is, from the reader's viewpoint, a monologue by Socrates, and reveals the private or inner as well as the outer responses of the narrator.

The problem is not with self-consciousness but with self-knowledge. This distinction is related to the Platonic distinction between being and thinking. Socrates regularly associates *epistēmē* with *technē* and the "work" of the latter with its product. He suggests that every science is productive and that its product is separate from or other than itself. Critias, his interlocutor in this section of the *Charmides*, objects that one can distinguish between theoretical and productive arts; *sōphrosynē* he says, is like arithmetic and geometry rather than like carpentry and weaving. Socrates grants the distinction but shows that it does not affect the difference between knowledge and the things known. Thus the odd and the even differ from arithmetic or knowledge of the odd and the even (165d–66b). Socrates thus accepts the distinction between theoretical and productive arts but not between either or both of these and *praxis* as is evident from his allowing the assimilation of *sōphrosynē* to arithmetic and geometry.[33] If theory is mathematical and practice is productive-technical, then there is no room for practical virtue or a nonepistemic type of knowledge. Similarly, the "fine arts," or at least poetry, which produces speeches rather than bodies, acquire a problematic status in the division just noted. Let us say merely that poetry and prophecy, classified in the *Phaedrus* under madness, have a subterranean and somewhat inconsistent connection to *sōphrosynē* understood as prudence or practical intelligence. And yet, the exclusion of nonepistemic or nontechnical knowledge is surely at odds with the general theme of the *Charmides*.

Let me rephrase the preceding conclusion. The thesis of the unity of virtue makes practical intelligence subordinate to, or a kind of, mathematical theory. In this case, knowledge is always of a determinate form. Consequently, there can be no knowledge of the whole, none of the soul, and therefore no self-knowledge. The connection with the impossibility of knowledge is as follows. Since knowledge is a condition or pathos of the soul, it is impossible to know without knowing that one knows, that is, to know oneself as the knower.[34] If this thought is developed, it leads to the Hegelian doctrine of Abso-

33. This is not an isolated occurrence in the dialogues. In the *Sophist*, the Eleatic Stranger divides the *technai* into the productive and the acquisitive (under which mathematics is included). In the *Statesman*, *episteme* is divided into the practical and the gnostic, but the practical arts are those which produce bodies (258d4–e7).

34. Cf. *Republic* 6:511d6–e4 and K. Oehler, *Die Lehre vom noetischen und dianoetischen Denken bei Platon und Aristoteles* (Munich: Verlag C. H. Beck, 1962), 96ff. Also *Phaedrus* 270c2–3: one cannot know nature altogether without knowing human nature.

lute Spirit as the excitation common to knower and known.[35] In the language of the *Charmides*, if *sōphrosynē* is the science of sciences, it must be the science of itself: to know oneself is then to possess epistemic wisdom. But Socrates, in a manner related to similar discussions by modern logicians, rejects this possibility. He conceives of sciences rendered determinate by analogy with the specific form each knows. A form of forms, however, is out of the question. In the language of the *Sophist*, every attempt to transform being into a *summum genus*, or to describe its attributes, leads to the negation of being or the mention of formal properties other than being. Hence the previously noted indescribableness of the good, but also, we may add, of *nous*, which, as receptive of form, could not have a determinate form of its own.[36] In sum, if *sōphrosynē* is knowledge, it cannot be science. But if it is nonscientific knowledge, then the unity of virtue (and the Platonic conception of *theōria* and *epistēmē*) is contradicted.

To return to the *Charmides*, Socrates takes for granted the separation between knower and known, or thinking and being. Even arithmetical beings have in modern parlance an objective status, independent of the subjective activity of knowing them. If *sōphrosynē* is knowledge of itself, it must therefore be separate from or other than itself. Since Critias grants this, he cannot sustain his contention that the prudent man knows himself in knowing the science of prudence (or temperance) (166b–c, 166e–67a). For if this were possible, then the prudent man, as the object of his knowledge, would be separate from or other than himself as knower or subject. We should not be prevented by the absence of the terms *subject* and *object* from grasping the fundamental implication of the *Charmides*; those terms follow from the distinction between knower and known. The attempt to acquire self-knowledge divides the self into subject and object. In the language of Fichte, the ego poses itself as the opposition between empirical ego (subject) and nonego (object). Plato no more than Fichte can overcome this opposition in theoretical or discursive science. Both in effect deny that the activity or work of soul renders visible the essence of soul. This is the precondition for the Hegelian synthesis of Aristotelian and Christian conceptions of noetic activity.

35. For a possible Platonic antecedent, cf. *Sophist* 248d10ff. The usual Platonic doctrine, however, is that thinking is receptive.

36. Cf. my article, "Thought and Touch, a Note on Aristotle's *De Anima*," now chapter 7 in my *Quarrel Between Philosophy and Poetry*. Note too that *nous* is not mentioned in the *Sophist* as one of the *megista genē*.

One might object that knowledge of knowledge, of the fact that X is knowledge of something or some kind, does not seem to be the same as self-knowledge. If I know something, I may well know that I know it, but it does not seem to follow that I must know myself. For if it did, then apparently every form of knowledge would be impossible, including arithmetic and geometry. Socrates in effect accepts this objection by distinguishing between technical knowledge and knowledge of the significance, which he calls utility, of technical knowledge. First, he distinguishes between the possibility of the self-reflexivity of knowledge and the utility of such knowledge, should it be possible (167a–b). If I merely know that I know what I know, then this surely entails that I am self-conscious. But it does not entail that I know myself, unless I am myself identical with what I know, and this is precisely what Socrates denies. But he puts the issue in a more complex way. Vision does not see itself; it sees visible things. Hearing hears, not itself, but what is audible. The senses as a whole do not perceive themselves, but what is perceptible. Socrates then establishes the same result in the cases of desire, will, love, fear, and opinion (167b–68a).

There are two ambiguities in Socrates' argument. The first is the distinction between technical knowledge and knowledge of utility. I prefer to prepare the consideration of this ambiguity by beginning with the second ambiguity. Let us grant immediately that the senses perceive their objects rather than themselves. This is in effect to treat the senses as capacities like that of mind, which are actualized only as their objects. But the Socratic thesis is at once open to the counter-thesis that there is no actual difference between the senses and their sensations. Just as it would be absurd to identify the sense of vision with the eyeball and the optic nerve, so too one need not identify the sensation or actualized sense with the object sensed qua external body. The "sensation" is the perceived body, that is its *eidos* or sensuous form: in a properly qualified sense, its *essence*. What I sensuously know of the object is indistinguishable from myself as sensuous perceiver. This argument would be easier to make in the case of thinking, but for various reasons I think it wise to show that the argument covers sensation as well. It is all very well to protest against the multiplication of entities or the interposition of sensations between the senses and their objects. However, the identification of sense and sensation is not such an act of interposition or multiplication but an *interpretation* of sense perception. The denial of sensations leaves a vacuum between the senses and their objects that can only be filled by identifying them in a kind of neutral monism, which quickly returns us to the puzzles of Eleaticism.

One could therefore say that Socrates' own doctrine of sense perception in one way contradicts, but in another is a precondition for, the modern doctrine of transcendental subjectivity. The contradiction arises to the extent that the perceiver (like the noetic thinker) forgets or loses himself in the content or object of perception. However, this self-forgetfulness occurs, not because the self disappears, but because it identifies with the form of the perceived object. As soon as we recollect the indisputable fact that the perception is indeed ours, self-consciousness and perceptual (or noetic) knowledge are combined within a single if indeterminate consciousness. The aporia arises from Socrates' inability to give a discursive or analytical account of indeterminate consciousness as the medium of forgetting and recollecting in the ways just indicated. The act of identification between knower and known is obscured by the doctrine of a radical difference between the *dunamis* of knowing and the *energeia* of what is known. The consequences of this obscuring stretch across the history of philosophy to the doctrines of Hume and Kant. We are therefore able to surmise why post-Hegelian epistemology, which defines itself as a return to Hume and Kant, leads so frequently to a rejection of self-consciousness or inner experience.

As the *Charmides* shows, Socrates regularly defines knowledge on the model of *technē*. He thus attempts to discover what *sōphrosynē* knows on the assumption that it is, "like all the other *technai*" what he later calls *homotechnical* or restricted to one kind of subject-matter and method. In his conclusion, after having explored the possibility that *sōphrosynē* is not a form of knowledge, Socrates returns to the identification of knowledge and *technē* and speaks regularly of the *epistēmē* of good and bad.[37] As Critias complains, Socrates tries to establish a homogeneity of all forms of knowledge (166b7ff.). Critias is surely right to protest that *sōphrosynē* is different from all other kinds of knowledge. To modify slightly his own formulation, *sōphrosynē* knows *somehow* not itself, but the temperate man, as well as the other modes of knowledge. This point is implicit in Socrates' own distinction between technical knowledge and knowledge of utility. Or rather, it is an explicit theme of the Platonic dialogues, running side by side with

---

37. 165c4ff. (esp. 165d6); 171c8 ("homotechnical"); 174b11ff. (esp. 174d5).

the doctrine of *epistēmē* as (ultimately mathematical) *technē* but never satisfactorily harmonized with it.

The issue of self-knowledge is rendered excessively obscure when posed in terms of the reflexivity of knowledge. It is true that the thesis of the identity of knower and known may be summarily stated in those terms. But the summary omits the doctrine of Absolute Spirit as the ground of that identity. Plato has no such doctrine; hence it is especially easy for him to ridicule the doctrine of a knowledge that knows itself. The absence of a doctrine of Spirit, together with the previously noticed distinction between (noetic or sensuous) perceptual capacity and form, makes it impossible for Plato to capitalize upon the implications of his own doctrine of *sōphrosynē*. These implications can easily be shown from Socrates' regular appeals to expertise or the need to appeal to the technician. The paradigm for a nontechnical knowing that knows both itself and the *technai* is practical intelligence, or *sōphrosynē* understood as prudence. To take a favorite Socratic example, the prudent man knows that, when he is ill, he must consult the physician. He knows that medicine is technical knowledge that applies to his own circumstances. Yet (unless he also happens to be a physician) he does not himself possess the knowledge or science of medicine. Socrates refutes Critias by ignoring this case in favor of the absurd contention that, since the known is other than the knower, just as sickness and health are other than medicine, so knowledge that medicine is a science is other than knowledge that it applies to sickness and health. All other considerations to one side, this argument is refuted by the fact that, when we are sick, we call the doctor.

The capacity of the prudent man to consult the appropriate specialist is a nonspecialized or nontechnical knowledge of the *useful*. Any effort to provide an epistemic analysis of prudence ends sooner or later in something like Bentham's hedonist calculus, or the transformation of utility into the value of a variable in a mathematical function. The Platonic dialogues may be compared in this context to a man standing at a crossroads who, when asked which way to go, points in two separate if parallel directions. The dialogues suggest the possibility of self-knowledge in a practical rather than a theoretical sense. Yet the analysis of practice they contain is such as to assimilate it into either theory or production. For example, in the *Charmides*, Socrates' main arguments against a science of science (and so of self-knowledge) rest upon this premise: whatever applies its own capacity (*dynamis*) to itself will have the essential being (*ousia*) of that to which its capacity applies (168b–e). Therefore, the exercise of sensuous or cognitive capacities immediately separates them from their source or principle: the sensing or cognizing man. Instead of inferring the necessary objectification of man by his own effort to know himself, Socrates leaves it to a higher authority whether anything can apply its capacity to itself without undergoing alienation. He distinguishes between science of science and *sōphrosynē* by means of a prophetic intuition concerning the utility and goodness of *sōphrosynē* (169a–b, esp. b4ff.). This suggests a distinction, previously suppressed, between theory and practice. But the suggestion is not developed, for the reason we have already established. If knowing how to do something is not the same as knowing its utility or goodness, then either we surrender the thesis of the unity of knowledge and virtue, or there is no knowledge of the useful and the good. Either alternative is disastrous for Platonism.

Socrates thus associates *sōphrosynē* even when considering its claim to be the science of science, with the practical, or with doing well in the domain of individual, family, or political life (171dff.). He criticizes science of science as useless even if possible, since it would know only that X and Y are sciences but not who knows them; it would in effect be an ignorance of all selves, or a loss of self-consciousness (170c–72b). Finally, he goes so far as to question the excellence of *sōphrosynē* itself, making use of a dream to convey his discourse. If *sōphrosynē* allows the mind to comprehend the sciences as well as to discern by prophecy the true experts and false prophets, this is still not the same as "doing well and being blessed" (172c1–73d5). Science and the epistemic function of *sōphrosynē* are not yet the good, not yet "knowledge of good and evil" (173d–74d). The distinction between theory and practice is thus somehow related to, or even contained within, *sōphrosynē*. But this means that the distinction is itself inaccessible to discursive theory.

In this concluding section, I want to consider briefly the Platonic doctrine of Eros as it relates to the connection between *sōphrosynē* and *Selbstbewusstsein*. One could almost say that Eros supplies *sōphrosynē* with the dimension of negative work it lacks in isolation. Unfortunately, Eros lacks even the degree of self-consciousness to be found in *sōphrosynē*. Eros lacks self-possession; hence its work at worst de-

stroys prudence, at best makes its exercise ambiguous. Let us begin
again with the *Charmides*. Socrates says there: "Nothing can be more
unreasonable, as I suppose, than to say that one knows 'somehow'
what he does not know at all" (175c4–8). Yet this is precisely what
Socrates has himself been saying, here as well as elsewhere in the
dialogues. To borrow a distinction from the *Sophist* (221c6ff.), Socrates
is an *idiōtēs* or private man rather than a *technitēs*. This role is entirely compatible with his professed erotic expertise. Eros is on the
one hand peculiarly private, on the other a knowledge of what one
lacks. It is a *technē* only in the metaphorical sense that the mind is an
eidos: In each case, there is a peculiar negativity or absence of formal
structure. Of course, the mind receives, whereas Eros desires; up to
a point, at least, one could say that the mind is passive and Eros is
active. But because Eros does not know what it wants (and is thus
not self-conscious), it must itself be directed, not by the noetic or receptive capacity of the mind, but by *sōphrosynē*. As we have seen, the
unanalyzable nature of prudence leaves the precise relation between
theory and practice unclear. Nevertheless, I believe that sufficient evidence has been presented to support the suggestion that Plato allows
for, if he does not himself assert, the eventual dominance of practice.
The reason is that, although Plato has discovered the role of negativity in cognition and in desire, or the condition for the assimilation
by Spirit of the objective environment, he cannot give an account of
his own discovery.

If Eros, *sōphrosynē*, and *nous* could be united, the result, I think,
would be tolerably close to Hegel's conception of *Geist* in its subjective
aspect. The impossibility of this union is perhaps best understood
with respect to Eros and is given dramatic illustration in the person
of Socrates. In the absence of a *logos* of Eros, Socrates turns regularly
to prophecy and charms. The deficiencies of prophecy are implied in
the ending of the *Charmides*, where Critias and Charmides, later to be
involved in the episode of the thirty tyrants, concoct a plot to over-
power Socrates by force.[38] The last line of the dialogue contains Socrates' surrender to false prophets: "Then I will not oppose you." The
Charmides is a comedy, because it shows Socrates conversing about
temperance and prudence with a future tyrant. But from a Hegelian
viewpoint it is also a tragedy, because the comedy rests upon an ironi-

38. *Charmides* 176b–d; Cf. *Republic* 1:327b4ff.

cal detachment from the domain of practice and is the prototype for the alienated resignation of Stoicism. However this may be, Socratic resignation is contradicted in the *Charmides* by two forms of intemperance. The first is with respect to the soul; as Socrates explicitly says, it is hybristic to question the goodness and utility of *sōphrosynē* in dialectical investigation (175d3–5). The second concerns the body, and in a way unparalleled in the dialogues. Shortly after meeting him, Socrates sees into Charmides' cloak and reports on his response: "and I caught fire and was not myself . . ." but a fawn consumed by a lion (155d3ff.).

Socrates moderates his Eros for dialectic with a prophetic confidence in the excellence of *sōphrosynē*. *Glauben,* we may say, is invoked in the absence of *Wissen.* But what of the corporeal Eros? In order to understand the issue, we have to ask why Socrates talks to Charmides at all. If Socrates is simply attracted to beautiful youths, then he is a fool. If the corporeal attraction is the necessary precondition for dialectic (as it cannot be, given the example of Theaetetus), then theory is subordinate, not merely to practice, but to desire. If the reference to corporeal Eros is an ironical indication of Socrates' interest in Charmides' soul, why should a philosopher express himself unreservedly in the irony of the flesh? Why should he discuss *sōphrosynē* with a potential tyrant? I suggest that the crucial answer to this question is to be found in the *Republic.* The philosopher is the erotic man par excellence, but Eros is in itself tyrannical, or leads, unless properly transformed, to the tyrant rather than to the philosopher.[39] The problem with respect to the body is therefore the same as the problem with respect to the soul. Psychic Eros terminates in the silence of prophecy, which is indistinguishable, so far as *logos* goes, from the silence of the body. Socrates is attracted to erotic youths because of their philosophical potentiality, but he is unable to reconcile the philosophical or theoretical with the tyrannical or practical dimension of Eros.

In Hegelian terminology, there is something unsatisfying about Socratic or Platonic Eros. It does not give stable results, whether in the choice of the beloved or in its pedagogic effects. This is because of

39. *Republic* 3:403a7ff.; 5:475b4ff.; 6:485a10, 490b2, 499b7; 9:573b6ff., 574d8ff., 575a3 and passim. Cf. my article, "The Role of Eros in Plato's Republic," now Chapter 6 in my *Quarrel Between Philosophy and Poetry.* It is essential to note that the *Republic* associates political ambition with Eros, not with spiritedness, which is subordinate either to intelligence or desire.

its unstable, indeterminate nature, which forever eludes *logos*.[40] In the *Symposium* (202d11–e1), Eros is described as a daimon, intermediate between the mortal and the deathless or divine. Its function is to unite these two domains, but in a very peculiar manner. On the one hand, Eros is poor, homeless, ugly, or lacking in the objects of his desire. On the other hand, as messenger between gods and men, or the eternal and the transient, Eros is filled up with both and "binds together the whole to itself." In short, Eros is neither mortal nor immortal, both waxes and wanes, lives and dies, "or is in between wisdom and ignorance" (202e3–203e5). As the bond of the whole, Eros is himself unstable or discontinuous; the whole is immediately dissolved into a heap of discontinuous parts. These parts die as they are born; even soul and knowledge participate, as mortal, in immortality by rebirth, not by continuous duration (207e1–208b4). The bond of genesis is indistinguishable from the negative excitation or posing of genesis by an invisible source. The presence of Eros is the ontological equivalent to the absence of essence. The whole, like its logical counterpart in the *Sophist*, is equal to, more, and less than itself; as the Eleatic Stranger says of *being* understood as the whole, it has no number or noetically accessible formal structure (245d8).

It would require a separate study to compare in detail the properties of Eros with the logical aporiai of the *Sophist* or *Parmenides*. I must rest content here with an indication. Eros is the Platonic equivalent to the Hegelian dialectic of reflection, or the process by which genesis is posed as a self-supporting totality. In Hegel, each moment of genesis contains the whole, and so too the source that poses the next moment and into which the present moment returns. The circle of becoming is the same as the circle of eternity, because the formation-process of the first is the life-pulse of the second. The logic of reflection thus provides us with the structure of self-consciousness: the reflection of self in other which is also an assimilation of both moments as preserved within a more comprehensive totality. Self-consciousness is transformed into self-knowledge, and hence into scientific wisdom or knowledge of the whole, by a complete account of the logic of reflection. In Plato, one may say that Eros is common to body and

---

40. According to the myth of Aristophanes in the *Symposium*, Eros is "stabilized" by the net of Hephaestus. But this is to make Eros subordinate to *technē* in a way that suppresses self-consciousness. Cf. my *Plato's "Symposium,"* 2d ed. (New Haven: Yale University Press, 1987).

soul, but it is separate from form, a completely indeterminate longing for the determinations it cannot genuinely possess. As separate, Eros is alienated from itself: it cannot give an account of itself and lacks self-consciousness.

The negative consequence of the separation of Eros from form or discursive thinking is shown in the *Symposium* by the characteristically negative description of "beauty itself," the representative of the Platonic Ideas. "Beauty itself" is silent or lacking in structural differentiation, apart from the minimum logical marks of self-identity (210e6–11b1). In one way, the logical marks of "beauty itself" are curiously reminiscent of the logical function of the "I think" which, according to Kant, is a necessary a priori feature of the synthetic unity of a manifold. Because these marks pertain indifferently to any Idea, they serve no role whatsoever in distinguishing one Idea from another. The vision of the Idea of beauty would seem to be nothing more than what Kant calls a limiting concept to sensuous intuition.[41] Diotima's account of immortality or the perception of eternity would thus be an account of the intellectual intuition of the Absolute as inaccessible to discursive reflection. This intuition arises from the logical analysis of reflection (the way up) but in such a way as to be concealed by it (the way down is then a *via negationis* terminating in *docta ignorantia*). Again, the similarities with the doctrine of Fichte are impossible to overlook.

The Socratic doctrine of form, which serves as the basis for the conception of science or knowledge throughout western philosophy, renders self-knowledge impossible. At the same time, however, Socrates introduces a conception of *sōphrosynē* or reflection upon the intentionality of Eros, which raises the possibility of self-knowledge in a nontheoretical sense. But this possibility is never fulfilled by Socrates and his students, because it contradicts the notion of knowledge as derived from arithmetic and geometry. One of the clearest signs of Socrates' confusion on this central issue is his vacillation concerning the thesis that virtue is knowledge. Common sense tells us that this thesis must be true, and yet the philosophical notion of truth tells us that common sense is mistaken. In somewhat different terms, knowledge is possible only because the mind sees or imitates the forms of things. The problem faced by the Socratics is how to preserve the

---

41. "Der Begriff eines Noumenon ist also bloss ein *Grenzbegriff*, um die Anmassungen der Sinnlichkeit einzuschränken." Kant, *Kritik der reinen Vernunft* B310.

stability of these forms from the erotic motions of the soul. Their solution, developed more fully by Aristotle but already evident in Plato, is to conceive of noetic vision as a limit case of psychic motion, in which self-consciousness disappears in favor of the forms of knowledge. Needless to say, there are tendencies of another kind, such as the assertion in the *Sophist* that the thing known is affected or moved by the activity of knowing. But these two tendencies are not brought together into a coherent doctrine of mind any more than the two doctrines concerning virtue are ever stabilized.

The general tendency in the Socratic school is, however, unmistakable. The subject is fulfilled by transformation into an object. Hence the ambiguous status of the experience of self-consciousness, or the human rather than the divine. This solution excludes or compromises those aspects of psychic excitation that are the basis for the practical or teleological activities underlying (or furnishing) the significance of noetic intuition itself. Platonism rests upon a connection between reason and the good that it is unable to substantiate. There is a disjunction within human nature between theory and practice, and an attendent vacillation as to which mode of activity is primary. In Plato, the vacillation is represented dramatically or poetically as Eros, and logically in the puzzles of whole and parts, one and many, and so on. This vacillation originates poetically in an inadequate conception of negative excitation, logically, in an inadequate analysis of nonbeing as a species of being. Thus, for example, the significance of that analysis is vitiated in the conception of noetic intelligence as receptivity or static emptiness: that is, a quasisyntactic negativity. Even the Aristotelian conception of *nous poiētikos* exemplifies the shortcomings of reflection, for its activity is the posing of forms which, in being thought, prevent intelligence from thinking itself, except as the activity of posing. The self-manifestation of the divine intelligence is therefore at once its concealment. Subjectivity is excluded from noetic activity by the very satisfaction of the erotic appetite for knowledge. One therefore finds in Greek thought the source of the Fichtean interpretation of reflective understanding, as well as the elements which, if properly developed, lead to the overcoming of Fichte by Hegel. This chapter has only presented one or two aspects of that extraordinarily complex process.

CHAPTER SIX

Theory and Practice in Hegel:
UNION OR DISUNION?

As my title suggests, I intend in this chapter to raise a question rather than to provide a definitive answer. The question is whether Hegel succeeds in establishing the union of theory and practice that is an essential ingredient in his system.[1] I shall limit myself here almost entirely to the *Encyclopedia* of 1830 which, however it needs to be supplemented, must stand as the one comprehensive and authoritative statement of Hegel's system. I am not concerned here with the various stages in the development of Hegel's thought but solely with its most mature presentation. It should go without emphasis that, in the format of a brief chapter, nothing more can be done than to explore part of the relevant evidence. To establish the legitimacy of questioning Hegel's success in uniting theory and practice, I will bring together a large number of passages from the *Encyclopedia*, almost none of which is contained in the section on objective spirit. However, it should be clear that these passages bear centrally upon that section of the *Encyclopedia*. This chapter may therefore be taken as a commentary on paragraph 513 of that section, which begins with the sentence: "*Sittlichkeit* is the completion of the objective spirit, the truth of the subjective and objective spirit itself."

I begin with certain passages that establish the connection between thinking and freedom in the *Encyclopedia*. According to Hegel, the highest interiority of spirit is thinking (11, 44): that is, spirit is satisfied in thinking.[2] This of course contains implicitly Hegel's intended union

This essay appeared in *Hegel's Social and Political Thought*, ed. D. P. Verene, © 1980 Humanities Press International, Inc., Atlantic Highlands, N.J., and Harvester Press, Ltd.
1. See also Rosen, *G. W. F. Hegel* (New Haven: Yale University Press, 1974), on whether Hegel succeeded in overcoming the alienation between the state and the philosopher.
2. Numbers in parentheses, unless otherwise indicated, are the paragraph and page number (in that order) from the Nicolin and Pöggeler edition of the *Enzyklopädie* (1830; Hamburg: Verlag Felix Meiner, 1969).

of theory and practice. Thus, for example, the thinking of true nature is in fact the production of nature by the thinking ego as *bei sich sein*, or as in accordance with the freedom of the thinking individual (23, 57). Freedom is contained immediately in thinking, which is always self-thinking or my thinking, but mine in the sense that I am simple universality. Therefore, in thinking nature, I am thinking myself: the process of self-knowledge develops coordinately with knowledge of nature. As Hegel states in the section on natural philosophy (245, 199), in practice, man applies the purpose contained within himself to the task of giving nature its form. One sees already the line of argument according to which practice unites itself to theory; in other words, it is practice that takes the initiative. Wisdom, however, requires us to go more slowly in building up the picture from its details.

The coordinate development between self-knowledge and knowledge of nature may also be called the coordinate development of interiority (*Wesen*) and exteriority (*Existenz*): the unity in this case is actuality (*Wirklichkeit*: 142, 140). Actuality, taken in its totality, or as *energeia* of the Absolute that exhibits itself in the structure of totality, is necessity (149, 144; cf. 156, 148). The "*truth* of *necessity* is thus *freedom*, and the *truth* of *substance* is the *concept*" (158, 148). In other words, "the *concept* is herewith the truth of *being* and *essence*" (159, 149). To paraphrase, the (self-) grasping (by Spirit) of the identity-within-difference of the pure spatio-temporal continuum and our reflective or discursive thinking of that continuum is the truth in question. Still more simply: The concept is the thinking of the coordination of substance and subject in the necessary structure of actuality (à la Spinoza). But it is also (potentially) freedom. This transition by thinking, within the concept, from necessity to freedom, is the hardest transition we have to make, namely, to think of freedom *as* necessity, as the coordination of actual subject and actual object in spirit. "The thinking of necessity is . . . the dissolution of this difficulty; for it is the coming-together of thinking with itself in the other—liberation (*die Befreiung*). . . . As existing for itself, this liberation is called *I*, as developed to its totality, *free spirit*, as feeling, *love*, as enjoyment, *salvation*" (159, 150). The passage just cited is of incidental interest, in view of those interpreters who exaggerate the religious or cultic elements in Hegel. For us, the point is slightly different. "The concept is free *power* as substantial for itself, and is *totality*" (160, 151). The concept is free because it grasps, or, as finally developed, is the self-grasping of, the whole. Nothing grasps it; there is no further transition to some more comprehensive level, but only development (161, 151).

We may pass by Hegel's analysis of the subjective concept and the object: "The Idea is the true, *absolute unity, in and for itself, of the concept and of objectivity*" (213, 182). It is the thinking of the whole in the judgments of the system. It resolves all finite dualisms of the understanding (214, 183). It is the atemporal, and so eternal, dialectic of differentiation and integration (214, 184), the essential process of the absolute and free concept (215, 184). Let us now draw a preliminary conclusion. In Hegel, freedom means thinking the whole. To do this, of course, requires that we be alive, and the life process must be assimilated into the activity of thinking. Hegel thus first discusses life, then knowing, and finally, he integrates these moments in the absolute Idea. One way to formulate the question of this chapter is as follows: What is the exact contribution of objective spirit to freedom in the comprehensive or highest sense?

I now turn to a more or less detailed survey of the union of theory and practice in the section of the *Encyclopedia* on logic. I begin with the transition from life to knowing: In itself, life is the identity of object and subject (part 3, section C [The Idea], 223, 187). In other words, life is intrinsically the union of theory and practice, and life, of course, is always of individuals. The process by which the identity in itself is made for itself is knowing (*Erkennen*), by which Hegel means a combination of knowing and willing (225, 188). As he puts this in a general statement: "Reason comes into the world with the absolute belief in its ability to pose identity and to raise its certitude to the level of truth, and with the instinct (*Trieb*) to render as nothing the opposition which, for reason, is in itself null and void" (224, 188).

More specifically, in the activity of *Erkennen* or (as we may call it) practico-productive theory, the opposition of one-sided subjectivity and one-sided objectivity is overcome. Initially, however, this *Aufheben* takes place only in itself. The identities are each finite; the circle of systematic theoretico-practical production of the totality of finite identities is not yet described. Hence the *Aufheben* falls apart into the distinct excitations of instinct (as reason is not yet working in a fully self-conscious way): (1) the one-sidedness of the subjectivity of the Idea is overcome by taking up the existent world into it as true objective content; (2) the one-sidedness of the objective world (which is mere *Schein*, a collection of contingencies rather than a necessary structure) is overcome by defining and shaping it through the *interior* of subjectivity, which therefore functions here as the true existing objective. Subprocess one is the instinct of *Wissen* toward truth, hence *Erkennen als solches*, the theoretical activity of the Idea. Subprocess two is the instinct of the good toward the completion of the good, or the practical activity of the Idea (225, 188f.).

We may now draw a more general conclusion. Theory originates in the process by which the world is assimilated into the subject, whereas practice originates in the process by which the world is formed by the subject. In both cases, the subject is active; there is no pure passive-receptive *Wesensschau*. That is, what Hegel calls the "theoretical activity of the Idea" is already practical, because *Erkennen* includes the practico-productive activity of will. It would perhaps be no exaggeration to say that, in Hegel's system, the unity of theory and practice is intrinsic to each as separate from the other. Thus the unity of the theoretical and practical Idea is already implicit in the purposiveness of reason. The separation of theory from practice is then the same as the separation of the objective from the subjective Idea in the necessary process by which the Absolute manifests itself in and as a world of extension and thought (the two principle attributes of Spinoza's substance). The purposiveness of reason, or the voluntative element in *Erkennen*, is the basis for what I called above the initiative taken by practice in its unification with theory. The unification of the theoretical and practical Idea is accomplished as the truth of the good, that which "the good accomplishes in and for itself," namely, by the practical activity of the Idea (235, 193). This practical activity is that of the subjective Idea, the will to define the objective world in accordance with its purposes (233, 193).

Hegel says this even more sharply: "The objective world thus is in and for itself the Idea, as it together eternally poses itself as *purpose* and produces its actuality through activity" (235, 193). In other words, as we noted above, the purposiveness of reason (and ultimately, of the Absolute) is present from the outset in objectivity. What we may then call the "reunification process" of subject and object, or practice and theory, must take place at each level of the externalization and development process of the Absolute. At the level of logic, the unity of the subjective and objective is *"absolute, total truth,"* but not yet as the whole; it is "the Idea that thinks itself, and indeed here *as* thinking, as *logical* Idea" or absolute Idea (236, 194).

The separation of theory from practice, although an essential part

of the unfolding process of the Absolute, is nevertheless in a fundamental sense an illusion. The overcoming of this illusion is equivalent
to the completion of history, or to the coordinate completion of eternity and world history, of which the pivot is the state (that is, the final
state or constitutional monarchy of Hegel's own time). On the other
hand, the union of theory and practice is essentially the same as the
union of objective and subjective, and it takes place in the Absolute.
If this is so, then how can the union of theory and practice take place
in the domain of objectivity, that is, in objective spirit or the state?
This is the question to which the balance of our analysis will lead us;
it is already visible in the structure of the analysis of the Idea.

There is another question, subordinate but related to our main
line of inquiry, for which a reply may perhaps be sketched. Does
Hegel make thinking into *poiēsis*? Is the practico-productive nature
of Hegel's theory a transformation of the Aristotelian distinctions of
theory, practice, and production into a single *energeia*? If we define
theory in the Greek sense as *looking* and *production* or *poiēsis* as *imitating* (natural forms or psychic ends), then a simple answer of "yes"
is impossible. For Hegel, thinking or theorizing is fundamentally an
assimilation process; it is a making only in the sense that it contains
will, and it could not be called an imitating in any sense. The distinction between original and image is not present in Hegel except
within the transitional stage of the reunification of subject and object
at all levels of Hegel's thought up to the final or comprehensive one.
From Hegel's standpoint, to call production *imitation* is to guarantee
alienation or dualism between original and image. One could also say
that the assimilative function of theory is analogous to the process in
Aristotle by which the intellect or soul becomes "somehow" the thing
thought. Hegel replaces the word "somehow" with the totality of his
system.

Similarly, one might wish to call willing a *poiēsis*, but again, this is
not altogether accurate, because subjective spirit produces but does
not imitate. Human production is the manifestation, not the imitation,
of divine creation, but not, of course, of the orthodox Christian creation *ex nihilo*. Even here a qualification is necessary. The Absolute, or
man, creates until such time as the truth is fully revealed and history
is completed or fulfilled (as distinct from terminated). Once Hegel
has finished speaking, it makes no sense to talk further of creation.
Henceforward, the task of man is to preserve what has been created.
With all these qualifications (and no doubt others could be added),

we may nevertheless agree that, in Hegel, the tripartite distinction of theory/practice/production is not maintained. It is present neither at the beginning nor at the end in Hegel's ontological eschatology. But one can scarcely say that Hegel confuses the Aristotelian distinctions. He transforms them by marrying them to the Christian doctrine of Spirit. If one wishes to criticize this aspect of Hegel's teaching, then it is the legitimacy of the marriage to which objection should be made.

I now return to our investigation of the union of theory and practice. We need not consider the section on natural philosophy in the *Encyclopedia* but go directly to the section on philosophy of Spirit. And again the theme of freedom gives us our bearings. The essence of Spirit is formally freedom or "absolute negativity of the concept as identity with itself." This means that it is immediate universality, or freedom from anything external to it (382, 313). Spirit must then develop or give content to itself as formal freedom. This development will have three stages: (1) subjective Spirit: freedom *bei sich,* or the self-referential (self-conscious) dimension of content; (2) objective Spirit: the world of reality, of freedom as "existing (*vorhandene*) necessity"; (3) Absolute Spirit: "existing in and for itself, and eternally self-producing *unity* of the objectivity of Spirit and of its Ideality" (subjective spirit: 385, 315). This corresponds to the process of unification of the objective and subjective in the absolute Idea (in absolute, total truth as logical Idea) (236, 194). Absolute Spirit is "Spirit in its absolute truth" and so is the unity of the Idea and nature, hence of the subjective and objective and of the practical and theoretical.

In man, this process occurs as the development of self-consciousness, which negates the one-sidedness of subjectivity and objectivity in the activity of satisfying instinct or desire (426–27, 350). The subjective Spirit is treated in three parts: anthropology, phenomenology, and psychology. The most important remarks about the unification of theory and practice occur in the section on psychology. As phenomenology is presented in the *Encyclopedia*, it is fundamentally about the development from consciousness to self-consciousness. This development makes the appearance of consciousness "identical with its essence, thereby raising its self-certitude to truth" (416, 364). So phenomenology, we may say, corresponds approximately to the section in the logic on essence.

We would anticipate that Hegel's analysis of the development of Spirit would be coordinate with his analysis of the Idea. Of course, the section on the Idea is the conclusion of the logic, whereas the section on Spirit is at the same level as that on logic. Nevertheless, it is in the development of the Idea that the subjective and objective are united in the Absolute. However, in the philosophy of Spirit, the subjective and the objective seem to be united in both the objective *and* the Absolute Spirit. Let us look at the details. I remind you that the initiative for the unification of theory and practice in the case of the Idea comes from the practical activity of the subjective Idea. When this unification is completed, we have the Absolute Idea. So the objective Idea is assimilated into the subjective Idea by the activity of the latter. But subjective Spirit is, as it were, *exteriorized* (rather than assimilated) into objective Spirit, that is, into the state and into world history. Are we then to conclude that the initiative for the unification of theory and practice in the domain of Spirit comes from the activity of the objective rather than (as in the case of the Idea) of the subjective element? And if so, is this activity theoretical rather than practical? What sense does it make to refer to the activity of objective Spirit as (primarily) theoretical?

It is true that subjective Spirit (rational will, the Idea in itself) wills to unfold its content into existence, the actuality of the Idea, or objective Spirit (482, 387). This unfolding is structurally coordinate to that of the subjective concept into the object world of theoretical science. The object is already the product of subjective desire or will, which motivates the unification of subjective and objective at this level. In the case of Spirit, however, the object is the state. Hegel's doctrine turns upon the assumption that there is not simply an analogy but an identity between the subjective dimension of the conceptualized object and that of the state. I find this assumption unacceptable. There is no reason to believe that the subjective dimension of the state (the satisfied ethical citizen) initiates a unification of subjective and objective Spirit in art, religion, and philosophy. Correspondingly, one might allow that a reasonable development of objective knowledge returns us to the knowing subject and hence to the unity of subject and object. But if "the reasonable development of the state" (whatever that is) is the unity of theory and practice in objective *Sittlichkeit*, is there not here a terminus of development (as perhaps in Maoist China)? How explain Absolute Spirit as a further consequence of that totality? In my opinion, the universality of the subject in objective knowledge is not even analogous to, let alone identical with, the universality of the subject in the objectivity of the state. Stated simply, complete knowledge is not analogous to complete political satisfaction because citizens are individuals, some of them philosophers, most of them not (to say nothing of other differences). Perfect knowledge may be divine, but God is not a citizen of Prussia.

Let us turn to some specific passages in the *Encyclopedia*. Just as consciousness has as its object the natural soul, so Spirit has consciousness as its object. Spirit develops by uniting objective content with its own Ideality, and is thus (1) theoretical: It treats the rational as its own immediate determination (the world of reality or necessity is known or assimilated); (2) will or practical: The rational determination is made subjective (not merely known but "owned"); (3) free: This is the *Aufhebung* of the one-sidedness of the theoretical and practical. This *Aufhebung*, or the unity of theory and practice, apparently occurs in the state, that is, in the free activity of objective Spirit (444, 358), or in *Sittlichkeit*, "the fulfillment of objective Spirit, the truth of the subjective and of the objective Spirit itself" (513, 402). Objective Spirit is one-sided because it has its freedom partly in external reality and partly in the good as an abstract universal. Subjective Spirit is one-sided because it defines itself abstractly in its inner singularity in opposition to the universal. These are *aufgehoben* through *Sittlichkeit*, and thus subjective freedom becomes "the self-conscious *freedom* unto *nature*" (ibid.). So the theoretical and practical remain as not yet unified within the domain of the subjective Spirit (444, 358); they are unified within the domain of the objective Spirit. In the case of Spirit, then, the unity of subject and object is initiated by objective activity or *Sittlichkeit*. As I have already claimed, if *Sittlichkeit* is itself motivated by the subjective element of purposiveness, this cannot be in the same sense as in the Idea. If it were, the result would be a universal homogeneous world state à la Kojève. This apart, once the subjective Spirit is fulfilled in *Sittlichkeit*, how does it move beyond objectivity and the state to the Absolute? That this is a problem for Hegel himself is suggested by the fact that there seem to be *two* unifications of theory and practice because two unifications of subjective and objective. Or else, if the final unification of subjective and objective takes place in Absolute Spirit, then the union of theory and practice is antecedent to it, again contrary to the dialectic of the Idea. Furthermore, we saw previously that freedom is thinking the whole, in other words, the Absolute Idea. But now freedom is the *Aufhebung* of the one-sidedness of the theoretical and the practical (via the objective and the subjective) Spirit, within *Sittlichkeit*, the completion of objective Spirit.

The intelligence of theoretical Spirit appropriates or assimilates the determinations of the world as immediate. Through the last negation of immediacy, intelligence poses within itself that its content is "for it": this is the transition to will or practical Spirit (468, 379). As will, Spirit steps into actuality; as *Wissen*, it is in the ground or foundation of the universality of the concept (469, 380). That is, practical Spirit is the enactment of purposiveness in the world as known theoretically. The completion of this enactment is freedom. Freedom as concept "is essentially nothing but thinking." So thinking must be united with willing; willing must raise itself to the status of "thinking willing." And this raising is the process by which practical becomes objective Spirit. In my previous formulation, subjective exteriorizes into objective Spirit and is thus truly free. And the actually free will—in other words, that of objective Spirit—"is the unity of the theoretical and practical Spirit." Again, "The will has this unity or universal determination as its object and purpose only insofar as it thinks, knows its concept, is will as free intelligence" (481, 387). To paraphrase, freedom is the thinking of politico-historical activity. In this case, it cannot be the thinking of art, religion, and philosophy, or the activity of Absolute Spirit.

We can sharpen the point as follows. Spirit that knows itself to be free is at first generally "the rational will, or in itself the Idea, and so only the concept of the Absolute Spirit" (482, 387f). That is, objective Spirit, or the thinking of politico-historical activity, is the Absolute Idea in itself (483, 389). Does it follow from this that subjective Spirit is the Absolute Idea for itself, and that the two are *aufgehoben* in Absolute Spirit? Apparently not; in the opening paragraph on Absolute Spirit (553, 440), Hegel says that it is the identity of *Realität* and the concept of Spirit as *Wissen* of the Absolute Idea. Subjective and objective Spirit, Hegel adds, are the way in which *Realität* builds itself up. The Idea was defined initially in the section on logic as "the true in and for itself, the absolute unity of the concept and of objectivity" (213, 182). *Realität* corresponds approximately to objectivity. Because objective Spirit is the Absolute Idea in itself, then so too is the subjective Spirit. In this case, it is the concept that corresponds to the Absolute Idea for itself. *The* Absolute, that is, Absolute Spirit, is then the union of Absolute Idea in itself (the union of subjective and objective Spirit) and for itself (the concept as *Wissen*). This proposal does not seem to correspond altogether with the definition of the Absolute Spirit as "eternally self-producing *unity* of the objectivity of Spirit and of its

Ideality" (385, 315). But we might try to reconcile them as follows. The Ideality or concept, as fully developed, is the Absolute Spirit for itself and so as not yet united with objective reality. The self-producing and eternal activity of unification is indeed the activity of the Absolute. The difficulty lies then in the apparently dual location of subjectivity. And this can be resolved by pointing out that objectivity is already a product of will; purposiveness and so subjectivity is an ingredient in the Idea from the outset.

I do not regard this as a very satisfactory resolution. The difficulty can be signaled by noting that, as the Absolute is union of the subjective and the objective, it must already be for itself as in itself. However, I want to state the whole issue in one last and more general manner. To my charges of structural incoherence, Hegel might defend himself as follows. The unity of theory and practice occurs decisively in objective Spirit and is a necessary precondition for Absolute Spirit or *the* Absolute: for the whole and knowledge of the whole. The unity of the philosopher and the state is then effected by the fact that the philosopher is a citizen and, in that guise, an element of the precondition for his identity as thinker of the Absolute. In other words, what looks like a dualism between citizen and philosopher is overcome at the level of the Absolute, where the philosopher sees the necessity of his citizenship as an ingredient in totality. In art, religion, and philosophy, the spirit rises above the state but only on the basis of the state. And the basis or ground is contained in the grounded.

In my opinion, such a defense could work only to establish the conclusion that, within the whole, there must be both citizens and philosophers, and that philosophers are also citizens. But this serves merely to internalize the dualism within the philosopher. As the philosopher or sage is the final manifestation of the Absolute, he naturally includes all elements of that manifestation. With the proper definition of terms, one could say that the philosopher is a tree or a star, a cow or a dog, as well as a citizen. Does it follow from this that the difference between the philosopher and, say, his dog is overcome? My point is not that one must first be a dog in order to be a philosopher but that knowledge of an object is not the same as union with that object. The difficulty lies in Hegel's suppression of the "somehow" in Aristotle's assertion that the intellect becomes somehow what it knows. In the given instance, and putting the point as simply as possible, if objective Spirit is the Absolute in itself, then the unity of theory and practice is unstable. Such a unity is carried out by objective Spirit, which cannot be practical because it is not subjective, and cannot be objective because it is not theoretical. Still more explicitly, the state is not a philosopher, but neither is it a citizen. And the completion or fulfillment of the state depends upon a uniting of citizen and philosopher that ought to result in the *Aufhebung*, or, in Marx's term, the withering away of the state. We therefore see how critical is the inversion, in the shift from Idea to spirit, of the order of initiative in the work of subjectivity and objectivity. This inversion is necessary for Hegel in order to exteriorize subjectivity in politico-historical activity. But it is accomplished at the price of a distortion in the symmetry of the structure of the system and by failing to answer the question as to the nature of the activity of objective Spirit. I realize that the answer seems to be *Sittlichkeit*. But this is defective, since there is no apparent reason why a satisfied citizen should become a philosopher. And there is every apparent reason why, once having become a philosopher, he should be a dissatisfied citizen.

We come finally to the question: What is freedom? Is it thinking, or thinking united with doing? I have suggested that if freedom is *Sittlichkeit*, then the Absolute must be beyond freedom. But if freedom is thinking, then there is no unity between theory and practice. It is by no means obvious that man can be free under any circumstances or in accordance with any philosophical explanation. I think, however, that if freedom is to have any meaning at all, there can be no union of physics and politics, to use somewhat old-fashioned terms. Man is free, if at all, only in the interstices of the split within nature between the cosmos and the state. But whether free or not, man remains man only as alienated from both cosmos and state. The suppression of a *Jenseits* may be effected by an act of extraordinary genius, as in the case of Hegel, or by obtuseness and self-forgetting. In either case, it is a philosophical error of the first magnitude.

CHAPTER SEVEN

Logic and Dialectic

Are logic and dialectic mutually exclusive enterprises, or is there an intimate relation between them? In this chapter, I shall defend the second of these alternatives. In so doing, I hope to contribute to the ongoing reconciliation between two major conceptions of rationality. My remarks are therefore not intended as an apologia for Hegelian dialectic; neither are they meant for some prominent school of the philosophy of logic. I will instead propose that logic and dialectic are joined together in the texture of everyday modes of reasoning. There is no natural competition between logic and dialectic, and my task is never to reduce one to the other. However, I do believe that the issue cannot be posed without making it evident from the outset that dialectic is the broader of the two functions of thought. It is surely noncontroversial to observe that there cannot be a logical justification of logic. Even such defenses as that by Aristotle of the principle of noncontradiction are dialectical, not to say ad hominem. The serious question, to my mind, is how to certify the rational, as opposed to the merely rhetorical, nature of the dialectical defense of logic.

Let us begin with the most generally held thesis concerning logic, namely, that it is the study of logical consequence. The circularity in this formulation is in effect acknowledged by contemporary authorities. According to Alfred Tarski, "the sentence X follows logically from the sentences of the class K if and only if every model of the class K is also a model of the sentence X." A few paragraphs later, Tarski adds the following remark:

> Underlying our whole construction is the division of all terms of the language discussed into logical and extra-logical. This division is certainly not quite arbitrary. If, for example, we were to include among the extra-logical signs the implication sign, or the universal quantifier, then our definition of the concept of consequence would lead to results which obviously contradict ordinary usage. On the other hand, no objective grounds are known to

me which permit us to draw a sharp boundary between the two groups of terms. It seems to be possible to include among logical terms some which are usually regarded by logicians as extralogical without running into consequences which stand in sharp contrast to ordinary usage.[1]

The paper from which I quote is addressed implicitly to the task of distinguishing logic from nonlogic. At least in the tradition to which Tarski belongs, logic is generally understood as the study of consequence, that is, of inference and, formally, of deducibility. This relation obtains among sentences—more exactly, between a set of sentences (or propositions) called premises and a sentence (or proposition) called a conclusion. In a subsequent section, I want to look more carefully at how we decide what it means to speak of *logical consequence*. Here, we may assume the consensus view of the concept. Let me emphasize two obvious features of Tarski's discussion. First: Tarski defines *logical consequence*, not *deducibility*. He acknowledges that "the formalized concept of consequence, as it is generally used by mathematical logicians, by no means coincides with the common concept."[2] In other words, one must go back to the common concept, or turn from formal deducibility and hence syntactics, not just to semantics, but to the semantics of natural language. This brings me to the second point: Tarski justifies decisions in formal semantics, and so definitions of logical consequence, with respect to common usage. The concept of logical consequence, even when rigorously defined, depends upon what we mean by a logical connective. And whereas what we mean by a logical connective is "not quite arbitrary" by the standards of common usage, it is not established in a precise manner by those standards. An important inference may be drawn from these two points, by us if not by Tarski. There is nothing unambiguous in the conception of the task of science as the replacement of primitive intuitions by formal theories. The intuitions cannot be simply replaced by theories, because the function of theories is to explain, and so to be measured by, intuitions. On the other hand, intuitions cannot be precisely captured in theories. It is almost immediately evident that the relation between intuition and logic is *dialectical*.

1. Alfred Tarski, "On The Concept Of Logical Consequence," in *Logic, Semantics, Metamathematics* (Oxford: Clarendon Press, 1956), 417f.
2. Ibid., 411.

Before developing the implications of this inference, let me cite a contemporary contributor to the tradition of philosophical logic. In his paper "What Is Logic?"[3] Ian Hacking is explicitly concerned to distinguish between logic and nonlogic: "My focus will be the demarcation of logic: What distinguishes logic from the extralogical?" (285). Hacking cites the paper by Tarski from which I have just quoted and indicates that the task of demarcation turns upon a clarification of the nature of logical constants, of which he proposes a definition (287). I cite Hacking here because, despite his attempt to resolve the problem outlined by Tarski, he makes it plain that the solution (based upon an attempt to infer semantical properties from syntactical ones, 300ff.) rests upon presuppositions that amount to an admission of the problem. I shall ignore his technical contribution, not because I consider it valueless, but because it is outside the perimeter of my present interests. What counts for us is Hacking's relativizing of operational rules for the definition of logical constants to a given language or semantic framework (318). In that context, Hacking says:

> There still remain the familiar questions as to what it is to grasp the meaning. Undoubtedly we understand some constants before formulating any rules, and even if we did not, there would be questions about following the rules. It may be, however, that certain positive conclusions are to be drawn from the theory of operational rules. For it is not as if they justify talk of logical *truth*. All we get from applying the rules are some sentences with the deducibility sign in front. To construe these as truths we require a semantics (318).

In his discussion of the semantic framework, Hacking apparently makes only two assumptions: that every sentence in the language must be either true or false but not both, and that one set of sentences is a logical consequence of another if, no matter what values are assigned to the members of the two sets, some member of the second set is true when every member of the first set is true. However, in earlier passages, Hacking states that "the operational rules at most *characterize* the logical constants in a certain way for a person that already has some logical ideas" (299) and "the operational rules 'fix the meanings of the logical connectives' in the sense of giving a se-

---

3. Ian Hacking, in *The Journal of Philosophy* 76, no. 6 (June, 1979), p. 318. Page numbers in parentheses in the text will refer to this article until otherwise stated.

mantics, only if classical notions of truth and logical consequence are already assumed" (300). It looks as though Hacking has two senses of *semantics,* one formal or technical, the other a presupposition about logical ideas or common usage. Since the technical semantics depends upon the pretechnical presuppositions, we are justified in restricting our attention to the presuppositions. There is then no syntactical procedure that enables us to generate semantical presuppositions concerning logical consequence or to dispense with these presuppositions.

Hacking's paper, which is, I think, a good representative of contemporary speculations on the nature of logic, thus provides us with a solid basis for drawing the same inference as followed from Tarski's paper. In Hacking's words once more, "I do not believe that English is by its nature classical or intuitionistic or whatever. Classical and intuitionistic truth are both abstractions made by logicians" (310). My inference is that English, or any natural language, is by nature dialectical rather than logical. Justifications for the semantics of classical or deviant logics are not arbitrary with respect to common usage; they simply appeal to different aspects of this usage. Natural language provides us with the source for all our intuitions about logical consequence; for this very reason, however, natural language also contradicts each of these intuitions. But this does not justify our rejecting natural language in favor of an artificial language. For which artificial language would we choose? To speak of different artificial languages for different purposes is implicitly to grant the priority of natural language, the source of our differing purposes, that is, of purposive activity altogether. By the same token, such talk implicitly grants the unreasonableness of making classical logic the paradigm for rationality in natural discourse. Please note: I am not denying that any sentence uttered in natural language can be analyzed in accord with the laws of classical logic. I am asserting that the decision to engage in this analysis must itself be justified by higher laws, and these laws are dialectical.

I would like to call this chapter a contribution to the semantics of natural language. In the sense I give to this expression, it includes such apparently deviant activities as an exposition of the motivating spirit of Hegel's logic, as well as more orthodox tasks like that of obtaining clarity about common usage. These two activities are not incompatible, since Hegel's logic attempts precisely to obtain clarity about common usage. Because Hegel is normally associated with the term *dialectic,* an extended remark on this topic may help to reassure those who fear that logic is endangered by any association with dialectic. Let me put the main point as simply as possible. For Hegel, what is normally called *logic* functions at the level of understanding, whereas dialectic (or dialectico-speculative logic) functions at the level of reason. This is not quite accurate, but it is not misleading, and it enables us to get to the heart of the matter with a minimum of technical exposition. For Hegel, dialectic is metalogical in the sense that it provides a sound conceptual account of the process of theorizing within language. Dialectic is thus the comprehensive theory of language and so of theory itself. Because all theory emerges from natural language, the rationality of theory depends upon the rationality of natural language. But classical logic cannot furnish a certification of the rationality of natural language. The dialectical essence of natural language demands a dialectical logic, one that is circular or presuppositionless in the specific sense that it grounds itself. In other words, Hegel claims to have discovered a logical analysis of our primitive intuitions that both reconciles their contradictory aspects and does not itself rest upon ungrounded intuitions.

The reader should note carefully that Hegel's semantics of natural language, as I am calling it, does not present us with a definition of logical consequence that serves as the semantical interpretation of logical deducibility. There is no concept, no definition, of deducibility as the paradigm of drawing inferences within natural language, which, as we have seen in a variety of ways, is broader than deductive reasoning. The concept of deducibility becomes intelligible only on the basis of restrictions placed upon natural language—restrictions, to be sure, that are motivated by intuitions themselves intimately connected with natural language. Hegelian semantics purports to show, or may be taken to attempt to show, how the complete analysis of the contradictions implicit in natural language uncovers the categorial structure of language. This structure is not mathematical because, in it, each category, as we think or attempt to isolate it, is continuously turning into its opposite, or indeed into all the other categories with which a logical understanding would wish to contrast it. I cannot undertake to explain here exactly what Hegel means by this. Suffice it to say that he intends to uncover the necessary conditions for the possibility of our saying *anything*. In order for us to be able to define *consequence,* there must be a coherent categorial (or rational) structure underlying this definition. Definitions and mathematical logics are discovered or constructed within a continuum of intelligibility. Whereas artificial logics are local or discontinuous, dialectical logic must be universal and continuous, exactly like the continuum of intelligibility. In the last analysis, there is no difference between this continuum and its logic. But there is a difference between, say, mathematical logic, or set theory, and the continuum of intelligibility within which logics and set theories are formulated.

I am not myself a Hegelian, however much I have learned from him. I hold to a much weaker sense of dialectic than he does. I have written elsewhere on my criticisms of Hegel at some length; it will suffice here for me to limit myself to the main point. In order to do this, I must first indicate a criticism of Hegel with which I do not agree. As Bertrand Russell has objected, Hegel's logic makes it impossible to understand any one definite object or property because of the claim of that logic that to understand anything fully is to understand everything. This objection is based upon a misunderstanding. Hegelian logic leaves science and mathematics untouched in their domains; what it tries to do is to provide an explanation of the context, effectivity, or presuppositions of science and mathematics. Hegel's contention that non-p is part of the definition of p is, to employ a Tarskian distinction in a different framework, metalogical, not logical. This contention amounts to the thesis that (metalogical) principles of logic, as expressive of the structure of the continuum of intelligibility within which logics are discovered or constructed, must themselves be continuous. To take what is perhaps the crucial point, in a classical or nondialectical logic, it is impossible to deduce or arrive at negation from affirmation. Even if we construct a logic with a single axiom, that axiom already contains both affirmation and negation, which must be understood as distinct in order for us to understand the operation defined by the axiom (as is obvious from the fact that such axioms are interpreted by truth tables). In Hegelian metalogic, position and negation are reciprocally-defining operations. This is not the same as to say that they are identical in the sense that they are two different names for the same operation. Hegel's point is rather that one cannot think, or write down a symbolical representation, of the law or predicate of identity except by a multiplication of our symbol for unity.

When we represent identity by the expression $x = x$ or $(x) (x = x)$, we double or triple the x. This is not simply a convenience of notation but shows something fundamental about thinking. We cannot think sameness except through the invocation or mediation of difference. Nor is there any confusion here of identity and predication. The logician wants to say that the x on the right-hand side of the equality sign is not different from, but the same as, the x on the left-hand side. The (Hegelian) metalogician's reply is that the sameness of the x can only be shown by indicating, through difference, the sameness of the x's. To put this in slightly different language, if we could conceive of identity without difference, it would suffice to think, say, or write down the symbol x. But to do this would be like claiming that we had discovered a logic with a single axiom, A. A single symbol means nothing; this is Plato's criticism of the Parmenidean doctrine of the One. What the logician is actually saying, then, might be paraphrased as follows: "Do you see those two x's in the expression $x = x$? Well, take them to stand for the same entity." However, we can perform this operation only by noticing that sameness is made cognitively accessible through multiplication or difference. The assertion A or x or anything else (*cow, man, number,* and so on) is in fact not an assertion, not a statement at all, but a noise, or a mark on paper. There is no conceivable way to define identity except through difference. This is Hegel's point about the reciprocal intelligibility of position or affirmation and negation. And it is from considerations such as these that Hegel arrives at his dialectical interrelationship of axioms. But none of these considerations is intended to have any bearing on the operations internal to standard or nondialectical logic.

My objection, then, does not lie along these lines. I cannot accept Hegel's claim to have expounded completely the categorial structure of the continuum of intelligibility. I have other disagreements as well, but this is the most serious, so far as Hegel's own doctrines are concerned. Hegel's logic, I repeat, is not deductive but developmental, and it is not linear-progressive (in the sense that it generates ever-new theorems) but circular. If Hegel's logic were not complete, it would fail to explain conceptually the continuum of intelligibility; there would be rents in the fabric of intelligibility. The links in the development would be dissolved. But how could we ever know that his logic is complete? How could we ever know that there is not still another category waiting to be discovered? Hegel's reply, of course, is that he has succeeded in explaining everything; but this claim is conservatism in its worst form. It assumes that what we know is all there is to know, in a way very much like that version of ordinary-language analysis that explains unorthodox or nonstandard utterances in terms of familiar or standard utterances. There is also the problem that a complete conceptual explanation must also assimilate or explain discursively our primary intuitions. But must we not see that such discursive explanations are sound and thus rely once more upon intuitions external to the demonstration? If our intuitions are explained by our discursive analyses, then there is no difference between Hegel on this point and those analytical philosophers who talk about "life-forms" and "linguistic horizons." My own view is different. It is a good Hegelian principle to observe that, in posing a restriction, we are already beyond it. This principle applies to Hegel as well as to ordinary-language or linguistic analysts. We must be beyond every discursive restriction in order to see what we are talking about. If our discourse were actually bounded by a linguistic horizon, we would never know it, never notice it, never be able to pose the problem. The capacity of posing limits or problems is rooted in, or is the same as, the capacity to transcend limits and problems. Those who claim to be able to conceptualize or axiomatize this capacity are not simply replacing intuition with discourse. They are claiming to be able to define the impossibility of our seeing what it is that they are defining.

A sympathy for dialectical logic is one thing, then; Hegelianism is something else. We may put to one side the question of whether my criticisms of Hegel are right or wrong. The important points are these: first, even a full-blown Hegelianism presents no danger to mathematical or nondialectical logic. And second, the intention of dialectic is to provide a rational basis for logic, one that it cannot furnish for itself. In other words, logic is powerless against rhetoric; and the distinction between logic and rhetoric leaves the way open for a doctrine of rationality with respect to rhetoric. Dialectic is such a doctrine. Dialectic is the attempt to discuss the continuum or fabric of intelligibility that makes logic possible. However, we can never be certain that we have completed our discussion of this fabric. Even if no rents are visible, it does not follow that we have made explicit the inner weave of the fabric. Finally, one may wish to call this weave by the term *structure*, but to do so is to run the risk of forgetting that such a structure cannot be logical in the usual sense.

We cannot distinguish logic from dialectic without arriving at some understanding of the nature of logic. The disputes among philosophers of logic should be enough to establish that we cannot arrive at this understanding merely by quoting from one or two fashionable treatises on logic. Tarski and Hacking hold that a sharp definition of logical consequence is prevented by the impossibility of providing a noncircular definition of logical constants. The question of the nature of logical constants aside, however, we have no precise understanding, in a conceptual or discursive form, of what it means to speak of logical consequence. Logicians are right to refer to intuitions of consequence, but they do not seem to me to take this point seriously enough. Perhaps the reason is their professional bias, which leads them to assume that the imprecision of intuition can always be replaced by the rigor of conceptual definition. I agree that such a replacement is possible. But the serious problem is quite different: how shall we justify the step from our intuitions to this or that rigorous definition?

For the sake of dialectical thoroughness (something different from logical rigorousness), let us begin our inquiry in a rather literal-minded way. Reference to standard treatises or textbooks on mathematical logic (Curry, Kleene, Shoenfield, or Mendelson may serve as examples) provides us with one version or another of the remark that logic is the analysis of thought, or the study of reasoning. I propose that we begin by taking this contention quite seriously. It will lead us to look at one or two problems that may seem superfluous to adepts but that in my opinion will help to make some valuable points. So we start with the question: what is a thought? Is it, for example, a concept? We might be encouraged to take this line of response by the frequent use of such expressions as "the logic of concept x." However, the meaning of these expressions is not clear. To be sure, Frege distinguishes between concepts and objects, but the syntax of "the logic of concept x" leads one to assume that x is a variable for names of concepts, which are thus treated as objects. But what would it mean to speak of the logic of an object? The reader will no doubt protest that concepts are not objects but properties by which we collect objects together and so distinguish them from objects lacking that property. In this case, I repeat my question with the appropriate variation: what would it mean to speak of the logic of a property? We would have to go altogether too far afield to come to close grips with the nature of the concept *concept*.[4] I want to bring out a simpler point just now. Neither a property nor an object—in more traditional terms, neither a sub-

---

4. Cf. Rosen, *The Limits of Analysis* (Basic Books: New York, 1980), chapter 1, 3B.

ject nor a predicate—has a logic. We have accepted as our beginning the intuition that logic deals with consequence. But nothing follows from a name, whether that name be of a subject or a predicate. To pronounce the name "love" or "causality" is very much like saying "Patricia" or "Max."

We may, of course, "analyze" concepts. In so doing, however, we shall require more than logic. For it is not logic that provides us with the senses, meanings, uses, or resonances of a concept or the name of a concept. Logic allows us to do something with these once we have them. It allows us to say, "this follows from that," where *this* and *that* stand for our initial acquisitions with respect to the concept. Even so, none of this is clear. Are we so sure that we know what we mean by saying that this follows from that or more generally that something follows from something? We agreed to begin on the basis of authority, and our authorities have told us that logic is (in sum) the study of reasoning thought. It therefore looks as though logic studies how one thought follows from another. Because thoughts presumably follow from each other only in the activity of thinking, "follows from" must also be a thought or an aspect of thinking. But again, what can this have to do with logic? We have to peek several lines or paragraphs ahead in the treatises by our authorities in order to find that logical consequence has something to do with necessity or at least with rules. However, experience shows me that I can think whatever I like; the stream of consciousness supports the thesis that any thought can lead to any thought. How do rules play any role here? The logician, of course, will tell us somewhat irritably at this point to distinguish between psychology and logic. But how are we to do so when we do not yet know what logic is? All we have been told is that logic is, or studies, the rules governing the sequence of thoughts. But either there are no such rules or, if there are any, they must be psychological, if psychology is the study of thought. In slightly different terms, how are we to interpret the curious fact that the word *logic* is clearly visible within the word *psychology*? If thinking is defined by the science of thinking, and the science of thinking is defined by logic, the distinction between psychology and logic may not be as clear as is often thought. A scientific account of thinking must take into account the fact that thinking is done by a thinker. In short, logic must take into account the bipolar structure of thinking. Is disregarding one of the poles a sound way of taking this structure into account?

There is nothing plausible about the assertion that logic has nothing to do with thinking. Such an assertion goes directly contrary to the views of our authorities. What they presumably mean, and what we need to understand, is that there is a purely logical aspect of thoughts. Unfortunately, we still do not know what *purely logical* means. We cannot resolve the problem with our initial intuition that logic means *follows from*, because *follows from* is an aspect of thinking, and in the activity of thinking, anything can follow from anything. Apparently we are not going to arrive at a preliminary understanding of logic until we can restrict the meaning of *follows from*. But how are we going to do this? We surely cannot restrict its meaning by our understanding of logic; we have no such understanding as yet. Of course, by peeking ahead, we noted that logical consequence has to do with necessity or rules. But as we have just seen, assuming that we understand those expressions, they do nothing to draw a distinction between logic and psychology. In the first section, we saw that we require intuitions about what is to count as a logical constant. We are now in the process of seeing that we also require intuitions about appropriate values of logical variables. *What* follows from *what*?

Once again, the reader may be tempted to interject: Logic is the study of the *forms* of thought. He or she may wish to introduce distinctions between statements and propositions, patterns of inference, axiomatics, and so on. "Why all this mystery-mongering and spinning of wheels to no purpose?" he or she will demand. The answer is that we are trying to think our way toward logic rather than simply engaging in an accepted convention. If to call logic the study of thought is to mean that one cannot think about logic, then thought becomes altogether arbitrary. On the other hand, to think about logic is to ask oneself, what is it? And fiddling with our logical machines provides no answer to this question. I shall therefore continue with my effort to think my way toward logic. And I begin again. It is plain enough that some speeches or deeds persuade us to do or say something, whereas others dissuade us. How does this happen? In some cases, we have to grant that we do not know. But if we never know why we are persuaded, then we do not know *that* we are persuaded. And in this case, our experience would have to be quite different from what it actually is. I am not attempting to construct a presuppositionless ontological system, so I have no qualms about accepting our common experience that persuasion is rooted in orderliness, in the way the world works. It is not just the case that some speeches are persuasive whereas others are not. If examples are required, here is one: the statement "this house is on fire" will persuade us to quit the premises as rapidly as possible (unless it persuades us to search for some person or possession that we want to rescue from the flames), whereas the statement "this house is blue" will not (unless we dislike blue houses).

The world works in certain ways. A close analysis of what we mean by *certain* would no doubt raise as many difficulties as our attempt to grasp the meaning of *follows from*. It may well be that, at bottom, the questions are the same. But there is an important distinction in the context. We do not need to possess conceptual knowledge of *certain* (meaning *regular*) in order to be persuaded by some speeches and not by others. However, we must possess conceptual knowledge of *follows from* if we are to claim to know the difference between logic and nonlogic and also to distinguish between logic and dialectic. A knowledge of causality is not necessary for me to be persuaded to leave a burning house. But a knowledge of logical consequence is necessary for me to make claims about the correspondence between logic and rational thought. If logic is nothing but a species of persuasion, then all talk about the rationality of logic is nothing but rhetoric. We may readily agree that logic is the study of those connections between statements that persuade us. But until we can distinguish between connections and associations (to use a Humean distinction), we will not have distinguished between persuasiveness and validity. We might, of course, commit ourselves to some definition of logical necessity. But what is the meaning of *commitment*? *Ought* we to stick by our logical commitments? And if so, why? Surely not for logical reasons.

I prefer to develop this difficulty in a somewhat different way. Suppose the suggestion is made that logic turns upon the distinction between formal and empirical components of our thoughts. To think is surely to have the experience of thinking. How can I think a component of thinking (namely, the formal component) without thinking, and so experiencing, it? If this is impossible, as it seems to be, then what sense is there in the distinction between the formal and the empirical components of thoughts? Of course, there might be some aspect of a thought which I am not actually thinking at some moment or another. But I cannot do logic without (by hypothesis) thinking of logical forms; and when I think them, I experience them. There is no point in saying that the term *experience* is being used in two different senses, because we have no theoretical basis for making that distinction yet. Let me lay my cards on the table at this point. I myself make the distinction by means of my intuitions. Those who reject talk of intuition in this context as meaningless or irrelevant, yet continue to insist upon logical forms, in my opinion simply do not know what they are talking about. They may, of course, mean to say that forms are theoretical constructions based upon empirical convenience. But if this is so, then there is in fact no distinction between the formal and the empirical components of our experience. And thus, the distinction between logic and dialectic is abandoned. Even worse, dialectic is abandoned, and its place is taken by rhetoric, whether of fashion or power.

We do not arrive at the conception of logical form by applying formal procedures to our cognitive experience. On the contrary, the development of formal procedures is based upon the conception of logical form. It is hardly irrelevant that even those who justify logic by means of nominalist or pragmatist doctrines continue to insist upon a notion of validity by virtue of form alone. Such terms as *canonical, standard,* and the like, continue to be employed by logical theorists to distinguish between the correct and the incorrect or the appropriate and the inappropriate way of interpreting validity, proof, and the like, as if our various stipulative or pragmatic definitions had a necessary basis in intuition, even when this is not explicitly granted, or when it is explicitly denied. We cannot, however, certify our stipulations by the articulation of a reason, if the sense and justification embodied in that reason are themselves the result of discursive stipulations. Sooner or later the sequence of stipulations terminates in how things look to us—in what *persuades* us. But our intention was to distinguish between the persuasive and the logically necessary. In my opinion, everyone knows that talk is rooted in cognitive perception. But philosophers are reluctant to give such perception or intuition as an explanation, because it is the nature of an intellectual faculty to have no structure, and this rules out any possibility of a theory of intuition in the modern sense of a discursive analysis. I should like to illustrate this point in a way that may seem to be a deviation from the discussion. Wittgenstein's later writings are filled with one passage after another in which intuition is first rejected, either explicitly or implicitly, and then a puzzle arises with respect to how we know some simple fact or another of our experience. For example, how do we know that someone is in pain? The answer, I think, is quite simple: sometimes we do not, but when we do, it is through an intuitive unification of a variety of perceptions, some visual, some aural, and so on. If we are not allowed to have an intuitive grasp of the sense of connected phenomena but are left with a person, his face contorted in a grimace, who shouts, "I am in pain!" then the puzzle arises whether the grimace and the shout are enough evidence for the inference that the man is actually in pain. And they are not enough evidence. This leads Wittgenstein to fanciful speculations about whether we require a "picture" of the pain as distinct from the grimace and the shout, or whether we would need to look inside the interior of the shouting person in order to try to see the pain, and so on. These speculations arise because the obvious answer to the problem has been ruled out. There is no analytical or theoretical account of how we know that certain symptoms show a man to be in pain, because we intuit this.

The same situation applies in the case of logical form. Stipulations have meanings, purposes, uses, and so on, which we finally perceive or do not perceive. The interposition of sequences of discursive explanations and justifications of the stipulation is itself an activity which, so to speak, holds up before the mind's eye one sentence after another, in hope that the addressee will "see" the point. Those who reject intuition are then at a loss to explain how we finally decide to do this rather than that, or how for that matter we understand any utterance whatsoever. To understand an utterance is not to understand some other utterance. When someone says, "we stipulate . . . ," he means to point out to his audience a logical form, pattern of inference, and so on. He is actually saying, "Look at this." An appeal to intuition is not an invocation of mysticism or speculative ontology. It is more like a shifting of one's stance than the taking of a new position. In such a shift, we just notice what we are doing all the time, and what, if we were not doing it, would be the consequences. There is nothing private about intuition, in the sense that we can certainly say something about what we see; that is the whole point of seeing of this kind: to enable us to say something. On the other hand, the public nature of intuition is not that of a definable structure. Intuition is not something to look at but rather the activity of looking. And how we look varies from case to case; it does not follow any rules.

I have now stated the basis upon which I myself distinguish between form and content within experience. Those who draw this distinction on the basis of some other capacity are free to refute me or to defend their own views. One view that will not stand up to criticism is that experience gives us the distinction between form and content. As we have now seen at sufficient length, we require some capacity for distinguishing between the aspects of experience relating to form and content. Pragmatic justifications amount to rhetorical interpretations of persuasiveness, not to a grounded concept of logical form. On the other hand, my reference to intuition has not served to justify some definite conception of logical form. I noted at the beginning of this essay that we have a variety of intuitions, which serve to justify a variety of forms, and so too more than one sense of logical consequence. However, I think it is reasonable to suppose that there is less controversy about logical consequence or the sense of *follows from*, than there is about the nature of logical forms. The quarrel between Platonism and nominalism is not about the sense of logical consequence but about the nature (or lack of a nature) of *what* following from *what*. We may be able to avoid a good bit of ontological controversy by shifting our focus from the question of logical forms to the question of logical consequence. Perhaps we shall be able to settle the question of the *what* once we have answered the question of the *follows from*.

We cannot begin with the textbook statement that forms of thoughts are expressible in formulae and so in formal patterns of inference. That is, after what has just transpired, we cannot answer the question about logical consequence by making use of the concept of logical form. Consider the following suggestion: "*b* follows logically from *a* whenever the truth of *a* guarantees the truth of *b*." In the first place, this leaves open the ticklish question of what to say when the truth of *b* is always conjoined with the antecedent falsehood of *a*. But this apart, the shift to symbols may have misled us into assuming that we know what *follows logically from* means. On the contrary, this is what was to be defined. In the suggestion just given, *follows logically from* is ostensibly defined by *guarantees*. But what does *guarantees* mean? What kind of guarantee does *a* offer for the truth of *b*, especially since the truth of *b* follows, in the usual logical schema, from the truth *or* falsity of *a*? In other words: we have begun our inquiry into the semantical justification in natural language for a concept of logical consequence. One might show, granted formal logic, or forgetting about the question of its justification, that certain symbols and certain operations upon these symbols necessarily, that is, thanks to the definitions, produce such-and-such results, and with no variations, so long as the definitions and operations are correctly and uniformly applied. But that was never in question. There is nothing controversial about the definition of inference or deducibility or theoremhood within a logical calculus, or within the metalanguage, in the technical sense of the term, of a calculus. Controversies arise when we apply this or that calculus to natural language. And of course, these controversies are already visible within natural language before we construct our calculus (and metalanguage).

So the suggestion in the previous paragraph is a nonstarter. This is not to say that it is absurd or meaningless. We can all understand the suggestion, thanks to our pretechnical experience, together with a minimum of technical information. What we cannot understand, at least thus far, is the license for moving from our natural linguistic or linguistically saturated experience to the suggested definition, thereby giving the latter the status of a rule that we *ought* to obey. I say *ought* rather than *must*, because there is no *must* about it. We can disobey this rule whenever we wish, if we are prepared to pay the price (or gain the reward). Sometimes philosophers talk as though it is impossible to disobey the laws of logic, but they never seem to be able to defend such an assertion in a noncircular way. Even if it were true that we could all agree upon, say, three universal rules that we could not disobey without ceasing to be rational, we would still be at liberty not to be rational. I do not say that this would be an easy thing to do; neither am I advocating such a course of action. My point is that it is impossible to define a rule except as something that we are free to disobey. No one says that it is a rule that animals must breathe. I am not referring here to the fact that human beings, at least, can voluntarily cease to breathe. I am calling attention to the fact that breathing is an essential ingredient in the activity of living. Are logical rules essential ingredients in the activity of thinking? Perhaps; but the problem is that there are a variety of rules and also a variety of kinds of thinking. Neither is there any point in being told that, if we wish to play such-and-such a game, then we must obey the rules. This is not in dispute. The question is which game to play, and no rule binds us to play one or another.

We now find ourselves in the following situation. In order to distinguish logic from dialectic (and so too from rhetoric), we need to explain what we mean by *logical consequence*. Roughly translated into ordinary language, it means that something follows from something. We were unable to decide what follows from what, so we agreed to shift our attention to *follows from*. But we do not seem to be able to take a single step in this direction. On the one hand, we have ruled out access to formal definitions, because our goal is to decide how we justify formal definitions. On the other hand, natural language, the language of pretheoretical experience, does not resolve the problem, because it furnishes us with many often conflicting intuitions, senses, purposes, desires, and so on. The whole problem is normally avoided by begging the question. It is assumed, in referring to natural language, that what we want is some pretechnical justification for the kinds of definitions to be found in the currently fashionable conception of logic. And, of course, such justifications can be found; natural language (by which I mean to refer to our everyday experience, which is saturated by language) is quite generous. It gives us whatever we request, which is to be expected, because it defines what we request of it.

One way in which to sum up these results is to say that logic is not metaphysically neutral. It is not an obvious and direct consequence of our everyday experience that we ought to move from informal reasoning to formalization. To state only the crucial point, formalization restricts us to one sense or another of logical consequence or validity, whereas natural language, and so everyday experience, sanctions a plurality of senses of validity. We grant that the world works in a more or less orderly fashion. But the strange thing about this orderliness is that it permits human beings to act successfully in quite disorderly ways. The orderliness of the world is compatible, to take the extreme case, with our paying no attention to logic. This is not to say that, when we pay no attention to them, logically valid arguments become invalid. They become irrelevant. If I live in a land without anteaters, no change transpires in the nature of anteaters, which continue to exist in their native habitat. Logical arguments, of course, are not like anteaters. But the difference is this: they cease to exist when we cease to make them. One might object that, without logic, rational thought is impossible, and so too investigations into the nature of logic, such as the present chapter. This, I think, is a more difficult case than the preceding one. But it is not as serious an objection as its devotees seem to think. So long as we do not know what logic is, we do not, by the terms of the objection, know what rationality or philosophy are, either. Hence we do not know whether this chapter is philosophy, poetry, or something else. However, it is not necessary to wheel through the galaxy of general objections to an inquiry into the nature of logic in order to see that no such objection could serve the purpose of explaining in a noncircular way what we mean by logical consequence and so by logic.

To come back to the denial of metaphysical neutrality, I am denying the claim that everyday experience certifies a canonical definition of logic as sharply distinct from dialectic and rhetoric. I propose that a dialectical treatment of everyday experience (or natural language) provides us with the basis for choosing a logic. The first point to be made is that "metaphysical neutrality" does not mean the same as W. V. Quine's expression "ontological neutrality." I am not interested here in the values of the variables of a first-order predicate calculus under a given interpretation. What interests me is the whole set of procedures called "first-order predicate calculus" and "a given interpretation." In other words, formalization is an expression of a metaphysical thesis or position. It is an interpretation of our everyday sense of what it means to be rational. Simply stated, it is the thesis that rationality is finally or ultimately a question of formal relations. The thesis comes to regard itself as metaphysically neutral when it forgets that formal relations have a being more fundamental even than the values of their variables. This forgetfulness is induced primarily by the redefinition of *being* as *existence* and the definition of *existence* on the basis of quantifiers, functional analyses of propositions, and variables as quantifiable and ranging over domains of objects. The formal symbolism thus assumes a cloak, not quite of invisibility, but of magisterial neutrality. It allows us to manipulate "what there is," but it is not itself to be included in that domain. Logic now assumes the status of the divine *logos;* it is beyond being (or existence). But this is either theology or nonsense; it is certainly not self-conscious and discursively-argued rationality.

The thesis that metaphysical problems disappear by the adoption of formalism is as old as Descartes. Descartes's version of this thesis leaves much to be desired in clarity and distinctness. Nevertheless, it is plain enough that in the *Regulae*, he says that we may express formally the ratios of things without taking into account their specific natures.[5] I use the term *ratio* to express the orders and measures of

---

5. Descartes, *Regulae*, ed. G. Crapulli (The Hague: M. Nijhoff, 1966), rules 3, 5 (especially p. 16) and 14.

both simple elements and geometrical shapes. The main point for us is that the Cartesian method is a generalization of mathematics, whose objects contain nothing of experience. They "consist of nothing but rationally deduced consequences."[6] They are, so to speak, a pure crystallization of reason. This purity, or the lack of empirical content, could be justified as metaphysical neutrality. However, in Descartes, purity is compromised by the fact that what counts as simple and complex (or absolute and relative) elements is dependent upon the investigator's intention. In other words, the order and enumeration of the elements is a function of the problem the investigator sets himself. We see here a striking anticipation of Kant's "Copernican revolution." Nature reveals her secrets to us if *we* formulate the proper questions. The modern mathematicization of nature has its roots in the proto-Idealism of Descartes. This is the link between Cartesian mathematical physics and Cartesian doctrines of subjectivity.[7]

To state this in another way, it is not clear whether man constructs the mathematical ratios of nature or intuits them. In a later passage, when responding to objections to his *Meditations*, Descartes contends that God's will is prior to his intellect and so that God could change the truths of mathematics and logic if he willed to do so. In the *Regulae*, it is difficult to distinguish between man and God. The problem of the relation between the will and the intellect casts its shadow over contemporary philosophy of logic and mathematics. On the one hand, we are told that there are canonical forms of rationality. On the other hand, we are told that logic is an empirical science or a free creation of the human intellect, and so too that which logic we choose is a function of our purposes, the problems to which we address ourselves, and so on. What we require, both in the case of Descartes and in contemporary philosophy, is a rational transition from primary intuitions and intentions to the canonical procedures of mathematics and logic. To argue the point in detail would take me too far afield, but I contend that Descartes presents no such transition. The *Meditations* is not a metaphysical founding of mathematical physics for (at least) the reason just given concerning the ambiguous relation between intellectual intuition and the will or human purpose. Descartes's formulation of the problem gives rise to the attempts of German Idealism to provide

6. Ibid., rule 2, p. 6.
7. Ibid., rule 6, p. 19; rule 7, p. 25.

a metaphysics of the will. But it also gives rise to the analytical attempt to cover over the problem with rhetoric and technical expertise.

The Cartesian project, in both its seventeenth- and its twentieth-century versions, intends primarily to make man the master and possessor of nature. But this cannot be accomplished unless man is free to restructure the traditional foundations of nature. Freedom of the will depends upon the contingency of structure. We may distinguish initially between logical and physical structure. However, if physical structure is contingent, the applicability of logic to nature requires a corresponding contingency in logical principles, rules, or categories. I do not believe that this point has been clearly and unequivocally grasped by those whom I am calling the Cartesians. An interesting example of this failure is the contemporary school of modal logicians who distinguish between logical and physical necessity. According to this distinction, whatever does not violate the principle of noncontradiction is physically possible. Another way in which to make this point is to say that thinking is implicitly conceived as distinct from being but at the same time as defining the structure of possible being. Let us call this a kind of logical Kantianism adapted to Cartesian goals. In order to retain logical necessity while at the same time making logic sufficiently flexible to deal with natural contingency, let us draw a tacit distinction between what I shall call logical and physical space. The heterogeneous appearance of nature, and so too of applied logic, is subjected to the uniformity of logical space. This is the assumption underlying the mathematicizing of nature. Mathematics is the universal articulation of logical space, the ultimate and comprehensive language of scientific thought. The problem in carrying out this program, at least at the theoretical level, is that the formal language of mathematics, with the normal exception of the principle of noncontradiction, has an ambiguous status. Does it belong to logical or to physical space? Is it necessary or contingent? Is it the transcendental language of nature or a human creation? If it is a transcendental language of nature, the distinction between logical and physical necessity is erroneous, and logical pragmatism or creationism is a false doctrine. If it is a human creation, we are now free to set our own questions but to a nonexistent or totally inaccessible nature. Logic and science are then indistinguishable from poetry.

The thesis of the metaphysical neutrality of mathematical science rests upon the distinction between logical and physical space. But that same thesis is challenged, not to say contradicted, by the ambiguous status assigned to logic (or more comprehensively, to mathematics). In my opinion, this ambiguity points to the metaphysical status of logic and mathematics, that is, to the metaphysical status of the assumption of a distinction between logical and physical space. In more traditional language, formalism rests upon a distinction between form and content that is either metaphysical or rhetorical. I prefer to call this distinction dialectical, but the choice of a name is obviously not the crucial point so long as the name we choose brings out the issues involved instead of concealing them. In subsequent sections, I am going to develop the issue from a slightly different angle. It seems noncontroversial to say that the principle of noncontradiction functions as the explicit or implicit axiom of logical space. But this principle is also the unchallenged axiom of natural language or pretheoretical experience. I shall argue that this principle, and so too natural language, is *dialectical*.

I summarize the results of this section as follows. Formalism in the general sense of the term (not to be confused with Hilbert's program) is already visible in Descartes's antimetaphysical metaphysics. According to this teaching, the forms and ratios by which we subjugate physical or natural heterogeneity all belong to the same genus. The conceptually heterogeneous space of Aristotelian science is replaced by the conceptually homogeneous space of mathematics. Problems, however diverse in phenomenal character, are reformulated or formalized so as to place them within logical space, thereby rendering them amenable to solution by *mathesis universalis*. Because logical space arises via the rejection of the ontological or metaphysical principles of Aristotelian science, it is asserted that mathematics, the language of this space, is ontologically or metaphysically neutral. Descartes pretends to ground his *mathesis universalis* in a metaphysical theology in order to persuade the theologians of his day to accept it in place of scholasticism. But the actual grounding of Cartesian science is in intuition, and by the nature of intuition, it is not amenable to a metaphysical or discursive theoretical grounding. Descartes in fact takes the step from intuition to the program of mathematical science by rhetoric: scholasticism is incapable of solving physical problems and satisfying man's desires. We do not need to examine the many ambiguities in Descartes's rhetoric here. Few if any contemporary Cartesians have any interest in his metaphysical theology, and not many students of Descartes, in our age of Cartesianism, have a clear perception of his rhetoric. Unlike the seventeenth-century theologians, we tend to accept Descartes's metaphysical theology as sincere. But whether we do or not, the fact remains that logical space is a human abstraction or a metaphysical interpretation of everyday experience, just as formal languages are abstractions from, and so interpretations of, natural languages.

One other point needs to be emphasized. To speak of the homogeneity of logical space is of course not to suggest that it cannot be articulated into diverse logical structures. Homogeneity refers to the principles of articulation, not to the absence of form. The forms are conceived as ontologically homogeneous; they obey common rules or are internally related with respect to their genesis, function, and possible transformations. They constitute a system, or more generally, are the basis of systematicness. Within logical space, we can define what it means for something to follow from something, because one stretch of logical space is continuous with another. In logic, what we mean by *follows from* is a rule expressing permission to move from one formal articulation of this space to another. This permission is not rooted in the formal articulations themselves, which are different and distinct from one another, but in the properties of homogeneity, which unite the articulated differences into a formal system. Hegel's dialectical logic is an alternative interpretation of logical space; this is why I called it a semantics of natural language. In my own version of dialectic, this semantics is the basis of definitions of logical consequence, just as it is in the metatheoretical justification of formal logic. However, I deny the possibility of a reflexive formalization of natural language. One can, of course, arbitrarily formalize any *fragment* of natural language. But one does so on the basis of the unformalized remainder, which provides us with the justification for the application of our formal techniques. This justification does not begin from a formal definition of *follows from*. It begins from intuitions that we express in natural language, and these intuitions are diverse and nonsystematic. It is the absence of a comprehensive or founding formal definition of *follows from* that allows a rational basis for formal construction or demonstration. We can always say what we are doing and why. The reasonableness of what we say lies in the fact that we can change our minds, or think of a better reason, or a more powerful formal definition, or a more subtle delineation of the presuppositions of logic. If rational thinking were grounded in an inviolable formal principle, none of this would be possible. The entire complex of problems would never arise, and if by some miracle it did arise, there would be nothing to say about it other than to repeat the principle.

I have thus far cast my lot with those who criticize the attempt to supply indubitable foundations to mathematics and logic by any kind of formalism. At the same time, however, I have defended a sense of intuition that may strike the reader as both too vague and too formalist. This would presumably have been the response of the late Imre Lakatos, if one may judge by his paper on "Infinite Regress and Foundations of Mathematics."[8] Lakatos offers in this paper an extremely powerful, if condensed and highly rhetorical, criticism of foundationalist thinking. He identifies as a crucial element in such thinking the recourse to intuition and, specifically, to logical intuition of ostensibly indubitable axioms. Stated somewhat more precisely, Lakatos takes intuition in a sense attributed to it by the rationalist tradition at least since Plato (although he himself begins his discussion with Descartes). Intuition is taken to be the immediate perception of simple or trivial elements or principles which, as so perceived, are indubitable. However, the history of rationalism, and specifically, of the Russellian attempt to combat skepticism by following Frege in the derivation of mathematics from trivial logical principles, is a history of continuous failure, retreat, and ultimate trivialization of (mathematical) knowledge.[9] I will summarize the well-known case of Russell's paradox, which enables us to bring out the main points in Lakatos's understanding of, and attack upon, intuition. In order to formalize mathematical reasoning, we require a perfect language, rooted in indubitable intuitions, and which is incapable of generating inconsistencies. Set theory was initially taken to be such a language, and the principle of abstraction was taken to be such a principle. It seems to be intuitively obvious that a set is a collection of objects sharing a common property and so that any property defines a set. However, we may form the set of all sets that do not belong to themselves, itself a natural consequence of our intuition that some sets belong to themselves (the set of concepts is itself a concept) and some do not (the set of apples is not an apple). And then disaster strikes: for if the set

---

8. Imre Lakatos, in *The Aristotelian Society*, suppl. vol. 36 (1962): 155–84.
9. Cf. ibid., par. 2, "Stopping Infinite Regrass by the Logico-Trivialisation of Mathematics," 165ff.

of all sets that do not belong to themselves does not itself belong to itself, then it does belong to itself, and if it does belong to itself, then it does not belong to itself.

Intuition leads us into contradictions. Russell's attempt to avoid these contradictions led to the theory of types and so not merely to highly nonintuitive procedures of formation but also to such non-intuitive axioms as the axiom of reducibility and, in general, to the "non-Euclidean" requirement for consistency proofs. In short, if we rely upon intuition, we contradict ourselves, whereas if we reject intuition, our axioms and formation-rules lose their indubitable status. The consequences of the rejection of intuitionism may be illustrated by Lakatos's criticism of "postulationism" or the thesis that axioms are not self-evidently true but are pragmatically justified by enabling us to achieve "postulated ends."[10] The question of foundation is then transferred to the domain of ends. Either there is an infinite regress of justifications of our ends, or these lose all rational certification through arbitrariness. In Russell's own fine expression: "The method of 'postulating' what we want has many advantages; they are the same as the advantages of theft over honest toil."[11] Lakatos's own formulation of this point deserves to be quoted in full:

> Of course, by "postulating" one can dissolve any problem. If one gives up intuition, despairs of certainty, *and* equates knowledge with certainty, then one may turn one's back on truth and play around with formal systems "unhampered by the striving after 'correctness'" and by outmoded Russello-Hilbertian ideas such as "a new language-form must be proved to be 'correct' and to constitute a faithful rendering of 'the true logic'" (Carnap: *The Logical Syntax of Language*, 1937, Foreword). It is sad how many 'logicians' followed this advice and soon forgot that logic is about truth-transmission and not about strings of symbols—even after Carnap started to realise his mistake. In their work the *technique* of logic overpowered its subject and started a perverted life of its own.[12]

I hope that these passages will suffice to bring out Lakatos's main attack upon intuition as a tool in the service of illicit foundational-

10. Ibid., 176; Lakatos is thinking of such theorists as Rosser and Ernest Nagel here.
11. Ibid., 176; quote from Bertrand Russell, *Introduction to Mathematical Philosophy* (1919), 71.
12. Lakatos, *Aristotelian Society*, 183 n. 31.

ism. His proposed alternative to the entire tradition he criticizes, is, of course, a kind of Popperian fallibilism, or the replacement of "indubitable" intuitions by guesses or refutable conjectures. "We never *know*, we only guess. We can, however, turn our guesses into criticisable ones, and criticise and improve them." And again: "The indefatigable sceptic however will ask again: 'How do you *know* that you improve your guesses?' But now the answer is easy: 'I guess.' There is nothing wrong with infinite regress in guesses." [13] But now my reply to Lakatos is easy: guessing is a kind of intuiting. Let me elaborate a bit on this. Most of the famous uses of intuition in twentieth-century philosophy do seem to fall into the Platonic-Cartesian tradition of a pure, immediate, intellectual perception of what is fully present, simple or trivial, and so indubitable. But this is not what I mean by intuition. Whereas I am not averse to including formal or categorial intuition as one type of intuition, I agree with Hegel that whatever we take to be immediate is actually mediated. Formal intuition is thus mediated by what Popperians might call "background knowledge" or a Platonist "opinion" (*doxa*). Opinions are formulated on the basis of everyday experience, itself saturated with natural language. If we try to analyze opinions more closely, we find that they consist of sense perceptions, fragments of tradition, habits, inferences, myths, dreams, intuitions, hunches, even guesses. And all of this is of course quite fallible. But just as Lakatos does not reject mathematics on the grounds of its fallibility, neither do we reject everyday experience or intuition, the "glue" of everyday experience, because it is fallible.

There is no more a rigorous analysis of everyday experience than there is of guessing or conjecturing. The fact that an intuition about set-formation leads to a formal contradiction does not lead us to give up intuition. Instead, it shows us that intuitions often conflict with one another, serve quite different functions, or are of different natures. I agree with Lakatos that there is no way to repair the contradictory consequences of some intuitions, in a rigorous or formalizable manner, by having recourse to other intuitions. The correct inference to draw from this is to give up the attempt to formalize natural language. If I understand Lakatos correctly, he would accept this, and indeed, this seems to be what he means by his criticism of foundationalism. However, he has misunderstood the nature of intuition, although not without considerable historical reasons. There are

13. Ibid., 165.

no "ultimate" intuitions because there is no immediate knowledge. To say this, however, does not banish what Lakatos means by "psychologism" from rational thought.[14] For Lakatos, reliance upon intuition is subjectivist because intuitions cannot be tested; unpleasant results of one's ostensibly ultimate intuitions can always be explained away through what Lakatos calls "rubber Euclideanism." However, he seems not to notice that guessing or conjecturing is just as subjective an activity as intuiting. Of course, guesses or conjectures may be tested, but so too may intuitions. I reject entirely the view that intuitions are immediate perceptions about which nothing rational can be said. On the contrary: I mean by an intuition a cognitive activity that makes it possible for us to say something.

An important element of my defense of intuitionism is my rejection of nominalism in all its forms. The sense of a proposition or statement cannot be another proposition or statement, because that indeed leads to an infinite regress, not of guesses, but of steps in the dark. But this is not the whole story: there is no apprehension of a formal structure when we see the point of an analogy, understand a joke, recognize a question as interesting or an answer as satisfying. I persist in using the term *intuition* to characterize these diverse capacities because a failure to do so leads, in my opinion, to just the kind of formalizing to which Lakatos objects. It leads either to infinite regresses or to the trivialization of meaning. The attack upon psychologism degenerates too quickly into a disregard for thinking and understanding; it therefore encourages us to disregard those features of sense or meaning that make intelligibility possible. However, I have discussed this topic elsewhere at some length. What requires emphasis here is that the discrimination of theories, or decisions concerning the satisfactory or unsatisfactory nature of our guesses, cannot be carried out on the basis of formally rigorous procedures. To claim otherwise would be to reintroduce foundationalism and dogmatism by the very procedure that was designed to extirpate them. One may agree that an infinite regress of guesses is not a formal fallacy. But it does serve to trivialize what we mean by scientific truth. A currently fashionable fallible conjecture is the empirical equivalent to an interpretation of mathematics as a meaningless manipulation of symbols in accordance with currently fashionable formal techniques. We have to perceive the desirability (fruitfulness, satisfactoriness, aesthetic excellence, and so

14. Ibid., 184.

on) of the direction in which our guesses are taking us. To explain this on the basis of physiology is to admit that what we call knowledge is defined by our perceptions. But because our perceptions are themselves interpreted on the basis of what we call knowledge, nothing seems to have been accomplished in the way of providing a noncircular, nontrivial account of rationality. As we know from his other writings, Lakatos tries to justify discrimination between guesses on the basis of the historical tradition of research programs. But such programs are an amalgam of opinions, hunches, habits, traditions, guesses, myths, and *intuitions*.

So much for Lakatos, whose views I have introduced only as an illustration of my own themes. Popperians in general strike me as relying upon the rhetorical force of their refutations as a justification of their conjectures. I do not find in their writings a clear distinction between logic and rhetoric. Despite all criticism of foundationalism and dogmatism, they retain an essentially traditional, mathematical conception of rationality. Having shown that mathematics cannot ground itself, they have nothing to put in its place. They do not recognize or explicitly state that background knowledge, research programs, and technical procedures employed in the testing of conjectures are not themselves simply conjectures but acquire a quasicanonical status on the basis of our intuitions. There is nothing conjectural about everyday experience, which is the source of conjecture. Theoretical reconstructions of ordinary or everyday experience must be judged in terms of that experience; otherwise, theory becomes indistinguishable from poetry. In sum: it is true that there is no formal semantics of natural language and no formalization of everyday experience. But it does not follow from this that everyday experience is replaced as the basis of science by historical tradition or fashion. That is, historical tradition itself reflects our intuitions. If we need not fear an absence of apodictic certainty within science itself, then we also need not fear the fallibility of intuition. The inconsistency of our intuitions does not annihilate the nature of everyday experience in the way that an inconsistency annihilates a formal deductive system. The justification of science is neither formalist nor conjectural in Lakatos's vague sense of the term; it is *dialectical*. One function of dialectic is to produce conjectures, but it does not do so in the dark, nor as a mindless reflex to historical fashion.

Lakatos assimilates intuition into tradition in much the same way that Wittgensteinians assimilate intuition into traditional language games.[15] On this thesis, what we attribute to intuition is just a habit induced by how we currently talk; and this in turn is decided by how we have been talking. For both Lakatos and the Wittgensteinian, a "revolution" in speech habits thus becomes inexplicable and irrational. Discontinuities in speech habits arise thanks to hunches of remarkable individuals. Even if this explanation were sound, it could not be sustained without an appeal to intuition. A shift in linguistic perspective is rooted in a different way of looking at the world. If this difference were in turn the consequence of antecedent language games or traditions, no shift in perspective could occur. Our capacity to discuss the shift in perspective, and so to perceive the difference between it and its antecedent, shows that the history of science is a web of intuition and language, not mere verbiage, but also not a surrealistic string of looks disconnected by blinks.

I want to claim, then, that the doctrine of intuition has been too closely connected in the history of philosophy with the intellectual perception of mathematical or quasimathematical forms. It is this connection, I suspect, that led Wittgenstein in his later stages to criticize intuition as an unnecessary shuffle, even as he was tacitly appealing to it, albeit under different names. He wished to emphasize that natural language has no formal semantics and that mathematics thus has no formalist foundations. This understandable intention led him to misunderstand the very language games he was in the process of describing. It is intuition that tells us which game to play and how to play it successfully. The suppression of intuition leads to a doctrine of the autonomy of rules and so directly to formalist accounts of rationality. As we have now seen at sufficient length, thanks in part to the assistance of Lakatos, there are no rules for the application of rules. If we cannot see which rule to apply, as for example in an inspired guess, then we fall into an infinite regress of discursive explanations of the application of rules; or else we reject explanation for arbitrary and discontinuous beginnings. In either case, we shall require dialectic to save us from irrational rhetoric.

So much for the defense of intuition; let us now return to the investigation of dialectic. Earlier I sketched out the notion of *logical space* or

15. The most recent is Richard Rorty in *Philosophy and the Mirror of Nature* (Princeton: Princeton University Press, 1979), 22, 34.

the intelligible continuum within which logics are differentiated. In the Cartesian tradition, these two are the same; that is, the continuum of intelligibility is structurally homogeneous. If this is so, however, then there must be a universal logic. But the existence of a universal logic can be supported neither by the facts of everyday experience nor by the constructive or creative behavior of logicians. In the dialectical tradition, logical space is a metaphysical interpretation of the continuum of intelligibility. Logical space is coextensive with the continuum of intelligibility in the sense that one cannot think or speak rationally without some intuition of logical consequence. On the other hand, logical space is not identical with the continuum of intelligibility, because our intuitions about logical consequence themselves require rational discrimination. In the balance of this chapter, I am going to try to clarify this initially obscure distinction by considering various problems associated with the principle of noncontradiction. I shall assume, or rather grant, that the principle of noncontradiction underlies all efforts to develop and defend a doctrine of rationality. If there are special logics in which contradiction is tolerated, they do not constitute a genuine exception to the previous assumption, because the special logic could not itself be constructed, let alone exhibit a sense of logical consequence, without a general obedience to the principle of noncontradiction. In other words, I assume or grant that what we mean by logic includes an allegiance to the principle of noncontradiction, and that we mean this because that is the way things are, not because we are playing a contingent language game.

Let me state in advance the comprehensive manifestation of our allegiance to the principle of noncontradiction. This manifestation is in the nature of predication. To state anything whatsoever is to say something of something. How we do this is by no means self-evident, but it is self-evident *that* we do it. It requires no "foundational" argument to assert that, when we wish to argue or persuade, we cannot do so by concomitantly asserting and denying that s is p, or, if the reader prefers, that Fa and not-Fa. This assertion cannot be denied meaningfully, because to attempt to do so would be to employ the principle asserted. If anyone were to say: "we do and do not obey the principle of noncontradiction," (with the usual qualifications of respect and time of utterance understood), he would not be making an assertion. One might wish to say that in one sense we obey the principle, whereas in another we do not. If this claim means that it is possible for us to utter rational statements (which play a constituent role in an argument or persuasive speech) which violate the principle of noncontradiction, then I deny it. To take the pertinent case, my defense of dialectic will be constructed of assertions, each of which is of the predicative form and so each of which obeys the principle of noncontradiction in the sense indicated. There is one statement that might be claimed to deny the principle of noncontradiction, and that is the statement of the principle itself. If we say: it is impossible to assert p and non-p of a grammatical subject at the same time and in the same way, then we have uttered a contradiction, in the act of instructing speakers to avoid such utterances; that is, the impossibility of the assertion of p and non-p is established, not simply by a syntactical rule, but by the antecedent tacit assertion of the intelligibility of the concept corresponding to the predicate "p and non-p." We have to understand that concept, and so violate the rule, in order to understand why it is objectionable and so directs us to construct the rule. However, what this statement shows is that contradictions are intelligible, not that we can construct arguments by using self-contradictory statements. Suffice it to say for the time being that the statement, as written above or in any other intelligible form, contains a non-self-contradictory act of predication. The predicate contains a contradiction, but not the sentence as an act by which a predicate is joined to a subject.

The principle of noncontradiction requires defending, but not in a sense that attacks the possibility of speaking logically by means of self-contradictory statements. What requires defending is recourse to logic. There is no such thing as self-contradictory logical speech and, in the sense just specified, there is also no such thing as self-contradictory dialectical speech. Instead, there is speech about the use and avoidance of contradictions. The fact that no rational assertion can be formed in violation of the principle of noncontradiction does not obviate the need to distinguish between rationality and irrationality. If it were not possible to distinguish between the non-contradictory syntactic structure of accounts of rationality and the semantic consideration of contradictions, then questions like those we are currently exploring could never arise. Let me give a very specific example of this perhaps initially ambiguous point. In book 4 of the *Metaphysics*, Aristotle engages in a well-known defense of the principle of noncontradiction, which he also calls "the most secure opinion."[16] This defense is dialectical and ad hominem. There is no "transcendental deduction" of the principle of noncontradiction from some higher principle. Instead, Aristotle points out the disadvantages that arise from our failure to obey it. (This is the more fundamental of Aristotle's two main defenses; the other is that those who pretend to disobey the principle are actually obeying it.) He does this because it is obvious that one *could* disobey the principle. In fact, the defense was necessary because Aristotle knew of contemporary thinkers who did at least claim to disobey it: the Heracliteans. I am not interested in the historical accuracy of this judgement. We can easily conceive of some other group of individuals who might challenge the authority of the principle of noncontradiction. One group might carry out its arguments by means of poems, woven together from self-contradictory statements. Another might refuse to argue at all and preserve the total silence of certain religious sects. No doubt other examples might be given, a task that I leave to the reader.

There is, however, one example in particular that I want to consider. One of Aristotle's main points is that contradiction must be avoided in deed if not in speech. He means to say that we cannot "securely" employ contradiction in speech because it violates predication, and predication reflects the structure of beings. Thus, if one approaches a hole in the ground, one must walk around it rather than attempt to fly over it; the properties of human beings and of holes are stable and of such a kind that it is flatly false to claim that human beings will and will not fall into holes if they attempt to fly over them. The nature of man and of holes will not change: this is the basis of predication, and hence of the security of the principle of noncontradiction. However, there is a very simple reply to all this. One may grant the thesis about human nature with respect to holes and nevertheless insist that, under other circumstances, one may still disobey the principle of noncontradiction with impunity. In other words, no one in his right mind would insist that the world never obeys the principle of noncontradiction. But it does not follow that the world always obeys the principle. And as a matter of fact, everyday experience, as we have already noted at length, produces intuitions which, if not mutually contradictory in a formal sense, certainly give rise to formal contradictions.

Now let me approach this problem from a slightly different angle. I

---

16. Aristotle, *Metaphysics* 4:1005b10ff. For the term *opinion,* see 1005b25ff.

will grant that it is always possible to reformulate any apparently self-contradictory statement in such a way as to show that, if the statement is intelligible, it contains no formal contradiction. I say that I will grant this, but I do not believe it. My view is rather that contradictions are often, if not always, and certainly in principle, intelligible. If this were not so, there could be no principle of noncontradiction. Nevertheless, I grant the point, in order to draw a further distinction, which I shall with some hesitation call the distinction between formal and existential contradiction. In order to explain what is involved here, I must proceed by way of examples. My first example is this: every living thing is also, and exactly as it is living, a dying thing. To be dying, of course, is not the same as to be dead. Hence we could say that, in the example, no formal contradiction has occurred. *Living* and *nonliving* are mutually exclusive predicates, as *living* and *dying* are not. I grant the validity of this observation so far as logical form is concerned. But I contend that it would be fatuous to overlook the existential and conceptual contradiction between living and dying, simply on the grounds that no formal contradiction has occurred.

One way in which to bring out the contradiction is to say that *living* and *dying* seem to be taking us in different directions. This is easiest to see in the case of children, who are "falling apart" or "breaking down" even as they are "growing up." We do not normally say that a healthy, growing child is dying before our eyes. Let us say that we do not play that kind of language game. To say this, however, serves to illustrate an intrinsic shortcoming in the doctrine of language games. Life and death go on regardless of what kinds of games we play. We may wish to avoid discussing the fact that life is dying, whether for ethical, religious, or aesthetic reasons, and we may arrange our conventional expressions accordingly. Thus we may refuse to apply the term *dying* to a healthy person until such a time when stipulated processes of decay are observable. But the problem is that these stipulated processes are in one sense always observable, whereas in another sense they are sometimes observable and sometimes not. How we arrange our terms may indeed interfere with our capacity to perceive the sense in which these processes are always observable. We may simply refuse to observe them. But that does not change the nature of living and dying; it merely makes us irrational.

I am trying to make two distinct but related points. The first is that there is indeed a distinction between a formal and an existential contradiction. The second is that, whereas we might be able to redescribe an ostensibly self-contradictory situation in such a way as to remove the formal contradiction, there are crucial cases in which to do this is to cover over, or to fail to understand, the situation. I am not claiming that any rational analysis of the self-contradictory nature of life could be carried out by means of sentences, each of which is formally self-contradictory. If anything, I am claiming that, at a certain point, the rational analysis of life terminates in the perception of a contradiction. It does not follow that we must stop talking at this point. Instead, we have to talk rationally, namely, by using sentences not syntactically self-contradictory, about a situation that is intrinsically self-contradictory.

To come back to my example, it is possible to say that in one sense I am living, whereas in another sense I am dying. But this is just the point. One might counter by saying that, just as under certain conditions in mathematical analysis we can disregard the minute ("infinitesimal") value of Δx, so too can we disregard the minute extension of my life in comparison with eternity, or whatever is meant by "all of time." A correct "integration" of my life with death shows that, for all practical purposes, I am already dead! I might reply in turn that on the one hand, there is no contradiction, but on the other, there is. However, this leaves unexplained the sense of a conjunction of an existential contradiction with a non-self-contradictory linguistic form. For example, if my ingenuity makes it possible for me to restate all ostensibly self-contradictory statements in such a way as to show that no formal contradiction obtains, is my ingenuity not also sufficiently extensive to permit me to restate every ostensibly non-self-contradictory statement in such a way as to show that a formal contradiction does obtain? If everything turns upon ingenuity, then things can turn in opposite directions. Those who try to make them turn out in such a way as to banish formal contradictions are doing so because of a commitment to logical rationality. Whereas we cannot say anything either in favor of or opposed to logical rationality that is both logical and self-contradictory, it does not follow that this demonstrates the universal excellence of logical rationality. How could logical rationality do more than provide the syntax for an explanation of the sense of a conjunction between an existential contradiction and a logically non-self-contradictory statement?

The logician says: "On the one hand, this; on the other hand, that. Hence there is no formal contradiction." The dialectician replies: "On the one hand, this; on the other hand, that. But both hands belong to the same body. Hence the contradiction remains." In other words, the absence of formal contradiction is not a sufficient criterion by which to distinguish between logical and dialectical speech. It is a mistaken notion of dialectic to assume that it proceeds by way of formally self-contradictory utterances. The example I have been considering is intended to show that dialectic proceeds by way of existential contradictions expressed in syntactically sound forms. It should be emphasized here that not every dialectical statement needs to turn upon an existential contradiction. I have purposely formulated my point in terms of the extreme case, in part because of the popular conception of dialectic, and in part because the characteristically dialectical cases do turn upon existential contradictions. I want also to underline that in my use, an existential contradiction is also a conceptual contradiction, whether formal or not. Those who tell us that it is a grammatical error to ask after the significance of existence are simply fatuous. It is not a grammatical error to ask this because no grammatical question has been posed. But neither has any error been committed in the syntax of the inquiry. The claim that life cannot properly be said to have a significance is a metaphysical doctrine, not a logical one. It may well be that the lives of those who hold to this doctrine lack significance. The rest of us, however, are entirely free to continue to be guided by our experience.

It may be, then, that we need two principles, one of noncontradiction and one of contradiction, or (to use my terminology) one formal and one existential principle. Certainly what we need is a rational account of why it is advantageous to use logic rather than to remain silent or to utter self-contradictory utterances. And this in turn is rooted in the need to account for the self-contradictory consequences of competing intuitions in everyday experience, which is the same basis upon which justifications for logic are constructed. We cannot rest content with the formal analysis without turning away from its existential instantiation, but it does not follow that we have to reject the formal analysis. The problem is rather to decide *which* formal analysis is sound.

Before I leave the example of living and dying, I would like to consider its generalized version. Experienced time, as distinct from its mathematical representations in physics, has irreversible directionality. No one lives his life, or patches of it, backwards; nor do natural phenomena occasionally enliven our experience by reversing themselves. And yet, it makes conceptual sense to say that each moment of time is moving simultaneously in opposite directions: namely, into the past and the future. I said "simultaneously," but that cannot be anything more than a metaphor. We cannot say that the self-contradictory motion is taking place at the same time, because time is "present" or accessible to us only in the moment itself. Neither can we say that part of the moment is receding into the past while part of it is advancing into the future, since a moment has no temporal parts. If it did, then the motion of these parts would have to be measured or defined with respect to another dimension of time and so relative to another moment. The same puzzle would then apply to this new moment. We experience time on the basis of a distinction between past, present, and future. This is not simply existential in the sense of a feeling, mood, or some other prerational pathos; it is conceptual, and the concept of three-dimensional time structures our discourse of all temporal experiences or events. And yet, there is no direct temporal experience (as distinct from memory or anticipation) of past or future time. To experience time is to live through it, and we live through each moment only once. Furthermore, what we are living through is the present. In whatever sense we experience the past and future, we do so as constituent dimensions of the unity of the present, which has no temporal parts yet is both receding into the past and advancing into the future. If we say that the present is receding into the past but not advancing into the future, or that the present moment is just replaced by a new moment, then we dissolve the continuity of time and so too the possibility of its mathematicization.

Perhaps these traditional puzzles can be suppressed by terminological distinctions. But the suppression of the puzzle is also the suppression of human experience. Is the puzzle a formal contradiction? Perhaps, and perhaps not; everything depends upon our ingenuity and our choice of formalization. If then we remove the contradiction, we destroy our own experience; if we do not destroy our experience, we raise the question of the basis upon which the contradiction has been removed, and so we are back at our dialectical starting-point. In sum: When the logician tells us that if p is the past, then non-p is not the future but rather the absence of the past, we reply: "What is the future, if not the absence of the past?"

Dialectic is rational speech about the whole. By "the whole" I mean human experience, but one could also restate this more abstractly as the relation between form and content. Dialectic is distinguished from logic in general terms as follows: logic is the study of those formal structures that exhibit one or another sense of *follows from* obeying the principle of noncontradiction. I say "in general terms," because I am under no illusion that the distinction between logic and dialectic can be stated precisely. On the contrary, if by *precisely* we mean *logically* in the sense of *formally*, then it is clearly impossible for logic to define itself. However, it is not clearly impossible for dialectic to define itself, because dialectic does not work with the sense of *precision* characteristic of logic. To say that definitions of dialectic are circular is not, then, to raise a valid objection to them. Everything we say about the totality of things is circular. We try to avoid this circularity, as well as other "defects" such as contradictoriness, by restricting our discourse to one or several technical languages. But the basis for the restriction continues to be the unrestricted whole or, as I have called it, everyday experience as articulated by natural language.

I have suggested that there may be two principles, one of non-contradiction, which refers to logical form, and one of contradiction, which refers to content. This suggestion needs to be refined, although it cannot be made precise for the reason just given. Once again we take our bearings by natural language, which I am not sharply distinguishing from everyday experience. Natural language is motivated by conflicting intuitions that give rise to contradictory utterances. We may be able to show that some of these contradictions are not formal; in other cases, the contradiction may be "sanitized" by showing that each half belongs to a distinct language game or segment of discourse. Nevertheless, some formal contradictions will remain. These are handled by mathematicians and logicians on an ad hoc basis; for example, if unrestricted use of the principle of abstraction generates contradictions, we respond by placing a restriction on the principle of abstraction. It is often said in this connection that the intuition underlying the unrestricted principle of abstraction—that we can form sets on the basis of any property whatsoever—does not simply produce the contradiction in question but shows the unreliability of intuition. I think that this is false. What the contradiction shows is that the given intuition is not strong enough to support an unrestricted principle of abstraction or set formation. If someone had not had the original intuition, there would have been no unrestricted principle of abstraction, in which case there would have been no restricted principle of abstraction. In other words, there would have been no set theory.

The problem here is the erroneous view that if there are any intuitions, they must be infallible. I have already explained why I reject this view. It is perhaps possible to say that nothing is "given," as human beings can say almost anything, but it makes no sense to deny that the language games which express consciousness are themselves intelligible on any basis other than the traditional subject-object, or knower-known, or thinker-thought paradigm. Objections to Cartesian dualism are one thing; an attempt to deny the experience of consciousness is something else again. But we have to distinguish between the givenness of the content of consciousness and the claim that this givenness is immediate and incorrigible. I therefore agree that the thesis of the immediacy of givenness is wrong; but it is wrong because the given is already a mediation. This is not the place to engage in a detailed discussion of the nature of thinking. It will suffice to say that the given is a mediation of intuition, language, history, local custom, physiological peculiarities, and so on. The given is therefore fallible and corrigible; it is subject to analysis. But analysis is *of* the given (in the sense of contents of consciousness). To say this is not to endorse Cartesian dualism or any other academic theory of the intellect. It is to endorse the principle that no theory of cognitive activity is satisfactory which deconstructs the very experience required to understand the theory in question.

Once we have sorted out the formal contradictions, or shown that in certain cases no such contradictions exist, we are left with the inconsistent nature of everyday experience, part of which manifests itself in the form of what I previously called *existential contradictions*. As popular wisdom wisely puts it, life is full of contradictions. We do not on that account attempt to replace life by a consistent formal calculus (or at least most of us do not). But neither ought we to delude ourselves into thinking that we have removed the existential contradictions when we rewrite attempts to state them in such a way as to eliminate formal contradiction. Coming at once to an example from mathematics, we read in every textbook that logic and set theory, the "foundational" disciplines, rest upon the basic distinction between the finite and the infinite. But in the technical development of logic and set theory, it is obvious that every ostensibly infinite set (including transfinite sets) is bounded by a still larger set, and so, in a quite definite sense, not of course that of extension, is finite. Infinite sets are both finite and infinite. Is this a formal contradiction? I suppose that it is theoretically possible to argue that such sets are finite in one sense and infinite in another, but how do we explain the relation between the two senses? Does the set have a definite nature or doesn't it? If it does, then there is a formal contradiction; if it does not, then the notion of a definite set, the basis of set theory, goes out the window.

In my opinion, the problem about the finite and the infinite is a generalized version of something that shows up at every level of set theory and no doubt of mathematics as well. The subject is grounded in conflicting and dialectical insights that can never be removed but that can be, so to speak, "pushed upstairs" or to one side by some technical innovation. Dialectic is the engine that drives mathematics; it is the impetus of its development. We progress by climbing the stair that our technical innovation has constructed just above the previous level of the subject. But we do this only by building yet another stair. This whole process, incidentally, was well understood by Hegel despite his erroneous belief that he had described it fully and rigorously. The "structures" woven together in the continuum of intelligibility are "alive" or marked by excitation; they are continuously transforming themselves into their neighbors. And this process can never be fully captured in a formal, nondialectical logic.

Another way in which to see the dialectical nature of logic is by noting that the principle of noncontradiction is not an axiom within the usual formalizations of the predicate calculus. For example, in Gentzen's natural deduction, the "law of contradiction" enters as an inference figure, negation elimination: from *a* and not-*a* we infer the false, and from the false, anything follows.[17] But this inference figure expresses a decision made by the logician in advance of constructing his logic—namely, to avoid contradictions. Similarly, in traditional axiomatic approaches to the predicate calculus, proof by contradiction is a derived rule of inference, following ultimately from consequences of the truth definition.[18] And the truth definition is a rendering precise of an intuition that contradictions are to be avoided. What we mean by *proof* is determined by our desire to eliminate contradictions, and this desire springs up on the basis of our everyday experience, in a way well described by Aristotle.

What Aristotle also shows us is that everyday experience requires

17. "Investigations into Logical Deduction," in *The Collected Papers of Gerhard Gentzen*, ed. M. E. Szabo (Amsterdam: North-Holland Publishing Co., 1969), 77–79.
18. Cf. E. Mendelson, *Introduction to Mathematical Logic*, 2d ed. (New York: D. Van Nostrand Co., 1979), 51f., 73f.

us to defend the elimination of contradiction, or to praise consistency. This defense and this praise are dialectical. Unfortunately, in the act of persuading us, they often cause us to forget the dialectical nature of the persuasion. And so we are catapulted by dialectic into logic, without remembering our starting-point. Or else, we are now able to view the starting-point only from within the perspective of logic. The dialectical features of everyday experience now strike us as illogical and something to be obliterated. Thus is born the desire to reconstitute everyday experience in scientific theories, as for example in the formalization of natural language. In the metaphor of the previous example, we no longer see the nature of the stair upon which we are standing as we engage in the unending task of reconstructing our experience.

I have been arguing that the presence or absence of formal contradiction in philosophical discourse is a matter of interpretation and, secondarily, of our technical ingenuity. In the process of formalization, we move from the philosophical speech to its technical restatement by a series of assumptions about meaning. The formalization is not given by the philosophical speech. Furthermore, once we achieve it, the dialectical nature of the original speech is not removed. I spoke above of the example of the finite and the infinite. This example can be stated in a fuller technical form.[19] According to the Skolem-Löwenheim theorem (or set of theorems), every consistent theory has a denumerable model, an interpretation for a countable domain of discourse, as an elementary submodel of any other model it may have. In simple English, this means that if a theory has an interpretation that includes an uncountable domain, it also has an equivalent theory with a countable domain. As Cantor showed by his method of diagonalization, the set of real numbers is uncountable. Given the assumption that the real numbers are countably infinite (in the domain of the model obtained by the Skolem-Löwenheim theorem), we can construct a real number that fits the definition of a real number but is not in the set of countably infinite real numbers because it is obtained by diagonalizing on that set. Again: another uncountably-many set is the set of all subsets of the integers. So any theory rich enough to contain arithmetic has a model with a nondenumerable domain. But by the Skolem-Löwenheim theorem, there is also an equivalent submodel of

19. Richard Mansfield provided essential help in formulating part of this example.

this model with a denumerable domain. This result is often called the *Skolem paradox*.

Is this paradox dialectical? Most philosophers of logic would say no. A typical way in which the paradox is avoided or dissolved is by distinguishing between levels of generality of discourse. The denumerable model m is constructed within a model m'. The set s, of all subsets of integers within m, is countable. But s is not the same as s', the set of all subsets of integers within m'. In m', s' is uncountable. Furthermore, there exists in m', but not in m, a mapping function by which we may establish a one-to-one correspondence in m', but not in m, between s and s'.[20] At first glance, it seems that we have a pure contradiction on our hands. The set of all subsets of integers is both denumerable and nondenumerable; or, alternatively, it is neither the one nor the other, as it has both a denumerable and a nondenumerable model. The contradiction is removed by the assertion that there are in fact two different sets here. Without going into all the details, there is a serious objection to such a procedure. It leads, not merely to one uncountable set of all subsets of integers, but to uncountably many such sets, because the move just described from m to m' can continue to m'' and so on forever, whatever *forever* may mean under such circumstances. We therefore never arrive at any set of axioms that succeeds in capturing the concept of the set of all subsets of integers. Each theory, corresponding to a distinct model m, has its own power-set axiom or prescribed method for forming the set in question. The concept of the infinite is thus bifurcated into two: we now have a countable infinite and an uncountable infinite. And we also have uncountably-many uncountable infinites. It also follows by the compactness theorem that we do not even capture the concept of finite via our axiomatic method, because every set of axioms with arbitrarily large finite models has an infinite model.

My example is intended to support two points. First: mathematical logic and set theory are intrinsically dialectical. The axiomatic approach fails to capture the mathematical concepts it was intended to explicate in a rigorous way. Other examples could be cited, such as the circularity of the attempt to provide an axiomatic foundation to

---

20. The sketch of the paradox and its usual resolution follows (with some modifications) Hilary Putnam, "The Thesis that Mathematics is Logic," in *Mathematics, Matter and Method* (Cambridge: Cambridge University Press, 1975), 15f.

set theory.[21] The second point is that it is philosophically misleading to restrict one's analysis of statements and arguments to the formal properties of contradiction and validity. In any argument rich enough to be philosophically interesting, if contradictions seem to exist, someone will always come along who is technically capable of providing a contradiction-free translation of the argument. But the exercise of technical ingenuity is made possible by the intuition into the initially dialectical situation. Therefore, even the decision that a given argument is formally invalid is disputable, because that decision depends upon our understanding of the argument in natural language. I would certainly not deny that one aspect of understanding a complex argument entails the application of formal techniques. What I deny is that this is sufficient, or even that it is possible in the absence of a preformal understanding of the argument. The maxim of computer technology, "garbage in, garbage out," applies also to the formalization of arguments.

In this chapter, I have not offered a theory of dialectic as the counterpart to a theory of formal logic. No such theory is possible, because dialectic is the explication of natural language, which is not formalizable. Neither have I presented a rigorous account of contradiction. Instead, I have suggested a distinction between formal and existential contradiction and so too that we need different kinds of principles to cover the two cases. What is usually called the principle of noncontradiction forbids us to speak logically in sentences containing formal contradictions. I accept this principle, and indeed I would be hard pressed not to do so, because what we mean by speaking logically is avoiding formal contradictions. At the same time, I have pointed out that what counts as a formal contradiction is often, if not always, a matter of how we interpret a stretch of natural language. In this connection, I have warned against the tendency to conceal existential contradictions by the procedures with which we avoid formal contradictions. I have used the expression *existential contradiction* despite its vagueness, because I wished to convey the link between dialectic and human existence as a totality. Dialectic addresses itself to this totality and so to the inconsistencies and contradictions that life produces. Dialectic is not a procedure for eliminating inconsistencies and contradictions but rather for making sense out of them. In order to

21. Cf. John Mayberry, "On the Consistency Problem for Set Theory," in *British Journal for the Philosophy of Science*, 28, nos. 1–2 (1977).

make sense out of them, it is necessary to take them one at a time, to examine each as it arises and within the context that gives rise to it. The problem was to try to distinguish between dialectic and logic and so to show the dialectical presuppositions of logic. I have no wish to reduce logic to dialectic any more than I would wish to reduce dialectic to logic. To do either of these things is to maim oneself. What is amusing, or would be if it were not tragic, is that in the bottom floors of the mansion of analysis, philosophers function as though the old problems of the preanalytical tradition were either dead or in the process of resolution by the new techniques of formal reasoning. Meanwhile, in the upper floors of the same mansion, the corpses are all dancing the dialectical round-dance of life.

CHAPTER EIGHT

The Limits of Analysis

LINGUISTIC PURIFICATION AND

THE *NIHIL ABSOLUTUM*

One of the most characteristic features of twentieth-century philosophy is the attempt to remove traditional metaphysical problems by a purification of the language in which they are expressed. The modern revolution associated with Descartes and his contemporaries, although it is itself a part of the metaphysical tradition, already exhibits this emphasis upon language, sometimes (but not always) expressed as allegiance to a new method. To be sure, the philosophical purification of ordinary language and the construction of new technical terms and methods is as old as philosophy, or at least as old as Plato. But the typically modern version of this philosophical tendency is linked to a new emphasis on the nature of the speaker: on the *ego cogitans*, the transcendental ego, the absolute subject, and so on.

One way in which to express the difference between ancients and moderns is to note the modern conviction that we know what we make. If philosophy is to succeed in its ancient goal of replacing opinion by knowledge, then imprecise speech must be replaced by precise speech. But speech becomes precise only when it is rule-governed, and rules are themselves known with precision only when we ourselves make them. This is the inner sense of the Cartesian shift from "natures" or "substances" to equations rooted in geometrical constructions that stand as surrogates for things in themselves. Unfortunately, whereas it may be true that we are able to know our constructions with precision, it is also true that we are able to make an apparently unending series of constructions, including those which mutually exclude or contradict one another.

The problem then arises: how can we choose between two or

This essay first appeared in *Etudes Phénoménologiques* (Belgium), no. 7, 1988.

more conflicting constructions? Has the attempt to replace opinion with knowledge not succeeded instead in replacing philosophy with poetry? As we shall shortly see, those who object to the rhapsodic character of traditional metaphysical thought and replace it by conceptual or logical analysis have in no way answered the first question and in no way escaped the dilemma implied in the second question. But the more general point is this: the history of the turn to purified or precise language from Descartes forward can be told in three sometimes overlapping stages. The first stage is connected with emphasis (of varying kinds) upon the nature of the speaker, that is, upon subjectivity. The second stage is marked by a turn away from the speaker, with primary attention paid to formal structure. The third stage exhibits the collapse of the distinction between speaker and discourse, or the triumph of subjectivity. In its late manifestations, this third stage quite erroneously regards itself as having gone beyond the subject-object distinction. Differently stated, late modernism goes beyond the object, but only by a comprehensive dissolution of objectivity into subjectivity. It is of no importance that the term *subjectivity* is no longer used. Terms such as *interpretation* serve the same purpose.

Despite the sophisticated etymologies of Heidegger, the fundamental distinction between ancient and modern philosophy lies in the conviction of the ancients that the noetic perception of pure or natural form is the basis of rational discourse. It does not follow from this conviction that a satisfactory discursive account of the perceived forms is possible. In fact, it is not difficult to show that Plato and Aristotle, to mention the two crucial cases, denied such a possibility. The case of Plato is too complex to be discussed here; I must refer the reader to my writings on the topic. Aristotle leaves the point at this: the psyche is or becomes "somehow" the things that are. His elaborate analyses of formal structure, whether or not one regards them as satisfactory, are all logically dependent upon this point. There is no doctrine of transcendental subjectivity, or of what Husserl called "categorial intuition," in Aristotle. But this is not to say that noetic intuition is to be explained as a doctrine of language. This tack, popular among some contemporary scholars, both falsifies the texts and makes nonsense of the doctrine of essence, which it defines from the outset in terms of the doctrine of predication. However, as I shall emphasize later, the doctrine of predication cannot itself distinguish between essential and accidental properties.

Personally, I think that Aristotle's audacity is at least the safest way to handle the problem of the indispensability of formal perception (or intellectual intuition, a term that is dangerous because it carries a quite different meaning in German Idealism). Because perception is an activity rather than an entity, and an activity that takes in rather than produces, it can have no formal structure of its own. All phenomenological descriptions or structural analyses of the perceptual activity of intelligence are in fact descriptions or analyses of the exteriorization of this activity as it manifests itself in the taking in of this or that formal element or structure. But the exteriorization of perception reveals itself as such only to perception itself. Those who lack such a perception, or in whom it is obfuscated by linguistic philosophies, are perfectly free to interpret the same descriptions and analyses as pertaining to the synthetic construction of the productive imagination, the absolute ego, or the historical individual. In other words, the attempt to describe intellectual perception leads to the reification of the intellect, with one of two further results. Either the subject is assimilated into the object, or the object is assimilated into the subject. The first result, incidentally, is inevitably followed by the second, as a glance at the history of twentieth-century philosophy will directly confirm.

The process I have just summarily described is that in which intellectual perception is replaced by, or dissolved into, language. In classical terminology, *noēsis* is assimilated into *dianoia* and *logismos*. There is very little question that twentieth-century philosophy in its principal movements is a consequence of this process. The greater part of this chapter will be devoted to examining some of the bad consequences within the domain of what is usually called "analytical philosophy" (even by those who deny that any such movement exists). First, however, I want to make some remarks about the situation within "continental" philosophy, as it is known in the American academy, or in another term, "phenomenology" (and I emphasize that these are terms of convenience, whose convenience stems from their at least partial accuracy).

The first thing to be said is that phenomenology is decisively marked by its Kantian ancestry. The reconstitution of the world, the discovery of a science of origins, depends upon the analysis of the structure of formal intuition. Thus Husserl distinguishes between the categorial form and the psychic acts by which the form is constituted in consciousness,[1] or between the *Wesen* and consciousness of the *Wesen*, which latter alone is produced (*erzeugt*).[2] However, the goal of phenomenology is the development of a universal science of the elements of intuition and of the categories and methods by which these elements are described. Whereas there is no end to the perspectives from which the *Wesen* is given, Husserl aims at a comprehensive description of the transcendental structure within which the unending stream of possible noetic intuitions occurs. This is his version of Kant's distinction between the transcendental structure of natural or empirical science and the unending progress of science itself.

Second, the foundational role assigned to "seeing" or noetic intuition is misleading to the extent that it gives the impression of Platonism. Husserl himself makes clear the difference between his essences and Platonic Ideas. The former are not actualities or metaphysical objects but the content of any intentional act, anything at all that can function as the subject of a true proposition.[3] Husserl's "Ideas" are *possibilia*, not actualities. The actual world is a special case of possible worlds.[4] Transcendental phenomenology is concerned with pure fantasy (*reine Phantasie*) and a priori possibility (*apriorische Möglichkeiten*).[5] Furthermore, the kernel of the *noema*, that is, the thing perceived noetically, or phenomenological essence, is a sense or meaning (*Sinn*).[6] But meanings—possible subjects of propositions—must be explicated by language.

I would restate the two preceding points as follows. Husserlian phenomenology is a new science, rooted in the intuition of possible meanings and developed by a radical reconstitution of philosophical language and methodology. As a science of possible meanings and of their formal structure, it is also a science of the universal structures of consciousness.[7] The initial root of intuition is thus scientifically accessible only through elaborate linguistic transformations. This amounts to the assertion that it is accessible only via the discursive analysis of

1. Edmund Husserl, *Logische Untersuchungen*, II/2 (Tübingen: Max Niemeyer Verlag, 1968), 175.
2. Husserl, *Ideen* (Tübingen: Max Niemeyer Verlag, 1980), 1:43.
3. Husserl, *Ideen* 1:11 (par. 3), 40–42 (par. 22); cf. 43 (par. 24).
4. Ibid., 88 (par. 47).
5. Husserl, *Cartesianische Meditationen* (Haag: Martinus Nijhof, 1963), 66–67.
6. Husserl, *Ideen*, par. 88 and 90.
7. See Husserl, *Ideen* 1, chap. 2.

intuition in the subjective and objective senses, that is, of the agent of intuition or of consciousness, as well as of the intentional correlate of consciousness. Science, including the science of phenomenology, is the language of possibility.

These remarks were necessary in order to justify the inclusion of Husserlian phenomenology within my general account of late modern or twentieth-century philosophy as fundamentally discursive: as a revolution in language. No such documentation is required in the case of Heidegger, who is clearly a philosopher of language in both of the major phases of his mature work, whether as a founder of the fundamental-ontological investigation into the *Sinn des Seins* or as the postontological thinker who is on the way toward language ("unterwegs zur Sprache"). I therefore accept Arion Kelkel's general remark that Heidegger's thought is a philosophy of language: "the explication of the implicit ontology of language," an expression that, with the appropriate modification of terms, applies to all stages of that thought.[8]

In a Husserlian phenomenology, the difficulty with which I am here concerned could be expressed as follows. Correct discourse is ostensibly rooted in noetic intuition. In fact, however, noetic intuition is certified by correct discourse. This problem is implicitly granted by Plato's employment of myths and metaphors to discuss the activity of noetic perception, and by Aristotle's virtual silence on the matter (a silence that covers the obscure chapters of book 3 of *De Anima*). Heidegger's revision of Husserlian phenomenology amounts to an admission of the impossibility of a science of intuition *or of Sinn*. However, instead of retaining the Platonic dualism or the Aristotelian assertion of its overcoming, Heidegger assimilates essences, forms, and meanings into language, which is thus itself transformed from scientific ontology to poetic *Andenken*, a discursive substitute for Platonic *anamnesis*. The result, oddly enough, is the same in both the ontological and the postontological periods: the triumph of interpretation (*Auslegung*) over theory (*theōria*).

Kant's search for the transcendental conditions of truth, goodness, and unity foundered because it was based upon the ostensible facts of science, the moral law, and the unity and purposiveness achieved by reflective judgment. These facts are not merely disputable; their facticity has itself come to be regarded as a matter of linguistic inter-

8. Arion Kelkel, *La légende de l'Etre* (Paris: J. Vrin, 1980), 16.

pretation. It seems that we can say anything we wish. The scientific phenomenology of the twentieth century has led to the same result: after Heidegger, a return to Nietzsche via deconstruction and post-modernism. To my mind, the results of the modern revolution are much worse than those of traditional metaphysics with respect to one crucial point. In each of its versions, the world of traditional metaphysics is defined by fundamental aporiai. But the world of post-traditional postmetaphysics is defined, if by anything, by an absence of foundations, and hence a fortiori by an absence of fundamental aporiai. The postmodern world is not a world at all, but chaos. What I have in Chapter 10 called Nietzsche's esoteric teaching has today become our exoteric teaching.

We find ourselves today in a Kantian world from which one crucial element is missing: Kant. This is why the world is indistinguishable from chaos. The missing element can also be described as noetic per-ception, not of pure forms, but in Kantian terms, as a recognition of the "interests of reason" that approaches Platonism, despite all differ-ences, as is perhaps most visible in the doctrine of regulative Ideas. From my present standpoint, Kant is an old-fashioned metaphysician in the sense that he does not attempt to assimilate completely rational belief into analytical discourse. On the other hand, Kant plainly does not rest content with Platonic myths, which he no doubt regarded as *Schwärmerei*. Instead, he engages in long, complex, and ambiguous re-flections based upon the use of hypotheses, postulates, and analogies, which reflections have given more than one reader the impression of a philosophy of *as if*, to use Vaihinger's famous term. In my opin-ion, however, this is a defect in Kant: It produces the impression of rationalization rather than of rationalism. It is on this point that Kant most clearly provides a paradigm of the modern tendency to replace metaphysical *aporiai* with technical artifacts.

So much for Kant and phenomenology. I turn to the so-called analytical philosophy to illustrate the unsuccessful efforts to remove metaphysical problems by a purification of language. Whereas I shall provide considerable detail, I will not attempt to document my argu-ments with references to specific authors, as these arguments are intended to apply to the movement as a whole. I draw no distinction between ordinary language and formal analytical philosophy for two reasons. First, the specific problem that will serve as my example is one that the formalist procedures seem to have eliminated. Second, despite important differences with the formalists, ordinary-language philosophers continue to rely, implicitly as well as explicitly, on such formalist doctrines as the theory of predication and a conception of analytical rationality that is formalist in essence. What one could call a central emphasis upon *phronēsis* is due, not to a rejection of analytical rationalism, but to a recognition of its limits. Nevertheless, the methods of analysis and standards of argumentation employed by the representatives of *phronēsis* are those of the modern scientific enlightenment.

The case of the later Wittgenstein represents an important exception but not one that was followed by the majority of his ostensible disciples. A satisfactory discussion of Wittgenstein's second period would take us too far afield and must be postponed for another occasion. Suffice it to say here that, in my opinion, Wittgenstein came to regard philosophy as both impossible and immoral. He therefore continued to employ implicitly analytical reasoning, but against itself, as it were, to give full rein to the aporiai of technical philosophy as agents of self-destruction. The positive side of Wittgenstein's later doctrine is thus the analogue to Plato's myths; or in another perspective, Wittgenstein's monologues are the analogue to Plato's dialogues.

The problem I have in mind is that of the *nihil absolutum*. The solution offered to this problem by contemporary analytical philosophy is in principle no different from that of Aristotle, who in turn develops and renders technically sophisticated a doctrine assigned by Plato in the *Sophist* to the Eleatic Stranger. Aristotle eliminates the ontological component of the Stranger's doctrine, namely, recourse to greatest kinds (*megista genē*) and in particular to the pure form of otherness. The nerve of Aristotle's approach is to transform otherness into privation and nonbeing into the syntactic operation of negation. I shall examine Aristotle's analysis in detail in another place and have studied the solution proposed by the Eleatic Stranger in my book on the *Sophist*. Here we need only to remind ourselves of the original historical event as recorded by Plato.

In the *Sophist*, the Eleatic Stranger cites Parmenides' warning not to think or discuss in any way "the altogether not" (*to mēdamōs on*). He then urges his interlocutor, Theaetetus, not to regard him as a parricide in view of what he is about to say. For over two millenia, the Stranger's request has been ignored, and he is, as far as I know, universally regarded as a parricide because of his revision of his master's teaching. The fact is that the Stranger does not commit parricide. He in effect obeys his master's warning, although he spells out in some detail the peculiarities of the warning itself, by replacing the altogether not with a quite different, and narrower, concept: otherness. I shall borrow an expression from Hegel and refer to this as *determinate negation*.

The Eleatic Stranger thus begins the long procedure, followed by the entire rationalist tradition of European philosophy, of keeping silent about the altogether not and talking instead about its presumed surrogate, finite negation or negativity—in other words, a *mixture* of Being and nothing. Still more succinctly, nothing is replaced as a topic of philosophical discussion by something: by a syntactical or semantical element, by a concept or discursive construction. The reason for this procedure is obvious. If philosophy is "giving an explanation," or replacing opinion with knowledge, and if no explanation can be given of what is not, philosophy cannot tolerate that what is not either participates in or gives shape or visibility to what is.

Not in its various manifestations within western philosophy is thus regularly explained in terms of Being or existence; correlatively, the *nihil absolutum*, ostensibly replaced by a finite nothing assimilated to or explained by something, continues to lurk unexplained in the negative dimension of the preferred technical construction. The work of analytical thinking, and in particular of logic and mathematics, continues to progress without visible harm from this metaphysical failure. But failure is something quite different from the successful rejection or destruction of metaphysics. Those who dismiss metaphysics will accordingly not be impressed by the considerations I am about to put forward. I ask them simply to consider whether my own analysis establishes or tends to support the thesis that they have not in fact resolved a central metaphysical problem. Stated differently, I assert that those who speak explicitly of the overcoming of metaphysics are fundamentally mistaken. Metaphysics cannot be overcome, because it is the thinking of insoluble problems, as even Kant understood.

I begin with a point of extreme simplicity. It turns upon a logical triviality, yet one which already contains the heart of the matter. Analytical discourse is based upon a small number of general principles, of which perhaps the most important is the principle of noncontradiction. I note initially that negation is mentioned explicitly in the *non* and implicitly in *contradiction*. It is accordingly impossible to understand the principle of noncontradiction unless one understands negation. More precisely, one cannot explain analytically the principle of noncontradiction unless one can explain analytically negation.

Instead of engaging in metaphysical speculation, let us turn directly to the representation of the injunction against contradiction in elementary logic: $-(p$ and $-p)$. The sense of this formula-schema derives from artificial rules defining legitimate concatenations of statement or predicate-variables by means of syntactic functions. The pertinent rule has the canonical truth-table form

p	$-p$	
T	T	F
T	F	T
F	T	T
F	F	F

The truth-table definition of the logical function " $-$ " is a formalization of ordinary-language negation. However, negation is defined in terms of falsehood, which means "not true," and therefore presupposes that we understand negation. Now let there be no misunderstanding here. I do not claim that we do not understand negation or *not*. I am asserting the logical "triviality" that *not* cannot be analytically defined except by the use of *not*, implicitly or explicitly; in sum, it cannot be defined in the strict sense of deriving it from positive elements alone. My contention is rather that in some sense, which cannot be rendered analytically precise, we do understand, and hence think, the altogether not, and most evidently in the simple act of thinking negation.

Given the fact that we somehow understand *not*, it is of course a simple matter to devise rules specifying its use in formal or informal language. The question at issue is how we understand the rules. One favored reply to my query is to say that we possess a "concept" of *not* that has sense but no reference. This reply fails to see that a concept, or a sense, is something, not nothing. But the Eleatic Stranger pointed out long ago that we cannot construct a concept of nothing, because nothing has (to use the modern terms) neither sense nor reference. The concept of *not* says, more or less, "Employ the negative particle under such-and-such circumstances." It does not explain either the sense or the reference of the negative dimension of the negative particle.

Nothing is gained by devising a set-theoretical concept to designate the sense of negation, since such concepts employ positive elements, such as the null class. The null class, however, already contains the notion of *not*, and in the doubly puzzling sense of "does not belong to," which also raises the metaphysical aporia of what it means to "belong to." It is metaphysically crucial that in set theory, the epsilon relation ("belongs to") is a primitive term. The reason for this was pointed out by David Hume: we cannot perceive necessary connections, and we certainly cannot establish them by using predicational discourse, which has no power to distinguish between "necessary" and "contingent," or between "belongs to" and "does not belong to." On the contrary, predicational discourse is itself rooted in our presupposition of such relations. Either Hume is wrong, and we do perceive or intuit these relations, or he was right. In either case, no analytical explanation is available.

I will return to the questions raised by predication in a moment. Let me first provide a second example, also quite simple, of the prediscursive nature of our understanding of *not*. The example is taken from Hegel's logic. However, I draw a non-Hegelian conclusion from the example. Philosophy, in its main or rationalist tradition, is the attempt to give a reasoned account of the whole. But the whole includes negation as well as position, difference as well as sameness, and so on. Furthermore, the positive elements are accessible as what they are only by virtue of not being what they are not. The difference of a human being from a bush or of a cow from a horse is not extrinsic to the entities involved in the sense that " − " is extrinsic to "*p*." Ontological difference is not a mathematical function, as we should see when we recall that " − " is different from "&" in a way that cannot be extrinsic to either or both.

The so-called ontological neutrality of mathematics (and hence of logic), to the extent that it obtains, is rooted precisely in the radical difference between beings and their logical relations, that is, between beings and relations considered as relations but not themselves as beings (a distinction that touches another metaphysical problem, to which I shall return below). A mathematical representation of the logical relations of beings, precisely to the extent that it is ontologically neutral, is ontologically *mute*. But no problems are resolved by silence. Instead, one metaphysics is silently replaced by another. To take the critical example of essences, alluded to above with respect to predication, formalization does not reveal these to be absurdities nor does it clarify their structure. Instead, essences are replaced at the outset by functions and relations; which is why, incidentally, philosophers of modal logic have not succeeded and cannot succeed in identifying any essences through the use of logical analysis.

I said that one metaphysics is silently replaced by another. Beneath the neutrality of logic lurk all the traditional problems of metaphysics, embedded within the technical machinery of their ostensible replacements. Determination of the validity or invalidity of arguments casts no light upon the nature of the entities about which the arguments have been constructed. This should be plain from the elementary distinction between validity and soundness, but it has been obscured by the tendency of analytical philosophers to explain soundness in terms of validity, or to copy, implicitly or explicitly, the mathematical procedure of constructing semantic entities from syntactical elements. As applied to philosophy, this leads merely to the identification of Being and syntax.

If a set of premises obtains, then a conclusion follows if it is logically implied by that set. The concept of essential necessity now refers to logical validity: metaphysical actuality is replaced by logical possibility in a way that is not so different from what we found in Husserl and could also show in Heidegger. Phenomenology to one side, this is perhaps the simplest explanation of why analytical philosophers tend to equate metaphysics or ontology with questions about the foundations of mathematics and logic. And those who, like W. V. Quine, equate ontology with the empirical sciences, nevertheless submit the results of science to logical analysis in order to verify the arguments in which scientific results are expressed. In slightly different terms, the empirical sciences rely upon logic for the necessity of their statements; this necessity is formal and has nothing to do with content. The empirical world is contingent; necessity resides in how we talk about contingency. When talk, including logic, is itself regarded as contingent, the result may be obscured by technical facility and the rhetoric of precision, but it is at bottom chaos.

Let us now come back more directly to predication. As long as we take our bearings by predication, there is no reason to say that a property belongs or does not belong necessarily to its ostensible owner. The concept of owner is ontological, not logical, and even in ontology its ambiguity can be obscured by speaking of the "bearer of properties." If necessity is a property of logic, then, because necessity and possibility are correlative terms, one would assume that possibility is also a property of logic. I put to one side the question of whether logical properties are not also contingent. What interests me now is that the empirical world, and therefore too our linguistic habits (considered as empirical facts), is from a logical standpoint relegated to the status of one of perhaps infinitely many possible worlds. This is the intersection of phenomenology and anlaytical philosophy. Logical and conceptual rigor leads to the result that we can say whatever we wish.

I do not deny that what we wish to say is restrained by what is the case, whether necessarily or contingently. My point is that analytical thinking cannot explain that restraint. In other words, one result of the historicizing of modern mathematics is that physics and logic have been separated. If it is not too cryptic a formulation, I should like to say that Being has been replaced by existence, which is in turn analyzed as an instance of something's belonging to something, namely, as the predicative analysis of the concept of which the existing thing is an instance.

Accordingly, the concept of necessity is transferred from existence to logic. And logic begs the question of necessity by defining it in terms of technical concepts which already presuppose that we understand what necessity means, as in the case of "necessarily belongs to." Apart from what has already been said, let us further consider that, in accord with formalist thinking, existence is given stability by the concept of counting. (In the case of transfinite sets, which do not concern us here, existence is given stability by naming, which depends implicitly upon counting, that is, upon identifying as a unit.) To exist is to be countable. Thus in standard predicative logic, existence is expressed as a quantifier. This is the sense in which logic is not ontologically neutral, as becomes quite clear when the question is raised whether concepts exist (or, in my earlier formulation, whether relations are beings). In other words, may we or may we not quantify over predicates?

The answer of the mathematician is surely that we can do whatever we wish, provided that we are able to furnish mathematically usable definitions. But the philosopher of mathematics is nevertheless deeply concerned with the ontological implications of our formal freedom. How are we to interpret it? And this is no longer simply a question of technical analysis. On the one hand, a concept (and so its representation as a predicate) is not the same as its instances. On the other hand, if to exist is to be countable, then there is no existential difference between concepts and instances. Quantification over predicates thus seems to open the doors of existence to infinite entities, including imaginary beings such as dragons and hippogryphs.

From a traditional standpoint, this problem arises from a failure to distinguish between Being and existence. The suppression of that distinction is due not merely to the desire to unify arithmetic and logic or to honor the ancient maxim, already visible in Plato, that to be is to be countable. It is rather motivated by the desire to suppress the metaphysical implications of the term *Being*. As a consequence of the arithmetical interpretation of existence by means of the Fregean functional analysis of propositions, the copula, that is, the traditional linguistic reference to Being, is assimilated into the predicate.

Being has no mathematical role to play, as is obvious from the form of a mathematical function $f(x)$, where f stands (in its logical employment) for a predicate and x for the domain of individual values or instances of the predicate. Strictly speaking, the formalism, whether employed in mathematics or in logic, makes no statement, either positive or negative, about existence, prior to the use of quantifiers, which must however themselves be interpreted. The quantificational interpretation of existence is philosophical, that is, metaphysical, not logical, and no less so if it is motivated by the desire to formalize or purify metaphysical language.

What I will call *logical existentialism* is thus a metaphysical interpretation of Being as the structure of the quantified logical proposition. The existing individual has no structure of its own independent of what is attributed to it by logical analysis. It is therefore neither necessary nor contingent and, strictly speaking, not even possible, apart from that analysis. The existing individual is an unidentifiable monad that becomes a possible existent, provided (to put it briefly) that we can attribute to it a logical structure containing no contradiction. But the intelligibility of this structure, and so the philosophical significance of the entire apparatus of mathematical logic, depends, as we have already seen, upon the antecedent intelligibility of Being and, more particularly, of nothing. What counts as necessary, contingent, and possible is dependent upon metaphysical considerations that are silently imported into the technical apparatus, which is then used to enforce a quite different technical or precise (as opposed to rhapsodic) understanding of these and related concepts.

Each philosopher may be free to choose his own rhapsody. My objection is directed to those who believe themselves to be dancing to the tune of stricter Muses than those of the metaphysical tradition.

The situation as thus far described is in fact still more complicated, as I must now indicate. The rhapsody of analytical philosophy, although on the one hand a monody of syntax, is from a slightly different standpoint a dualism of arithmetic and syntax. This occurs if we interpret existence statements (for example, "Socrates exists") as incomplete versions of identity or predication statements. Even if we do, however, there is still the fact of quantification, and hence the question of whether numbers are themselves syntactical devices. I leave it to the reader to decide between nominalism and Platonism in the philosophy of mathematics. My point is that monody, or monism of the syntactical variety, not merely reduces Being to syntax but deprives syntax of meaning. Why not be frank and simply say that the destruction of the "metaphysical monsters" of "meanings" simply leaves philosophy meaningless?

We note that, whereas the copula disappears into the predicate in the functional analysis of the proposition or statement, *not* remains separate from it as a truth function. In the statement "Fido is not a human being" (where "Fido" is the name of my dog), the predicate is taken to be "_____ is a human being," not "_____ is not a human being." There are (in the normal interpretation) no negative predicates for much the same reason that Plato and Aristotle denied that Being has a contrary. To argue otherwise is to import "nothing" into existence. This raises the extremely difficult question of how to analyze negative existential statements. I can touch upon only one aspect of this cluster of issues and must refer the reader to my book, *The Limits of Analysis*, for further discussion.

The denial that existence (the logical surrogate for Being) has a contrary is closely connected to the independent status of *not* as a logical function. This raises the peculiar question of the difference between truth-functional statements about real and imaginary beings. As soon as this question is raised, we see, or ought to see, that the attribution of existence is in fact not at all determined by our logical apparatus. The analytical treatment of existence is thus circular or incoherent. On the one hand, existence is determined on empirical grounds (for example, does Santa Claus exist?). On the other hand, what we mean by *existence* is determined on technical or logical grounds.

Perhaps one could also say that *not* is given an independent status in logical analysis that is denied to existence, and so surreptitiously to Being, which is defined in terms of quantification, identity, and predication. I therefore risk the closing suggestion that nothing, the altogether not or *nihil absolutum*, has a deeper and, in ghostly terms, more prominent role in analytical philosophy than does existence or Being. There is a doctrine of Being of sorts in analytical philosophy, whether that doctrine is monism or dualism. But there is no doctrine of nothing, despite the independence of *not* and its explanation as a truth function. The explanation is circular or, as one could say, impredicative. Analytical philosophers have thus obeyed the command of Father Parmenides. But they do so by refusing to face up to the question of whether truth functions exist.

I have written this chapter not with the intention to hypostatize Being and nothing but rather in defense of the thesis that, whereas Hegel is correct to say that everything is a mixture of Being and nothing, he is wrong to assert that there is a complete conceptual explanation of this mixture. I myself am a partisan of the thesis that we understand Being and nothing but that we cannot explain them in a rigorous, consistent, noncircular manner. If I am accused of succumbing to rhapsodic speculations, I can only say that, whether my critics are listening or not, the music plays on.

CHAPTER NINE

Rorty and Systematic Philosophy

What is the connection between Richard Rorty and systematic philosophy? It depends upon what we mean by systematic philosophy. A *systema* is literally a "standing together." On Rorty's account, things stand together depending upon how we (that is to say, influential intellectuals) talk about them. Because talk is conventional or historical, and still more precisely, because knowledge is the social justification of belief (170ff.), systems are in effect unmasked as ideologies.[1] This view leads Rorty to his own deconstructive *systema* of social pragmatism, ordinary-language analysis, and post-Gadamerian versions of the hermeneutics of intersubjectivity.

One might still defend systematic philosophy as the study of the structure of ideologies. In a sense, this is a fair description of Rorty's own professional activities. However, we must add at once that Rorty does not so much analyze structures as interpret them. As I have indicated, analysis is connected with one form or another of truth and, in a properly qualified sense, with epistemology. Rorty, however, is a hermeneuticist, and by hermeneutics he means "an expression of hope that the cultural space left by the demise of epistemology will not be filled—that our culture should become one in which the demand for constraint and confrontation is no longer felt" (315).

One cannot analyze a structure except with technical tools. For Rorty, however, as I have already indicated, *technē* is a pseudonym for ideology or, let us say, rhetoric. Rorty cannot make official use of transcendental arguments because he rejects, or at least denies us access to, the domain of the transcendental. Neither can he appeal to principles, grounds, or categories, as these all rest upon the controlling assumption of an order that, if it is not eternal, cannot itself be an ideology without generating an infinite regress of interpretations, or in other words, what is today called postmodernism.

1. Numbers in parentheses, unless otherwise indicated, are page references to Richard Rorty, *Philosophy and the Mirror of Nature* (Princeton: Princeton University Press, 1979).

Rorty thus places himself in the line of twentieth-century liberators from the domination and spiritual distortion of systematic philosophy. However, his emphasis is upon society rather than upon spiritual freedom. The result, perhaps not unlike the case of John Dewey, is that liberation is silently transformed into social domination. Rorty avoids facing this problem because he has next to nothing of substance to say about the structure of a liberated society. He is an intellectual, not a social or political thinker. In another formulation, Rorty is more concerned with boredom than with freedom. He requires interesting conversation, but he seems to forget that interesting conversation can take place in prison—for example, in the prison of academic conformity, masked as deconstruction.

The reduction of philosophy to ideology, and hence of notions like that of element, form, unity, and structure to the level of psychological fantasy or social tyranny, has necessary implications for Rorty as well as for systematic philosophy. On its own grounds, Rorty's hermeneutics, which he styles as "edifying" and "reactive," is also an ideology. Rorty, like all postmodernist liberators, is an epiphenomenon of the Enlightenment, but he is no less an Enlightenment figure for that reason. He tacitly subscribes to the Horkheimer-Adorno thesis about the Enlightenment as the domination of reason, but he fails to take seriously the domination of linguistic fashion. As an edifying reactor, Rorty is also a quisling.

Rorty proposes to enlighten us by entertainment. He prepares us for the entertainment of fashionable conversation by attempting to convince us that traditional philosophy, in his view "systematic philosophy," is boring. To cite a typical passage, "By sketching a little of the history of discussions of the mind, I hope to show that the problem of reason cannot be stated without a return to epistemological views which no one really wishes to resurrect" (37). Rorty's point is thus not that traditional philosophy, or epistemology, is wrong, but rather that we are no longer interested in it (cf. 351, 359). In another formulation, it is an optional way of viewing philosophy (136).

Rorty's view that "the problem of reason" is the same as, or is necessarily connected to, epistemology, is most evidently refuted by the example of Hegel, about whom Rorty has nothing "interesting" to say. I suspect this is largely due to Rorty's tacit acceptance of the Heideggerean thesis about modern philosophy as the quest for certainty (61). Heidegger, of course, extends this thesis to cover all of western metaphysics, or Platonism. Rorty does not go quite as far. Instead, he treats Plato as the inventor of the canonical form of the doctrine of the soul as a "glassy essence" (42ff.), or in other words as a mirror of eternal Ideas (which Rorty himself somehow knows to be mere names: see page 32 for his nominalism). Plato is therefore the "father of the *logos*" or the grandfather of epistemology.

Rorty cannot refute traditional philosophy, whether in its Platonist or its Cartesian version, without himself becoming a traditional philosopher. His actual procedure is quite different from an attempted refutation. It consists of the continuous mockery by caricatures of traditional philosophy, by Rorty's account a series of uninteresting or outmoded views to which no one would wish to return. It is crucial to understand from the outset that Rorty's book contains no single instance of what professional philosophers call a genuine argument purporting to refute the traditional thesis, either in its own terms or on the basis of Rorty's own theoretical position.

The reason in both cases is the same. An ideology or a psychological error cannot be refuted in its own terms, because these terms are false or meaningless. Rorty has no theoretical position of his own but only an alternative ideology, so he is at bottom asking us to exchange our ideology for his. Like all clever esotericists of the modern epoch, Rorty alternates between the advocacy of a revolution and the regular assurance that "our" ideology (namely, the ideology shared by the leading academic schools of our time) is in fact the same as his.

Rorty's book is propaganda, not argument. In my opinion, this is not in itself a sufficient reason for condemning the book. Much of what passes for argument in professional philosophy is in fact propaganda. Professors argue; philosophers employ rhetoric to determine the goals and nature of argumentation. Rorty, like all philosophers, exemplifies the master-slave dialectic. Whether he is in fact a philosopher thus turns upon the question of whether he is a master or a slave. To think that it turns upon the validity or invalidity of his arguments is to have misunderstood his book as well as the nature of philosophy.

Arguments are a dime a dozen. Rorty, however, like all prudent persons, clearly believes that a penny saved is a penny earned. To be more explicit, because Rorty wishes to show that systematic philosophy is impossible, or undesirable and uninteresting, he can hardly proceed in a systematic manner. The assertion that traditional philosophy rests upon the image of the glassy essence and the Platonic reflection therein is itself supported by Rorty's interpretation of the history of philosophy. Exactly as in a Platonic dialogue, the interesting part is not the argument but the myth.

Rorty tells us a story that consists of two parts. The first part is his description of Platonism and Cartesianism, or the history of philosophy as it culminates in Kant. The second part is Rorty's account of post-Hegelian philosophy, in its Continental and analytical manifestations. After the story there is a moral, namely, Rorty's version of edifying and reactive eclecticism, or how to keep the conversation going.

Because the conversation is itself simply the ongoing flow of history, it is immediately apparent that Rorty's book is no more theoretical than it is systematic or, for that matter, antisystematic. Rorty has written an untheoretical and unsystematic philosophy of history. I call it untheoretical because the general presuppositions of Rorty's reading of history are those of what may for the sake of brevity be called ordinary-language analysis. In other words, despite his laudatory references to such figures as Dewey, Heidegger, and even Donald Davidson, Rorty belongs to the school of those who engage in the *haut vulgarisation* of the fragmentary remarks of the later Wittgenstein.

Those who engage in the deconstruction of Platonism are quick to assure us that they do not refer to Plato but only to his unfortunate influence. In the same spirit, I distinguish between Wittgenstein and his academic disciples. Whereas it is not at all clear what positive recommendations are being put forward by these disciples, there can be no doubt that they object to metaphysics or systematic philosophy and thus to the application of scientific procedures of theory construction to philosophy.

The *haute vulgarisation* of Wittgenstein is normally associated with moral intensity. In Rorty's case, however, morality is, so to speak, "laid back"; anything goes, even the discourse of Rorty's more formally or ontologically inclined contemporaries. The one thing that is not permitted, of course, is Platonism, or systematic philosophy: more specifically, the view that there are definite philosophical questions with correspondingly definite answers.

Rorty's version of the philosophy of history is thus propaganda on behalf of tolerance. This is not the worst principle to which to dedicate one's talents. Furthermore, Rorty is right to believe that systematic philosophy is antithetical to tolerance. What cannot be included in the system must be excluded. Or, if everything can be included, it must be in the form dictated by the system. One could go farther and say that every philosophy, systematic or not, is intolerant to the extent that it distinguishes between the noble and the base as well as between the true and the false.

To the extent that Rorty is opposed to philosophy, and not simply to traditional or systematic philosophy, his exercise of tolerance is at the same time an exercise of intolerance. Because arguments are ideologies, Rorty must enforce the rejection of philosophy by the strength of his own interests, which in turn acquire dominance by rhetoric and political manipulation. It is amusing to watch certain elements of the academic community, who exercised the same will to power for forty-odd years, objecting to Rorty's great prestige and influence among contemporary intellectuals.

To use one of Rorty's favorite words, I find his success *uninteresting*. It is a trivial consequence of the democratization of the doctrines of Nietzsche and Heidegger together with the growing awareness of the inner unity between these doctrines and those of the later Wittgenstein. I do, however, regard it as interesting to consider the problem Rorty faces in his attempt to become a master, or, if a slave, *primus inter pares*. Rorty claims both that he has correctly understood the history of philosophy and, by extension, past human experience, and also that there are no correct understandings of human experience and certainly no correct philosophical accounts of that experience.

To say this in a more fundamental way, there cannot be for Rorty any correct understanding of the world, because *world* is a technical term and refers to a structure. On the other hand, Rorty allows for "linguistic structures" or "horizons" that themselves enforce this or that conception of the world. Rorty thus knows that the world is in all cases a linguistic structure, a perspective or (to use my own terminology) a false image of chaos. He evidently does not know that this commits him to a view of the ground of the world as discursive.

Rorty, like so many contemporaries, is a kind of Fichtean. He is committed to the postulation of an inaccessible transcendental speaker that disguises itself in the very act of emitting a positive discourse or linguistic horizon. One such positive discourse is that of transcendental philosophy, as for example the philosophy of Kant. I said that these discourses are false images of chaos. But the chaos is itself an image, namely, the result of every human effort to grasp discursively what I have just identified as the transcendental speaker.

Rorty, of course, would like to reject the transcendental dimension as just another linguistic construction. But that is precisely the point: to insist upon our inability to emerge from the determinate world of a specific historical linguistic horizon is to render discursivity transcendental. Discursivity is the condition for the possibility of linguistic horizons. To describe these horizons as contingent human creations is to beg the question, not to answer it. It is to say nothing more than that discursivity, the bound of the world and hence its structure, is incarnated in historical individuals. But this is exactly the thesis of German transcendental philosophy.

Rorty differs from Kant and approaches more closely to Fichte by denying that we can grasp the categorial structure of transcendental discursivity in a theoretical discourse that is not itself a false image of chaos. Like Fichte, Rorty places the emphasis upon practice or the act of the will. Unlike Fichte, Rorty's act of the will is in the service of difference rather than of unity or identity. This is the point of contact between Rorty and Derrida.

Rorty's antitranscendental transcendentalism has many consequences, among them the fact that, on Rortyan grounds, there can be no such thing as the correct reading of a text. As I noted previously, no reading of a philosophical text can be justified by reference to the text itself, which has already been identified as a fantasy or an error. It is entirely correct to interpret a fantasy in any way we wish, that is, in any way that persuades us or our audience. To say otherwise, of course, is to appeal to an objective reality and the genuine transcendence of linguistic perspectives, or to what Rorty ridicules as *flatus vocis* (43) reflected in the mirror of the mind.

Strictly speaking, once this is understood, there is no further need to consider Rorty's views in any detail. One has merely to pronounce them uninteresting and can then proceed to the infinitely more gratifying effort to enforce one's own hermeneutical mastery. This procedure would be approved by Rorty himself, or at least by his discourse. Rorty's views are today conventional among intellectuals and not the least among professors of philosophy. But Rorty informs us that the role of the hermeneutical philosopher is "to perform the social function which Dewey called 'breaking the crust of convention'" (379). The politics of liberation is thus for Rorty the cutting edge of metaphysics. Rorty, of course, speaks of the social rather than the political; like so many intellectuals, he believes that the social rather than the political is the sphere of liberation.

This, however, is a subtlety, and Rorty has encouraged his fellow

Americans to philosophize with a hammer. For our purposes, we may regard his emphasis on the social as a consequence of the doctrine of intersubjectivity that in Rorty's case is called "conversation." In Rorty's substitute for ontology, to be is to be talked about; by the same token, "I converse, therefore I exist."

According to Rorty, conversation was previously (in the "tradition") taken for monologue. Hegel justifies the dominant monologue of each age as the expression of its spiritual development. Strictly speaking, monologue is transformed into dialogue only with the advent of the comprehensive Hegelian discourse. This dialogue is not between Hegel and his predecessors but rather between Hegel and God. Rorty, on the other hand, is conversing with well-placed professional colleagues.

How are we to account for this coarsening in theological ambition? The first thing to be said, and I can only assert it here, is that there is no doctrine of intersubjectivity in Hegel and hence no conversation between merely human beings. On the other hand, Hegel in no way accepts Rorty's paradigm of an eternal essence reflected in the mind's mirror. In an amusing keeping with the Jewish revelation, Hegel takes his bearings by speech, not by vision. One may add parenthetically here that the contemporary objection to a metaphysics of presence, as mediated by such Israelites as Heidegger and Derrida, is a fundamentally Hegelian enterprise.

More accurately, it is the consequence of Hegel's successful attack against intellectual intuition, whether in its Greek or in its German forms, as well as of the failure of Hegel's attempt to replace philosophical monologue by what Heidegger calls onto-theo-logical dialogue. Hegel, unlike Rorty, correctly understands that the Platonic Idea, like the Aristotelian form, is not accessible to the precise systematic discourse of ontology. Hegel's objection to intuition is not that it produces erroneous speech but that it produces no determinate speech at all.

To say that Hegel talks to God is finally to say that he attempts to assimilate formal structure entirely into conceptual logic, that is, into systematic discourse. To say that Plato remains at the level of monologue is finally to say that, for him, form, as inaccessible to systematic discourse, is reflected in the mind only as a false image. In this sense, Rorty, although he does not know it, is a Platonist. The difference between the two is that for Plato, the falsehood of the image does not cancel its power to convey a perception of the truth.

Plato's dialogues remain an image of his unwritten monologue, and precisely of a monologue that is engendered by the impossibility of systematic philosophy.

This last paragraph was no doubt too cryptic to be immediately persuasive. Let me give a more accessible example of how Rorty gets Plato wrong. Rorty attributes to Plato the thesis of an eternal order whose structure is reflected in the mind. Rorty compares the mind both to an eye and to a mirror. He does not seem to notice the difference between these two metaphors. An eye, so to speak, sees its objects directly, whereas a mirror sees nothing, but presents a reverse image to whoever looks into it. The significance of seeing the world unfold in reverse order is presented by Plato in his myth of the reversed cosmos, as narrated by the Eleatic Stranger in the *Statesman*.

Given the circularity of the motion of the cosmos, there are no "visual" consequences of the reversal of direction. The shift from east to west and vice versa cannot be seen by the residents of either cosmic cycle, and its consequences are presented with respect to genesis and time, or what the deconstructors call *historicity*. There are thus no Platonic Ideas in the *Statesman* and no discussion of the mind as a mirror or an eye. In this dialogue, vision is a derivative of hearing, as for example in the hearing of a myth.

This Hebraic motif in the *Statesman* is not the only evidence of the poetic wisdom of the old view that Plato was a student of Moses. The last word in the *Statesman* on mind and knowledge is that rules and *technai* or the arts and sciences are entirely subordinate to *phronēsis* or sound judgment, which is free to disregard these rules and *technai* entirely.

Essentially the same point is made in the *Phaedrus* by Socrates when he presents his great myth of the soul. There is a discontinuity between Eros and the Ideas or hyperuranian beings that makes ontology impossible. The charioteer of the philosophical soul raises his head only above the surface of the cosmos "and is carried around by the revolution, disturbed by the horses and viewing the beings with difficulty" (248A). In other words, ontology, or systematic speech about the structure of being, is ruled out by cosmic kinesis. Philosophical vision is perspectival, but the structure of the perspective is defined by the hyperuranian beings. To see with difficulty is not the same as not to see at all.

These two examples are not intended to sustain a comprehensive interpretation of the Platonic dialogues. They are offered as evidence of what is missing from Rorty's ideological account of Platonism. Nor should we be under any misapprehension concerning the importance of the historical discussions in Rorty's book to his overall enterprise. Rorty makes this clear enough, for example, on page 34: history is needed in order to explain "how we got the intuitions which make us think that there *must* be a *real*, indissoluble, philosophical problem *somewhere* in the neighborhood."

The historical sketches (I prefer the term *cartoons*) are designed to sustain "the claim (common to Wittgenstein and Dewey) that to think of knowledge which presents a 'problem,' and about which we ought to have a 'theory,' is a product of viewing knowledge as an assemblage of representations—a view of knowledge which, I have been arguing, was a product of the seventeenth century. The moral to be drawn is that if this way of thinking of knowledge is optional, then so is epistemology, and so is philosophy as it has understood itself since the middle of the last century" (136).

Platonism thus constitutes the prehistory of epistemology, to which it ostensibly furnishes the essence-mirror structure, as well as the conception of philosophy as a set of problems with technical answers. I have only been able to indicate why Rorty's account of Platonism is nonsense. But it is surely well known that Hegel, who lies on the other side of epistemology, rejected it at least as decisively as Rorty, not because (as Rorty weakly holds) it is optional, but because it is incoherent.

In order to understand the nineteenth-century view of philosophy and hence the various schools of the twentieth century, one must certainly possess an accurate understanding of Hegel and thereby an explanation of why Hegel was replaced by neo-Kantianism. One of the weakest features of Rorty's book is that it contains not even a cartoon of Hegel's system. This observation brings me back to the point at which I began my excursus on Plato. Rorty has no light to cast on the decay from conversation with God to conversation with philosophy professors. Surely it is not a testimony to spiritual power to say that one finds philosophy professors more interesting than God.

Not only did Hegel anticipate Rorty's rejection of epistemology; he also set the stage for postmodernism, or the advent of the post-anthropological, postphilosophical, and posthistorical epoch. Rorty, to be sure, is too much of a humanist to be a representative spokesman for postmodernism. Nevertheless, it is not merely his eclecticism that makes him an ally of this latest version of Enlightenment decadence. The fact is that Rorty, for all his self-styled Lessingian humanism (377), cannot tell the difference between a human being and a machine.

I want to illustrate this charge, and thereby conclude, by considering the essential points of Rorty's interpretation of Kant's doctrine of synthesis. Rorty's treatment of Kant epitomizes his hermeneutical procedure: It shows very clearly how his arguments are in fact rhetorical exercises. This will serve to confirm the thesis, already arrived at, that there is no connection between Rorty and systematic philosophy.

Differently stated, there are no arguments in Rorty to refute, and it is missing the point of his book to argue with him as though I were commenting on a paper at a meeting of the American Philosophical Association. Rorty's theoretical account of philosophy is a myth—as I see it, an uninteresting inference from an interpretation of the history of philosophy that is not merely optional but false.

I take my bearings from the following passage devoted by Rorty to Wilfred Sellars. "To sum up, Sellars's psychological nominalism is not a theory of how the mind works, nor of how knowledge is born in the infant breast, nor of the 'nature of concepts,' nor of any other matter of fact. It is a remark about the difference between facts and rules, a remark to the effect that we can only come under epistemic rules when we have entered the community where the game governed by these rules is played" (187).

Whatever Sellars might say about this account, Rorty intends by it to express his approval and, whether intentionally or not, he arrives at an identity between Sellars and the later Wittgenstein. Still more important, the distinction between facts and rules is Kantian. However, for Kant, rules are facts in the sense that there are unique rules expressing the nature of rationality. Kant is not a psychological nominalist, as are Sellars and Wittgenstein in the interpretation Rorty gives to them. Rorty, like the majority of his analytical contemporaries, but also like advanced continental philosophers such as Apel and Habermas, is a post-Heideggerean neo-Kantian. I mean by this uncouth expression that he replaces the transcendental ego with an intersubjectivity that is in turn derived from linguistic history.

Rorty arrives at psychologism, or historicism, because he belongs to that school of neo-Kantians that cannot justify synthesis. Rorty contends that synthesis is a mistaken interpretation of what is better explained by a doctrine of predication (154). Not unsurprisingly, Rorty is totally silent about the structure of predication. But even nominalists owe us an account of the intelligible unity of the proposition. If no analytical account of that unity is forthcoming, then the intelligibility of the proposition itself constitutes an argument, not for nominalism, but for synthetic unity of the Kantian variety. Unfortunately for Rorty, this leads directly to the transcendental ego.

Rorty never takes seriously Kant's account of synthesis. Instead, he offers passages such as this one: "What we want to know is whether concepts *are* synthesizers, and it is no help to be told that they couldn't be unless there were a lot of intuitions awaiting synthesis" (154). Unfortunately, Rorty's remark is also of no help, since it does not contain Kant's case for synthesis. Kant never proceeds in the circular and irrelevant manner contained in Rorty's flippant caricature. Instead, he addresses himself to the fact of unity in the structure of the proposition, whether the content of that proposition be empirical or a priori.

In rejecting synthesis as the work of a transcendental ego, Rorty notes that Kant could have done the same had he gone directly to a view "of knowledge as a relation between persons and propositions" (152). This comment makes clear Rorty's allegiance to the doctrine of linguistic intersubjectivity. However, by the terms of that doctrine, intersubjectivity is itself a proposition or set of propositions, that is, a syntactic function that requires explanation.

If the relation between persons and propositions is itself a proposition, then we have an infinite regress. If it is a function, then the unity of the function requires accounting for, as for example in a Kantian manner. Rorty offers no such accounting. Instead, he says that Kant might have regarded "a person as a black box emitting sentences, the justification for these sentences being found in his relation to his environment (including the emissions of his fellow black boxes). The question 'how is knowledge possible?' would then have resembled the question 'how are telephones possible?' meaning something like 'How can one build something which does that?' " (152).

Despite Rorty's confusion of human beings and black boxes, he believes that physiological psychology provides us with the answer to the question just cited. This in turn shows that the reference to black boxes is irrelevant. Knowledge of how to build a telephone casts no light upon the unity of the propositions containing the instructions for building a telephone. It casts no light upon the intellectual powers of the builder.

As to physiological psychology, descendants of the Enlightenment have attempted to explain thinking in precisely the same manner. But their question is not that of unity. They begin from the synthesizing or unifying function and use it nonreflexively as they analyze the physiological components of intelligible thoughts or utterances. From the proposition "A human being can build a telephone by doing x, y, and z," it follows trivially that a human being can build a telephone. It does not follow, however, that a human being *is* a telephone. And even if a human being were a telephone, or a computer, nothing would follow concerning the unity of the functions of the telephone or computer.

Rorty's linguistic neo-Kantianism here goes hand in hand with his adherence to the Cartesian version of Enlightenment—see his remark on "the (entirely justified) notion that the preservation of the values of the Enlightenment is our best hope" (335f.). Rorty is not interested in philosophy but in natural science; or rather, he is not so much interested in natural science as he is willing to abdicate to its authority as the replacement for traditional philosophy. Unfortunately, this respect for science is hard to sustain when one regularly speaks of the philosophical significance of nature as does Gertrude Stein of Oakland: "There is no there there."

In a footnote on page 155, Rorty claims to restate an important step in Kant's justification of the Copernican revolution. "To put the point another way, Kant's own transcendental idealism cuts the ground out from under the 'Transcendental Deduction'—for either the machinery (synthesis) and the raw material (concepts, intuitions) described in the 'Deduction' are noumenal, or they are phenomenal. If phenomenal, then, contrary to the premises of the 'Deduction,' we can be aware of them. If noumenal, then nothing (including what the 'Deduction' says) can be known of them."

Contrary to Rorty's interpretation, the distinction between the noumenal and the phenomenal, whatever its defects, applies to objects, not to the machinery or raw material of the deduction. For Kant, the possibility of making the distinction between the noumenal and the phenomenal is a consequence of the possibility of a transcendental deduction, or in other words, of the Kantian version of the fact (not of the concept or the argument) that we are, and experience ourselves as, *ego cogitans*.

In other words, it is not the case that for Kant, the mind has what Rorty calls "privileged access" to its own machinery. Rightly or wrongly, Kant claims that the mind *is* its machinery. A transcendental deduction is then not a free construction of the imagination, or a hypothesis inferred from experience at the level of experience. It is not a language game or a response to one's environment but instead Kant's revision of what Aristotle called "thought thinking itself."

To sum up, Kant is not in the business of providing instructions on how to build a telephone. He is concerned to account for unity. Rorty in effect tells us that unity is provided by adherence to the rules of the game. He simply cannot see that the rules of the game are themselves the product of unity. Differently stated, logic, the generalization of syntax, tells us nothing whatsoever about unity. Instead, it defines identity, a relation, which is already dependent upon the unity of the structure of its elements.

Richard Rorty situates himself in the Wittgensteinian version of the attempt to philosophize without foundations. If we trace this attempt back to its source, I suggest that we will find it in the misunderstanding of the nature, as well as the failure, of Hegel.

One way in which to formulate Hegel's intention is to say that all previous thinkers attempted to establish a foundation for philosophy that is necessarily external to it. Whether the foundation is a principle, a set of formal elements, a table of categories, transcendental subjectivity, a veridical God, or everyday experience, it was not possible to certify that foundation by assimilating it into the system it was intended to support. To say this in another way, the evidence or arguments designed to certify the principle could not in turn be certified by the principle itself.

The disjunction between the foundation of the principle and the principle as foundation leads finally either to mysticism or to discursive relativism; that is to say, it leads in both cases to the abandonment of philosophy: to silence or to its discursive equivalent, infinite chatter. Hegel's attempt to resolve this failure is to transform the disjunction itself into a self-certifying, that is, circular and complete, concept.

I will state this point very concisely: whereas all other philosophies begin from or terminate in nothing, and further in a static or vacuous *nihil absolutum,* or attempt to disguise this eschatological nihilism by a technical translation of the *nihil absolutum* into a finite negation, Hegel's initial step is to attack nothingness head-on. Hegel's speculative dialectic, his logic, is in its entirety an attempt to state conceptually the sameness of Being and nothing. Hegel insists from the outset that the ostensible *nihil absolutum* is a determinate negation.

The essential content of this assertion is as follows: let us grant a fundamental nihilism; if we do not merely surrender to it but attempt resolutely to understand it or master it by thought, we will see that nothingness has an internal dynamical and productive structure. This structure is the whole (*das Ganze*).

For our present purposes, the main point is that Hegel's system has no foundation. There is nothing external to Hegel's system, and if one points to this absence of externality as the annihilating *nihil absolutum*, Hegel replies that the threat is specious, because we have only to think it in order to assimilate it into the whole or to transform it into a determinate negation, that is, to transform the static nothingness into what he calls "the terrible labor of negativity."

Unfortunately, Hegel was very quickly misunderstood as the most extreme case of the traditional philosophical attempt to construct a system on the basis of an absolute principle, namely, the Absolute. There can be no doubt that, if Hegel attempted to build a philosophical system on the external foundation of the Absolute, he failed absolutely. The net result, to come directly to our own time, was the conclusion that, if philosophy is to be a legitimate enterprise at all, it must proceed without foundations.

From here, it is a short step to the further conclusion that a philosophy without foundations is not a philosophy at all, or that philosophy is, not complete, but "finished," to be abandoned. It is Rorty's merit that he understands this and does not attempt to conceal it from himself by outbursts of technical virtuosity that, if they have any significance at all, are intrinsically Hegelian demonstrations of the structure of the terrible labor of negativity. What Rorty does not understand, and what may not be intelligible, is that if philosophy is to be preserved, it must return to Hegel in this minimal but indispensable sense: it must come to terms with the *nihil absolutum*.

CHAPTER TEN

Nietzsche's Revolution

Stylistic caution. *A: But if everyone knew this,* most *would be harmed by it. You yourself call these opinions dangerous for those exposed to danger, and yet you express them in public? B: I write in such a way that neither the mob, nor the* populi, *nor the parties of any kind want to read me. Consequently these opinions of mine will never become public. A: But how do you write, then? B: Neither usefully nor pleasantly—to the trio I have named.*

—FRIEDRICH NIETZSCHE
Human, All Too Human, translated by R. J. Hollingdale

Friedrich Nietzsche is today the most influential philosopher in the Western, non-Marxist world. The scope of this influence cuts across the traditional lines of theory and practice by which intellectuals and political activists are usually divided. Furthermore, in apparent contradiction to Nietzsche's own assertion that he does not write for the mob, his doctrines have been disseminated throughout the general public, and not the least among people who have never heard his name or read a page of his voluminous writings.

It is a remarkable fact that Nietzsche, a self-professed decadent, nihilist, atheist, anti-Christ, opponent of academic philosophy, scourge of socialism, egalitarianism, and "the people," who espoused aristocratic political and artistic views, insisted upon a rank ordering of human beings, and went so far as to advise men to carry a whip when they visit the women's quarters, is today one of the highest authorities, if not *the* authority, for progressive liberals, existentialist theologians, professors, anarchist speculators, left-wing critics of the Enlightenment and bourgeois society, propounders of egalitarianism and enemies of political and artistic elitism, the advance guard of women's liberationists, and a multitude of contemporary movements,

This essay appeared in the November 1987 issue and is reprinted with permission from *The World and I*, a publication of *The Washington Times Corporation*, copyright © 1987.

most if not all of which seem to have been castigated by Nietzsche's unparalleled rhetorical powers.

Although it is not discussed explicitly by statesmen and political commentators of the mass media, Nietzsche's dominance is a political fact of the highest importance. One might go so far as to say that the degree to which we become aware of Nietzsche's revolutionary stature, as he intended it rather than as he presented it disguised by a variety of rhetorical masks, determines whether we belong to the mob or to those whom Stendhal, a favorite of Nietzsche, called "the happy few." To understand Nietzsche is far from simple, but it is not impossible. The importance of such an understanding, not merely for scholarly reasons but with respect to the health of the Republic, amply warrants our making the effort.

In this chapter, I attempt to articulate the essential elements in Nietzsche's revolutionary politics, with sufficient textual citations to support my analysis but without the kind of comprehensive development of detail that requires a lengthy book. Before I begin to unfold the general story, let me state the fundamental political result of Nietzsche's teaching. An appeal to the highest, most gifted human individuals to create a radically new society of artist-warriors was expressed with rhetorical power and a unique mixture of frankness and ambiguity in such a way as to allow the mediocre, the foolish, and the mad to regard themselves as the divine prototypes of the highest men of the future. A radically new society requires as its presupposition the destruction of the existing society; Nietzsche succeeded in enlisting countless thousands in the ironical task of self-destruction, all in the name of a future utopia. Without pressing the point here, one may note the extraordinary similarity between Nietzsche's program and that of Karl Marx.

It is important to begin with a reminder that whereas both Nietzsche and Marx speak of violence, and Nietzsche even more unrestrainedly than Marx, the first step in the destruction of the West is not war, and not even armed insurrection, but the initiation of the process of transforming human values. As Hegel wisely remarked, we understand a people by the gods they worship. Nietzsche identified himself as a disciple of Dionysus, the pagan god of intoxication. That he may have done so ironically, namely, as a concealed disciple of Apollo, the pagan god of lucidity, does not mitigate the disastrous consequences of the public assertion, nor does it warrant our confusing or attempting to identify the two gods. The Socratic contention that philosophy is divine madness is not to be confused with the mingling of intoxication and lucidity. The lucidity of the drunkard is unable to distinguish the precision of fantasy from that of truth.[1]

One other preliminary observation is indispensable. My study of Nietzsche should not be understood as intentionally unsympathetic or as a gesture of comprehensive repudiation. We cannot understand Nietzsche without grasping his genius. Furthermore, we cannot appreciate the dangers of his political program if we do not perceive the validity of much of his diagnosis of Western society. Nietzsche's power arises from his unique combination of psychological profundity and literary subtlety. He would not have achieved his influence over us all if he were nothing but a charlatan. A serious criticism of Nietzsche is necessarily at the same time a criticism of part of oneself.

It is often said or implied that Nietzsche was a political conservative. This is understandable, as we are about to see, but it is not accurate. In order to establish that he was not, I begin with the following citation:

> *Whispered into the ear of the conservative.*—What one did not know previously, what one knows today, could know —, a *backward formation*, a return in any sense and to any degree is entirely impossible. . . . No one is free to be a crab. There is no avoiding it: one *must* go forwards, that is to say, *step by step farther into decadence* (—my definition of modern "progress" . . .). One can *hamper* this development, and by hampering it, dam up and collect the degeneration, make it more vehement and *more immediate:* one can do no more than this.[2]

This passage is helpful for two reasons. Not only does it distinguish Nietzsche's position from that of the conservative; it also states concisely his revolutionary procedure. Nietzsche intends to accelerate the process of self-destruction intrinsic to modern "progress," not to encourage a return to some idyllic past. The more persons who can be convinced that they are modern progressives (or even postmoderns),

---

1. In this connection it is important to read par. 10 of "Raids of a Non-contemporary Man," in *Twilight of the Idols* (Götzen-Dämmerung), in which Nietzsche identifies the Apollonian and the Dionysian as two forms of intoxication.
2. *Götzen-Dämmerung (Streifzüge eines Unzeitgemässen)*, in *Nietzsches Werke*, ed. Karl Schlechta (Munich: Carl Hanser Verlag, 1954), vol. 2, par. 43, 1018–19.

the quicker the explosion.[3] Nevertheless, Nietzsche is a revolutionary of the right in his radical aristocratism and antiegalitarianism. It is true that assertions such as the following are fundamentally aesthetic: "Where the people eat and drink, even where they venerate, it usually stinks. One should not go to church if one wants to breath *pure air*."[4] But it is obvious enough that aesthetic sensibility, when it is as violent in its antipathies as Nietzsche's, has direct political consequences.

For explicitly political formulations of Nietzsche's "conservatism," one should perhaps examine his denunciation of socialism, which he saw as a direct consequence of the secularization of Christianity and modern progressive liberalism, with the resultant destruction of vitality and creativity. Socialism is in his eyes the younger brother of modern European despotism, which it desires to replace. Socialism seeks complete power for the state, and strives to negate individuality:

> Socialism itself can hope to exist only for brief periods here and there, and then only through the exercise of the extremest terror-ism. For this reason it is secretly preparing itself for rule through fear and is driving the word "justice" into the heads of the half-educated masses like a nail so as to rob them of their reason . . . and to create in them a good conscience for the evil game they are to play.[5]

Nietzsche's thought is too complex to reduce to a single thesis or a simple political formula. It should not be inferred from the aesthetic foundation of his critique of socialism, for example, that Nietzsche wished to encourage the straightforward institution of "cultivated" societies. Cultivated societies of the usual liberal sort (liberal in the late nineteenth-century sense of the term) are exactly what Nietzsche wished to destroy. As is especially evident in *Human, All Too Human*,

3. See *Ecce Homo*, "Why I am a Destiny," tr. Walter Kaufmann, in *On the Genealogy of Morals and Ecce Homo* (New York: Vintage Books, 1969), 326: "I am no man; I am dynamite." In the same section, after speaking of his enterprise as the "revaluation of all values," Nietzsche says: "I am by far the most terrible human being that has existed so far; this does not preclude the possibility that I shall be the most beneficial." Nietzsche is referring to the fact that, as is stated by his character Zarathustra, whoever wishes to create must first destroy.

4. *Beyond Good and Evil*, tr. Walter Kaufmann (New York: Vintage Books, 1966), 43, par. 30.

5. *Human, All Too Human*, tr. R. J. Hollingdale (Cambridge: Cambridge University Press, 1986), 173f., par. 473.

he never tires of assertions such as this: "A higher culture can come into existence only where there are two different castes in society: that of the workers and that of the idle, of those capable of true leisure; or, expressed more vigorously: the caste compelled to work and the caste that works if it wants to."[6]

Passages of this sort should be compared with texts in which Nietzsche praises "the blonde beasts of prey," the noble conquering and master races such as the Romans, the Arabians, the Germanic and Japanese nobility, the Homeric heroes, and the Scandinavian Vikings: warriors rather than artists.[7] The same point is made in the following remark about the Greek city-state: "*The evolution of the spirit feared by the state.*—Like every organizing political power, the Greek *polis* was mistrustful of the growth of culture and sought almost exclusively to paralyse and inhibit it. It wanted to admit no history, no development in this realm. . . . This culture evolved *in spite of* the *polis*."[8]

The point of these passages is double-edged. On the one hand, Nietzsche is opposed to the state and hopes ultimately that it will "wither away" to be replaced by a united Europe.[9] On the other hand, he requires states of savage "aristocratic" warriors in order to complete the destruction of decadent Europe and to revitalize the human race. A high culture will then evolve *in spite of* the savagery or repression of the state. These two points do not fit neatly together. The "good European" in Nietzsche seems to allude to a gradual process of development that is contradicted by the need for dynamite.

———

I am about to suggest a way in which to make sense out of conflicting elements in Nietzsche's writings. My hypothesis has nothing to do with the usual scholar's dodge, historical development. Such a hypothesis would not work in the present case in any event, because the two elements can be found in the same published works. By way of anticipation, my hypothesis is that Nietzsche has a double rhetoric corresponding to the two stages of his overall revolutionary strategy.

In order to explain and justify my own hypothesis, I must first state as clearly as possible Nietzsche's fundamental objection to nineteenth-

6. Ibid., 162, par. 439; cf. 165–66, par. 452.
7. *On the Genealogy of Morals*, 40, pt. 1, par. 11; 86, pt. 2, par. 17.
8. Hollingdale, *Human, All Too Human*, 174, par. 474.
9. Ibid., 174–75, par. 475.

century liberal society. This is easy enough to do, as it is perhaps the best-known and most explicit aspect of his mature writings. We have already had occasion to refer to Nietzsche's judgment of nineteenth-century European society as decadent. According to Nietzsche, modern scientific and technological progress is accelerating political and social democratization by a flattening of spiritual perception and a homogenizing of experience. The European is undergoing a steady decline in vitality and creativity, or what Nietzsche calls the will to power, as a consequence of which he is slipping deeper into nihilism, or the condition that obtains when all standpoints are regarded as being of equal validity, with the consequent devaluation of each.[10]

This devaluation is misunderstood as a sign of progress: of egalitarianism and fair play. In fact, "morality is today in Europe the morality of the herd-animal."[11] Progress, viewed spiritually, is mediocrity, or progress toward spiritual death. At the same time (and there is always another side to the issue in Nietzsche), the decadence of society is accompanied by a kind of loss of illusions, and this has a paradoxically favorable potentiality for the would-be revolutionary.

In a long fragment from the *Nachlass* of Nietzsche's unpublished sketches for his intended but never completed masterwork, we read:

> *The naturalizing of mankind in the 19th century* (-the 18th century is that of elegance, refinement and generous sentiments). - . . .
>
> We are coarser, more direct, full of irony against generous feelings. . . .
>
> Our standpoint toward *morality* is more natural. Principles have become laughable; no one permits himself any more to speak of his "duty" without irony. . . .
>
> Our standpoint toward *politics* is more natural: we see problems of power, of a quantum of power against another quantum. We

---

10. These central themes are present in most of Nietzsche's writings but are perhaps most easily accessible in Kaufmann, *Beyond Good and Evil*, of which the reader should consult especially pars. 208, 219, and 224; for the critique of Christianity, see Kaufmann, *On The Genealogy of Morals* and *The Antichrist*. Nietzsche's last thoughts on decadence understood as nihilism are strikingly recorded in the posthumously-published fragments published in English as *The Will to Power*, tr. Walter Kaufmann (New York: Vintage Books, 1968).

11. Kaufmann, *Beyond Good and Evil*, 115, par. 202.

do not believe that a right will prevail if it does not rest upon power: we perceive all rights as conquests.

I will cite only one more paragraph from this fragment:

In summa: there are signs that the European of the 19th century is less ashamed of his instincts; he has taken a good step toward admitting his unconditioned naturalness, i.e., his immorality, without bitterness.[12]

This is a very important text, which brings out very well how Nietzsche plans to "dam up" (his expression) the decay of his time in such a way as to accelerate the instant of destruction. To expand only one aspect of the total situation, immorality is on the one hand a result of relativism brought on by scientific progress and historical sophistication; on the other hand, it is the detachment from decadent values that is the necessary precondition for their destruction and the production of new values.

The term *nature* thus plays an ambiguous role in Nietzsche's thinking. Despite Nietzsche's rejection of the Stoic invocation to a life in accord with nature, he retains the normative function of a nature that is derived fundamentally from Newtonian physics.[13] Power politics may be criticized when it is a question of evaluating the brutality of Bismarck's policies or the sacrifice of the higher spirits to the needs of the nation.[14] But at a deeper level, all politics is for Nietzsche power politics. One can criticize the absence of power, but not its expression. A correct understanding of life in accord with nature is thus already contained in Spinoza's maxim that might makes right.[15]

In paragraph 203 of *Beyond Good and Evil*, there is a clear and forceful statement of Nietzsche's goal, which should be called *political*, provided that we understand this term in its broadest philosophical sense: the attempt to transform human nature. Nietzsche has often been called a prophet, and this is in a way accurate, but we must remember that he combines the inverse of Christian rhetoric with the

---

12. Schlechta, *Werke* 3:615–17.
13. See Kaufmann, *Beyond Good and Evil*, 15, par. 9.
14. See Nietzsche's denunciation of *Grosse Politik* in Hollingdale, *Human, All Too Human*, par. 481.
15. For Nietzsche's (generally) high opinion of Spinoza, see his letter to Overbeck, 30 July 1881, in Schlechta, *Werke* 3:1171f.

law-giving function of the Hebrew prophets. In other words, Nietz-sche's attack on Christ certainly includes an attempt to take the place of Christ, but always as adapted in terms of the Jewish Scripture.[16] The law-giving function of the philosopher is possible because man is the not-yet-completed animal; this is a corollary to the pervasive thesis that creation is destruction.[17]

In the aforementioned paragraph (203), Nietzsche asserts that "the democratic movement is not only a form of the decay of political organization but a form of the decay, namely the diminution, of man, making him mediocre and lowering his value."[18] The only hope for human salvation lies in the destruction of the old and the creation of new values. This can be done only by new philosophers, that is, not by the academic civil servants or professional philosophers who are spokesmen for the established order, but by an entirely new breed of free spirits or philosophers of the future.[19]

Nietzsche does not say so explicitly here, but we may say on his behalf that these new philosophers must themselves be produced by Nietzsche's teaching. This difficult point has to be explicated in two stages. First and simplest: Nietzsche's devastating attack on modern European society is intended to free the higher human types from the decadence, stultification, and false sense of optimism engendered by nineteenth-century scientific liberalism. But second: free them for what?

This question has two different answers; I now suggest that they correspond to Nietzsche's own distinction between the esoteric or higher and the exoteric or lower presentation of the truth.[20] The exo-teric answer is the recommendation to return to the cruel creativity of the Renaissance city-state or to the *polis* of Homeric (more gener-ally, pre-Socratic) Greece. Cruelty is linked with creativity, as we saw

16. Nietzsche preferred the Old to the New Testament; see esp. Kaufmann, *Beyond Good and Evil*, par. 52. In par. 211 of the same work, Nietzsche asserts that genuine philosophers are commanders and lawgivers: they create values as an expression of the will to power.

17. Kaufmann, *Beyond Good and Evil*, 74, par. 62; cf. *Thus Spoke Zarathustra*, pt. 1: "Of the thousand and one goals."

18. Kaufmann, *Beyond Good and Evil*, 117, par. 203.

19. Nietzsche says that national or academic philosophy is laughable: the state is never concerned with the truth but only with truth that is useful to it. *Schopenhauer as Educator*, in Schlechta, *Werke* 1:361.

20. The clearest statement of this position, already implicit in the passage serving as epigraph for this chapter, is to be found in Kaufmann, *Beyond Good and Evil*, par. 30.

from Nietzsche's praise of such warrior races as the Scandinavians and Romans, not only because to create is also to destroy, but because the initial stage of the new epoch must be parallel to that of all archaic societies, or those like the Italian city-states that emerge against the background of the decadent Christian middle ages, namely, a stage of domination by aristocratic warriors.[21]

To continue with the exoteric reply, what is the philosopher of the future to create? Neither copies of the works of the past (which will presumably be destroyed by the revolution in any event) nor simply spontaneous expressions of difference or individuality: "My philosophy aims at an ordering of rank: not at an individualistic morality. The ideas of the herd should rule in the herd—but not reach out beyond it: the leaders of the herd require a fundamentally different valuation for their own actions, as do the independent, or the 'beasts of prey,' etc."[22] In considering this point, we should bear in mind another fragment from Nietzsche's unpublished notes: "What determines rank, sets off rank, is only quanta of power, and nothing else."[23]

Whereas Nietzsche associates the rejection of the natural order of rank with nihilism,[24] he also teaches at all stages of his thought that "the total character of the world is . . . in all eternity chaos."[25] This brings us to Nietzsche's esoteric or deeper teaching. Succinctly stated, it is as follows. Since what the traditional philosophers call Being or nature is in fact chaos, there is no eternal impediment to human creativity, or more bluntly put, to the will to power.

Creativity is not properly human at all but natural in the sense that it is the cosmological expression of chaos as lines of force. We live at the intersections of these lines of force (and the reader may think

---

21. In addition to other texts already cited on this point, see *Zarathustra*, preface, the sections entitled "Of Reading and Writing," "On the Tarantulas," and "On Redemption"; cf. the reference to "Caesar with Christ's soul" in Kaufmann, *The Will to Power*, p. 513, no. 983, as well as p. 330, no. 616. The inconsistencies in Nietzsche's exoteric teaching, taking it apart from the esoteric teaching, become visible when one thinks through the contradiction between Nietzsche's praise for archaic culture on the one hand and Renaissance culture on the other (to say nothing of his admiration for Goethe, Stendhal, and Dostoievski).

22. Kaufmann, *The Will to Power*, p. 162, no. 287.

23. Ibid., p. 457, no. 855.

24. Ibid., p. 14, no. 13; p. 24, no. 37.

25. *The Gay Science*, German text in Schlechta, *Werke* 2:115. For further discussion of this crucial point, see my *Limits of Analysis* (New Haven: Yale University Press, 1985), 193ff.

here of Lucretius), which we now call *history*, and which "express" us, although we believe that we express (or create) them. The "natural order of rank" is thus in fact the expression of power as chaos, (mis)perceived by us from our shifting perspectives in a way for which Nietzsche never offers any ontological or metaphysical explanation but which makes life possible, even though life is an illusion.

Except from a merely quantitative standpoint, this order, and so the values it expresses (my term) together with all of human creation, is intrinsically worthless in any but a subjective and hence entirely illusory sense. I repeat: life is an illusion. Nietzsche's esoteric teaching thus comes to precisely the doctrine for which he criticizes Platonism and Christianity: it empties human existence of intrinsic value. However, Nietzsche claims that this step is the necessary preliminary to genuine creation of value for human life, as sustained by the will to power of the creator. But because this is just an illusion, as the subjective or perspectival image of cosmic chaos, the final result is the same.

The doctrine that is much too dangerous for "the people" (see the epigraph at the head of this chapter), namely, the "truth," is thus impossible to distinguish from the base or debilitating nihilism of decadence, according to which "everything is false! Everything is permitted!" [26] Truth, even Being, is *interpretation* (after Nietzsche, the crucial term of our century).[27] In other words, life itself is an illusion, and this is why "art is worth more than the truth." [28] Art not merely enhances but produces life: art is the illusion by which we are inured, or rather charmed, into living a noble lie.

To summarize, Nietzsche advocates a return to the natural order in a sense, but not in a Platonic or Aristotelian sense. His paradigm at this level of his thought is instead Newtonian and Spinozist. Nature is power and, still more fundamentally, chaos.[29] Health, vitality, and creativity are intrinsically quantitative. Nietzsche in effect draws the last bitter consequence from the modern scientific Enlightenment: The

26. Kaufmann, *The Will to Power*, p. 326, no. 602.

27. This point is made over and over again in the *Nachlass*, in *Sämtliche Werke. Kritische Studienausgabe*, ed. G. Calli and M. Montinari (Berlin: Walter de Gruyter, 1980), e.g., 12:38 (1:115); 12:39 (1:120); 12:161 (2:190). See also Schlechta, *The Gay Science* 2:249f.

28. *Nachlass*, in Schlechta, *Werke* 3:693, 709, 738.

29. See footnote 14.

search for truth leads directly to nihilism and the death of the spirit. There cannot be the slightest doubt that, on Nietzschean grounds, theology, metaphysics, and ontology are all utter nonsense. Unfortunately, the same can be said of science and scientific philosophy, because these lead to the negation of sense and of the significance of human existence. The only consolation is art.

Because Nietzsche regards truth as a lie, there is no point in asking him for a philosophical explanation of the possibility of stable perspectives or, in other words, of the relative stability of illusion. The moment we understand that we are inhabiting a lie, we must forget or be destroyed. Nietzsche's constant insistence upon his own honesty is not inconsistent with this advice: honesty compels Nietzsche to reveal his esoteric teaching, to expose it to public view and thus to transform it into an exoteric teaching.[30] Nietzsche mitigates this risk by coating the bitter medicine of honesty with the sugar of creativity or of art.

But why is Nietzsche honest? One can say that this is a philosophical imperative; even Plato reveals that the so-called just city is founded upon a noble lie, in contrast to the lie in the soul.[31] However, Nietzsche is a rhetorical Platonist, so to speak, not a "metaphysical" Platonist. He is required to tell the truth in order to justify the destructive revolution that is the necessary precondition for the salutary or noble lie to take effect. The truth is necessary in order to motivate the exertion of the will to a power that produces the salutary illusion of vital art. We can triumph over the truth precisely because we know that Being is chaos. Nietzsche's esoteric teaching is the bluntest version of the modern Enlightenment.

This point is well brought out by Nietzsche's imperative to live dangerously: "That which has value in the contemporary world, does not have it in itself, according to its nature—Nature is always worthless —but one has at some time given, donated worth to it, and *we* were these givers and donators! We human beings have first created the world that pertains to human beings!"[32] When Nietzsche says that God is dead, he means not simply that we no longer believe in him

---

30. For a discussion of honesty, see Kaufmann, *Beyond Good and Evil*, par. 227. Cf. Schlechta, *The Gay Science*, par. 335.

31. Plato, *Republic* 2:382b1ff.; 3:389b2ff.; 3:414b8ff.

32. Schlechta, *The Gay Science* 2:177, par. 301. For living dangerously and the consequent praise of courage, see 165–66, par. 283. Courage is the lowest of the Aristotelian virtues but the highest of the Nietzschean virtues.

but that God never existed, except as an illusion created by human beings to delude themselves (albeit in an initially, or potentially, salutary manner).[33] In times of decadence, it is necessary to shout what others are merely whispering, to make public what is admitted behind closed doors: that no God stands between us and the void. Hence courage is the necessary precondition for creation. We must be brave enough to be atheists and immoralists in order ourselves to become gods and fashion new moralities.

The value of life thus depends upon its valuelessness. But this takes us to a still deeper stratum of Nietzsche's teaching. The exaltation of the artist-warrior is itself an exoteric doctrine. It is not we who have created the world at all. The world is a work of art giving birth to itself.[34] Art is the perspectival, human, and illusory perception of chaotic transformation. What looks to Nietzsche's Dionysian disciples like freedom is to Nietzsche's Apollonian vision *amor fati*—the Spinozist acceptance of fate, or what we may bluntly call *slavery*.[35]

Nietzsche's vision of human existence is of a dream in which from time to time certain individuals, by the strength of their will, determine the shape of the illusion. In the nineteenth century, the peculiar mixture of elements that hitherto dominated the dream in a positive sense are undergoing a complex process of deterioration. If this process is not terminated, the deterioration will ultimately produce a thousand-year domination of what Nietzsche calls, in the preface to *Thus Spoke Zarathustra*, the last men. The sterility of these men is indicated by the fact that their vision is punctuated by blinking and their speech by the clucking of tongues.[36]

In this light, we are able to appreciate the dual significance of one of the most frequently-cited passages in Nietzsche, "How the 'true world' finally became a fable."[37] In this text, Nietzsche gives a condensed history of the process by which the belief of the wise man in the true world is gradually destroyed, thanks to the combined influ-

---

33. This regular theme is first mentioned in Schlechta, *The Gay Science* par. 108; cf. paragraphs 127, 205.

34. G. Colli and M. Montinari, *Nachlass* 12:119.

35. *"Amor fati:* from now on, let this be my love!" Schlechta, *The Gay Science*, 2:161, par. 276.

36. The persons in the marketplace are anticipations of the last men, of what the future holds unless the entire process of life, as described in the preface, is aborted. *The Viking Portable Nietzsche*, tr. Walter Kaufmann (New York: The Viking Press, 1954), 128ff.

37. Schlechta, *The Twilight of the Idols* 2:96.

ence of Platonism, Christianity, and modern science. For all of these, the world of genesis is unreal because it is not the locus of value. It is interesting to note that Nietzsche thus interprets scientific laws as a species of Platonist Ideas, very much as does Hegel in *The Phenomenology of Spirit*. For Nietzsche, of course, this means that they are poems or projections of the human will. "The passage culminates in the following lines: We have abolished the true world: which world remains? perhaps the apparent world? . . . But no! Together with *the true world we have also destroyed the apparent world*! (Noon; moment of the shortest shadows; end of the longest error; high-point of humanity; INCIPIT ZARATHUSTRA.)"[38]

The end of the longest error coincides with the high-point of humanity; that is to say, in a Hegelian expression, that the owl of Minerva takes flight at dusk. Extreme decadence gives birth to Nietzsche, the most extreme of decadents, who is also vouchsafed an insight into the nature of life, and hence the opportunity to recreate it by instigating a transvaluation of values. The culmination of this "error," which is also the truth, plays the same role in Nietzsche as does the proletariat in Marxism: complete negation is the necessary precondition for a radically new affirmation. Unfortunately, Nietzsche's doctrine of negation is not sufficiently Hegelian; it does not culminate in a comprehensive and eternal or circular concept, but at best in the eternal return of the same. Shortly stated, Nietzsche replaces Hegel's concept, which is identical with Spirit and hence with God, with a myth. The prophet or poet replaces the conceptual philosopher.

It is against this complex background that we have to understand Nietzsche's most famous and also most obscure book. I offer only a few remarks on essential points. The first thing to be said is this: in my opinion, the great obscurity of the book is due not so much to its possessing a hidden meaning that requires elaborate decoding, but rather to the fact that the meaning is intentionally and necessarily incomplete as well as self-contradictory. It is incomplete because it is a prophecy of a radically new situation that not only cannot be clearly described but that may never come about. It is self-contradictory because, as we have now seen, the esoteric teaching contradicts the exoteric teaching. The contradiction can be removed only by seeing

38. Ibid.

that, at bottom, there is no essential difference between the esoteric and the exoteric teaching: the book implodes into chaos.

In Nietzsche's mature estimation, *Zarathustra* "stands altogether apart" from the other writings of mankind.[39] The fundamental idea of this book, according to Nietzsche, is the eternal return.[40] The meaning of this doctrine is the task common to Zarathustra and to himself, the act of saying yes "to the point of redeeming even all of the past."[41] " 'Was *that* life?' I want to say to death. 'Well then! Once more!"[42] Zarathustra and Nietzsche teach us to restore value to human existence, to overcome the split between heaven and earth induced by Platonism and Christianity (Platonism for the masses) by repudiating our resentment at the pains and troubles of life.

This yea-saying, however, is not to be confused with traditional Stoicism or oriental passivity. It is another aspect of the precondition for exercising the will to power. If we do not accept that this world is the locus of value, we will not be able to create. But at the same time, we must accept that this world is worthless in order to recognize that we ourselves create value, not nature or Being. Because we ourselves are modifications of the same chaotic process that results in the world, or differently stated, becasue the world is just a projection or perspective of the will to power, Nietzsche, underneath the extravagant poetic language of inspiration imitative of the German translation of Holy Scripture, is propounding a noble lie.

The affirmation of the eternal return, with the coordinate "love of fate," is certainly in conflict, or as I believe, in contradiction, with the equally pervasive doctrine of the artist, the creator of new values.[43] The ambiguity of their relationship may be effectively studied in the section from the third part of *Zarathustra* entitled "The Convalescent." Zarathustra's animals—in other words, not his human disciples but various aspects of (what must be) finally illusory interpretations of nature—speak to him of the eternal return as follows:

> O Zarathustra . . . to those who think as we do, all things themselves are dancing: they come and offer their hands and laugh and flee—and come back. Everything goes, everything comes

---

39. Kaufmann, *Ecce Homo*, 304.

40. Ibid., 295; Kaufmann translates *Wiederkehr* as "recurrence."

41. Ibid., 308.

42. Kaufmann, *Zarathustra*, "The Drunken Song," pt. 4, p. 430.

43. Sample passages in *Zarathustra*: 139, 143, 156, 171, 197–200.

back; eternally rolls the wheel of being. Everything dies; everything blossoms again; eternally runs the year of being. Everything breaks, everything is joined anew; eternally the same house is being built.

And so on.[44]

Throughout this section, it is the animals that interpret the doctrine of the eternal return. Zarathustra refers to them as "buffoons and barrel organs," by which he indicates that their version of the eternal return is popular, appropriate to a circus, comical. His restatement of the doctrine places emphasis upon his freedom from nausea at the sight of human misery: at the smallness of human evil, as Zarathustra puts it.[45] But that freedom is evidently fragile; Zarathustra tells the animals, "I must sing again, this comfort and convalescence I invented for myself. Must you immediately turn this too into a hurdy-gurdy song?"[46]

The only real difference between the animals' statement of the doctrine of the eternal return and the statement of Zarathustra is this: the animals make the doctrine public or popular, whereas Zarathustra sings it to himself. In my opinion this is a clear sign of the ambivalence in Nietzsche's own heart about the possibility of saving mankind. In order to do so, the truth must be published; but publication of the truth debases it into the coin of the realm.

All this is evident enough in the text. In the last analysis, Zarathustra does not converse with his animals but with his own soul.[47] As he puts it in an earlier passage: "In the end, one experiences only oneself."[48] We can infer from these texts that Zarathustra does not genuinely converse with independently existing disciples: these, like his animals, are his own creations or interpretations. They are like the characters in the Platonic dialogues with whom Socrates converses. So too Socrates is a figment of Plato's imaginative reinterpretation of human existence: Plato, like Nietzsche, is talking to himself, but in such a way as to benefit eavesdroppers. And this is why *Zarathustra* is intentionally imcomplete. Whereas the eagle and the serpent, who stand for the will to power and the eternal return, are the right

44. Ibid., 329–30.
45. Ibid., 331.
46. Ibid., 332.
47. Ibid., 333.
48. Ibid., "The Wanderer," 264.

animals for Zarathustra, "I still lack the right men."[49] This is Zarathustra's last word on the subject.

Zarathustra has no genuine disciples because he still lives in a time of decadence. In order to produce genuine disciples, Zarathustra must first destroy his own time, but hence too himself. How this can be done while allowing Zarathustra's positive doctrine to remain is never explained, nor in my view could it be. The most one could say is that Zarathustra, like Nietzsche, must throw himself into the revolutionary maelstrom as an act of creative exaltation—or if one prefers, of faith. This, incidentally, is the direct paradigm for the Nietzscheanism of the Left.

I want to provide one more textual example—the final speech of Zarathustra, in which he first expresses and then rejects pity for the higher men:

> "Pity! Pity for the higher man!" he cried out, and his face changed to bronze. "Well then, *that* has had its time! My suffering and my pity for suffering—what does it matter? Am I concerned with *happiness*? I am concerned with my *work*."

I interrupt the citation to comment upon the strikingly Hegelian nature of this rejection of happiness in favor of work. Those who insist upon a sharp juxtaposition between Hegel and Nietzsche have understood neither the one nor the other.

> "Well then! The lion came, my children are near, Zarathustra has ripened, my hour has come: this is *my* morning, *my* clay is breaking: *rise now, rise, thou great noon!*"
>
> Thus spoke Zarathustra, and he left his cave, glowing and strong as a morning sun that comes out of dark mountains.[50]

What is Zarathustra's work? Despite the doctrine of the eternal return, Zarathustra can neither passively await nor reproduce the anticipated epoch of world history. As we have seen over and over again, he must first destroy his own time. This cannot be done without disciples, who must themselves also be created—by rhetoric. However, the crucial point is this: the destructive disciples cannot possibly be the same as the creative disciples. The minions of the revolution (and

49. Ibid., 437.
50. Ibid., 439.

this necessarily includes Nietzsche's disciples of the twentieth century) must perish on the barricades of a creative future, a future to be
created by a child: "But say, my brothers, what can the child do that
even the lion could not do? Why must the preying lion still become
a child? The child is innocence and forgetting, a new beginning, a
game, a self-propelled wheel, a first movement, a sacred 'Yes.'"[51] The
meaning of this section is not that the same individual who was initially a lion next becomes a child, but that the human spirit undergoes
this metamorphosis (just as the lion was previously a camel). This is
Nietzsche's philosophy of history.

Nietzsche claims that Zarathustra is stronger than he, and hence
has a right to the future as Nietzsche does not.[52] But this, I believe,
means only that Zarathustra is the rhetorical creation by which Nietzsche hopes to prepare the way for the "fated" future, by which he
hopes to identify with fate and thereby to influence its outcome. The
difference between the lion and the child is fundamental; it is the
difference between the destroyer and the creator. And the difference
between Nietzsche and the lion is certainly not that between the camel
(the first of the three spiritual types) and the lion. Nietzsche is outside
the normal categories of human typology; he is, as he says of himself,
one of the "posthumous men—who are harder to understand than
contemporary men, but who are better *heard*."[53]

In what sense is Nietzsche a posthumous man? As the initiator
(granting him his grandiose self-conception) of the destruction of
Western bourgeois society, does not Nietzsche also guarantee the
vulgarization of his own works? Will he not come to life as a self-
constructed Frankenstein? And still more radically, will he and his
works not perish, if they fulfill their intention? Are not Nietzsche's
genuine disciples precisely his spurious or popular disciples?

A second question remains open: what new values will future creations bring? This is the same problem faced by Marx with respect
to the posthistorical utopia. Nietzsche, like Marx, belongs to the long
line of Enlightenment reformers going back to the origins of the modern epoch who either assume that progress will be salutary or who
insist that it must be better than the defective present. In the nineteenth century, confidence finally metamorphoses into hysteria.

51. Ibid., "On the Three Metamorphoses," 139.
52. Kaufmann, *On the Genealogy of Morals*, 96.
53. Schlechta, *Twilight of the Idols*, "Sayings and Arrows," vol. 2, no. 15.

There is a third question that emerges from our study, to which we can give at least a partial answer. According to Nietzsche, every text has endlessly possible interpretations. Furthermore, the philosopher of the future will say "*my* judgment," not "Nietzsche's judgment."[54] How then can we arrive at a valid understanding of Nietzsche's texts? The only way in which to answer this question is by denying the thesis that the author's intention is not discernible within the various readings a text allows. The closest we can come to bridging the gap between determinate sense and infinite interpretation is by the contention that Nietzsche's crucial themes are intentionally ambiguous. As directed against the present epoch, they are negatively intelligible; for example, Nietzsche's critique of moral ressentiment is not in fact a praise of ressentiment. But as directed to the future, such key themes as the eternal return and the will to power are compatible with whatever the most powerful will chooses to make of them. Nietzsche's positive meaning depends upon the persuasiveness of his interpreter.

When Nietzsche says that everything deep loves the mask,[55] or that "every philosophy also *conceals* a philosophy; every opinion is also a hide-out, every word also a mask,"[56] he must be understood in two senses. First, Nietzsche conceals by publication; I mean by this that the esoteric teaching is stated simultaneously with the exoteric teaching. But the exoteric teaching is so much more attractive that it charms the majority of Nietzsche's readers, whereas the esoteric teaching is intended to persuade the right persons to facilitate the work of the charmed multitude. Second, Nietzsche means that there is no criterion by which to identify a profound interpretation of Nietzsche. Readers find their own level of understanding, depending upon the "rank" to which they belong.

By way of conclusion, it is useful for us to remember that Nietzsche rejects too much. Dishonesty cannot be distinguished from honesty, or honesty from chaos, unless there is a natural distinction between the noble and the base. Otherwise, there can be no distinction between the noble and the base nihilism, or between life-enhancing and life-debasing immoralism. On this delicate point, the will to power is too coarse to illuminate us.

We should also understand that Nietzsche's appeal to his heteroge-

---

54. Kaufmann, *Beyond Good and Evil*, 53, par. 43.
55. Ibid., 50, par. 40.
56. Ibid., 229, par. 289.

neous constituency contains both radical and conservative elements. These are united by a common rejection of modern progressive liberalism. There is a very difficult lesson here, which should not be accepted without the most elaborate precautions. Nietzsche tells us more forcefully than any other serious thinker that "fair play," or "seeing the other person's point of view," necessarily weakens our commitment to our own point of view. Especially today, we do not like to see that if everyone is right, no one can be. The only exit from this dangerous dilemma is to understand that democracy is not vapid egalitarianism but itself an expression of nobility and hence of the difference between the noble and the base.

I would like to restate this last point. Life is not mathematics, in which universal correctness is, at least in principle, attainable. We cannot apply mathematical science uniformly, in an unlimited manner, to human existence, in the service of a political doctrine that is dedicated to freedom, justice, and the distinction between the noble and the base. When we try to do so, correctness tends inevitably to be defined quantitatively, in terms of formal validity, or as a function. The content becomes irrelevant. The radical sees this as clearly as does the conservative. Both oppose the reification of the human spirit, but on quite different principles. The conservative wishes to preserve tradition as the reservoir of nobility; the radical wishes to express his nobility in the act of creation. But preservation as well as creation entails destruction.

By leaving the content of his revolutionary doctrine undefined, except as a stirring appeal to Dionysian intoxication, Nietzsche is able to recruit disciples from the entire diapason of antiliberal sentiment, left as well as right. There are incentives for all to regard themselves as constituting the highest rank. But we need merely apply Nietzsche's own critique of egalitarianism to this doctrine to see that none of Nietzsche's interpreters can be genuinely creative, inasmuch as "everything is permitted." The noble nihilism is indistinguishable from the base nihilism. The only step taken by Nietzsche's clever disciples today is to speak of interpretation instead of morality.

I close with a final question. How can we make sense of Nietzsche? My suggested answer: not as an ontologist or unconscious Platonist, and not as a reactionary spokesman for the high culture of archaic Greece or the Italian Renaissance, but as a product of the very Enlightenment he purports (for the most part) to castigate. Nietzsche is a late disciple of Descartes, Newton, and Voltaire. He illustrates very well the inconsistency of the characteristic elements of the Enlightenment; namely, the transformation of nature from friend to enemy, the virtual identification of reason and mathematics, and the degradation of God from agent of personal salvation to clockmaker.

But Nietzsche is also a disciple of Goethe and of Stendhal, who venerates the artist and who himself possesses an aesthetic sensibility of ravishing precision and subtlety. Excessive psychological refinement: "All that is rare for the rare."[57] Refinement, yes; but decadence as well, and a loneliness that isolates rather than unites him with his fellow higher men and modern revolutionaries. On this point, Nietzsche may more profitably be regarded as a great novelist-statesman, in some ways comparable to Proust, but who fashions his daydreams in such a way as to allow him to imagine their ultimate actuality. Nietzsche's loneliness is to be overcome posthumously, precisely because this overcoming is political in the grand sense of the term. Proust's loneliness can never be overcome, because it is directed to the past in its search for assuagement; it remains a fantasy forever, leading to nothing but understanding, like Platonic recollection.

57. Ibid., 53, par. 43.

CHAPTER ELEVEN

Poetic Reason in Nietzsche
DIE DICHTENDE VERNUNFT

Phèdre: Qu'est-ce donc que tu veux peindre sur
le néant?
Socrate: L'Anti-Socrate.
Phèdre: J'en imagine plus d'un. Il y a
plusieurs contraires à Socrate.
Socrate: Ce sera donc . . . le constructeur.

—PAUL VALÉRY, *Eupalinos*

The German expression *die dichtende Vernunft* is to be found in Nietzsche's *Dawn*. We shall be concerned with the relevant passage in due order. As this expression is intended to provide us with a thread that extends across Nietzsche's thought from his predecessors to his progeny, we begin with a comment about its meaning. Nietzsche's thought is certainly a labyrinth; whether we have selected an Ariadne-thread, and whether a Minotaur has been identified, let alone slain, is for the reader to decide.

The German verb *dichten* means "to write or compose", and by extension, "to write poetry". It is in no way fanciful to remind the reader that the same verb in another context may mean "to tighten," as for example in caulking a seam or making a roof weatherproof. Poetry is thicker or denser, in the sense of purer or more concentrated, than prose. One thinks of a parallel discussion by Martin Heidegger in which he asserts that the poem is pure speech.[1] There is certainly a connection for Nietzsche between *dichten* and protection against nature.

More directly, however, the Nietzschean text establishes an intrinsic relation, perhaps an identity, between *dichten* and interpretation.

---

1. "Rein Gesprochenes ist das Gedicht." The statement occurs in Martin Heidegger, "Die Sprache," in *Unterwegs zur Sprache* (Pfullingen: Günther Neske Verlag, 1959), 16.

We may reasonably regard it as paradigmatic for subsequent discussion of Nietzsche's influence in our own century, and especially for our own generation, which is so haunted by the interpenetration of writing and hermeneutics in the process of world-making. Finally, we note that *dichten* is not, as employed by Nietzsche, synonymous with "poeticizing," which is to be understood here as the creating or writing of verse. As was also well conveyed by Valéry, who supplies the epigraph for the chapter, the writing of poetry is an example, not the essence, of *die dichtende Vernunft*.

In sum, we may translate *die dichtende Vernunft* as "poetic reason," provided that we understand "poetic" to mean "constructive" or "productive." Even this, however, will not preserve the sense of writing or textuality that is an essential dimension in Nietzsche's use of the term. In addition, such terms as "constructive" or "productive" must not delude us into forgetting that Nietzschean *dichten* is no more identical with the productive reason of classical German philosophy than it is with the Greek *poiein*. Nietzsche's interpretation of his own thought as "reversed Platonism" (*umgedrehter Platonismus*, which might without excessive irony be translated as "misinterpreted Platonism") leads him to reject the classical German thinkers as well, all of whom, in his view, together with the entire Western tradition of theologians and metaphysicians, are Platonists in the decisive respect.[2]

We begin our entrance into the labyrinth with the following passage: "My philosophy *reversed Platonism:* the farther from true beings, all the more purer more beautiful better it is. Life in illusion as goal."[4] On Nietzsche's account, Platonism produces the intelligible world of Being (Ideas, essences, categories, rules) as a consequence of the moralizing repudiation of the sensuous world, which is called *illusion*

2. "Seit Plato sind alle Theologen und Philosophen auf der gleichen Bahn." *Jenseits von Gut und Böse*, in *Sämtliche Werke. Kritische Studienausgabe*, ed. G. Colli and M. Montinari (Berlin: Walter de Gruyter, 1980), 5:112, par. 191; cf. same edition: "Seit Plato ist die Philosophie unter der Herrschaft der Moral." 13:259, fragment 7 [4], 1886–87. From now on, unless expressly stated, all citations from Nietzsche will be from the Colli and Montinari edition. References to the *Nachlass* will follow the form just employed: volume number, page number, fragment number, and date of notebook entry.

3. The German text reads: "Meine Philosophie *umgedrehter Platonismus*: je weiter ab vom wahrhaft Seienden, um so reiner schöner besser ist es. Das Leben im Schein als Ziel." 7:199, 7 [150], 1870–71. The reader who is unfamiliar with the *Nachlass* should know that Nietzsche's entries into his notebooks were often elliptical and fragmentary; my translations in the text attempt to be as close as possible to the syntax as well as to the sense of what Nietzsche wrote.

(*Schein*). Nietzsche identifies this production as itself an illusion or work of art. It is neither pure Being nor the transcendental structure of Kantian appearance (*Erscheinung*).

The distinction between appearance and illusion, whether in a Kantian or Hegelian sense, disappears for Nietzsche because "Being satisfies itself in complete illusion"[4] and not, as for Hegel, in complete appearance. At this level of our analysis, each world or human perspective is for Nietzsche a work of art, not in the sense of an intentional product of technical creation like a poem or a symphony, but rather in the sense of a representation (*Vorstellung*) produced by the fantasizing or "poeticizing" reason.[5] Such a work of art is an illusion of a true or eternal world: "The true essence of things is an invention of representing Being."[6] As an illusion, however, it is necessary for life, which *is* representation,[7] or the projection of order onto chaos, the ultimate substratum. We may therefore refer to the illusion as *Being*, namely, as the human face of chaos but not as the structure of appearance in the Kantian sense.[8]

We are now in a position to discern the ambiguity in, not to say the labyrinthian nature of, Nietzsche's goal of "life in illusion" (*das Leben im Schein*). The illusion is twofold, to say the least. Human beings must live in illusion or create their own worlds. But they must also regard this creation as Being. To perceive the illusory character of one's world is to succumb to decadence and the base or enervating nihilism.[9] Life requires, or is the same as, an illusion about illusion. It

---

4. "Das Sein befriedigt sich im vollkommenen Schein." 7:200, 7 [157], 1870–71.

5. "Vielleicht stellt die Phantasie dem wirklichen Verlaufe und Wesen etwas *entgegen*, ein *Erdichtung* die wir *gewohnt* sind als das Wesen zu nehmen." 9:445, 11 [12], 1881. Cf. 9:432, 10 [D85], 1880–81.

6. "Das wahre Wesen der Dinge ist eine *Erdichtung* des vorstellenden Seins." 9:569, 11 [329], 1881. Cf. 9:532, 11 [238]; 11:146, 25 [505], 1884; 13:53, 11 [113], 1887–88; 13:332, 14 [148], 1888.

7. 12:153, 2 [172], 1885–86.

8. See 12:253, 7 [2], 1886–87.

9. Most important here: the beautiful description of the historical decline from the true world to a "fable" or perceived illusion, in "Wie die 'wahre Welt' endlich zur Fabel wurde," *Götzen-Dämmerung*, 6:80–81, par. 6 (cf. pp. 78–79). In the poetical language of *Also Sprach Zarathustra*, the invocation to the creation of new values (e.g., pt. 3, "Von alten und neuen Tafeln") is not the same as the need of the lion to become a child: "Unschuld ist das Kind und Vergessen, ein Neubeginnen, ein Spiel, ein aus sich rollendes Rad, eine erste Bewegung, ein heiliges Ja-sagen" (pt. 1, "Von den drei Verwandlungen," 4:31).

is therefore not immediately obvious how the celebration of creativity and of the overcoming (*Überwindung*) of mankind ("der Mensch eine Brücke sei und kein Zweck"),[10] so influential in our own time, is to be made compatible with the preservation of creativity itself. We note in passing the tension between the end (*Ziel*) of life as illusion and the denial that man is an end (*Zweck*).

Seen from within (namely, to a resident within illusion), what Nietzsche calls "life within illusion" is the intersection of artistic creativity and health or "the will to power." We cannot help thinking of Nietzsche's own struggle with illness when we read his assertion that he has experienced in his own life "that art is *worth more* than the 'truth.'"[11] The deeper sense of this statement, of course, is not autobiographical and is to be found in *Twilight of the Idols*[12] and in the following more expansive fragment: "Art and nothing but art. It is the great potentiator of life, the great seductress toward life, the great stimulus to life."[13]

Why do we require to be seduced toward life? Like so many of the questions addressed to Nietzsche, this one has two answers of differing degrees of profundity. At a more external level, residents of the late nineteenth century, Nietzsche included, have been enervated by the decadence of rationalism.[14] More fundamentally, life, understood as health and still more fundamentally as intoxication,[15] *is* art, that is, not knowing but making:

> Will to power as knowledge
> not "knowing" but schematizing, superimposing as much regularity and as many forms onto chaos as suffices our practical needs.[16]

This terminology reminds us once more of Kant. In Kant, space and time are the forms of understanding (*Verstand*), and schematizing takes place within time. In Nietzsche, *die dichtende Vernunft* schematizes chaos. One wonders whether "chaos" is not a product of Nietzsche's own poeticizing and so a part of his interpretation of

---

10. *Also sprach Zarathustra* 4:31, pt. 3, par. 3.
11. 13:227, 14 [21], 1887–88.
12. *Götzen-Dämmerung*, "Streifzüge eines Unzeitgemässen," 24 in 6:127.
13. 13:194, 11 [415], 1887–88.
14. 13:265, 14 [86], and 13:626, 24 [1], 1888.
15. *Götzen-Dämmerung*, "Streifzüge," eight in 6:116.
16. 13:333, 14 [152], 1888.

life as divine creation. Chaos would then be the Nietzchean reversal of the Kantian noumenon; the schematizing function of imagination would then be exercised by *Phantasie* or invention (*Erdichten*). Kant's theoretical reason is thus entirely assimilated into practical reason. It becomes, so to speak, a historicized version of Fichte's "activity" (*Tathandlung*) and thereby an example of nineteenth-century praxis.

There is an unmistakably Kantian resonance within Nietzsche's reversal of Platonism. Human consciousness, whether interpreted as representation, instinct (*Trieb*), or will to power, produces the world. Nietzsche, however, takes a radical step beyond Kant by abolishing the distinction between transcendental structure and personal perspective. In this sense, Being is life, and life is at every level art, that is, illusion: "We live indeed through the superficiality of our intellect in a continuous illusion, that is, in order to live, we need art at each moment."[17]

In his later period Nietzsche identifies the artistic or constructive essence of life as itself a manifestation of the will to power, which thus assumes the function of a comprehensive force that is, as it were, both transcendental (my term) and immanent: "Life itself is *essentially* appropriation, violation, overpowering of strangers and the weaker," and so on.[18] It is a trivial consequence of the comprehensive status of the will to power that, as we noted previously, the distinction between appearance (*Erscheinung*) and illusion (*Schein*) is abolished.[19] The will to power thus serves as the middle term or essence of Being and art: "The will to illusion . . . to deception, to Becoming and to change function here as deeper and more fundamentally 'metaphysical' than the will to truth, to actuality, to Being: — the last is merely a form of the will to illusion."[20]

I have employed the term *comprehensive* rather than *universal* to characterize the will to power because it is a force, each point of which has its own perspective, that is to say, "its entirely definite valuation."[21] Being is Becoming, namely, "excitation" (*Bewegung*), and each excitation or alteration is "an encroachment of power upon another power"

17. 7:435, 19 [49], 1872–73.
18. *Jenseits von Gut und Böse* 5:207, par. 259.
19. See esp. the fragment entitled "Gegen das Wort 'Erscheinung,'" which identifies *Schein* as "die wirkliche und einzige Realität der Dinge. . . . Ein bestimmter Name für diese Realität wäre 'der Wille zur Macht.'" 11:654, 40 [53], 1885.
20. 13:229, 14 [24], 1888.
21. 13:371, 14 [184], 1888.

or a center "from out of which the will increases" (*um sich greift*).[22] The comprehensive process of world production is thus a process of the production of local perspectives. The comprehensiveness of the world is therefore an illusion: every apparently stable unity, whether a subject or an object, is in fact a diversity. The inner excitation of Hegelian logic has been poeticized and so robbed of its conceptual structure. In a representative text: "From each of our fundamental instincts there emerges a different perspectival evaluation of all events and lived experiences. . . . *Man as a multiplicity of 'will to power': each with a multiplicity of means of expression and forms.*"[23]

Because the intoxication, will, or constructive genius of the artist is in fact an illusory unification of the endless self-differentiation of the will to power, Nietzsche seems to have deprived himself of the ability to explain the presence of a world. This, incidentally, is a problem that has not been noticed, let alone solved, by contemporary acolytes of difference. A world, like an individual subject or object, is said by Nietzsche to be an illusion. But on Nietzschean grounds a stronger statement is required: A world would seem to be impossible. The illusion of unity must itself be unified in order to function as an illusion, as *this* illusion. Conversely, an illusion is an illusion only to a unified consciousness, one which is unified as conscious of the aforementioned illusion. The production of illusion, at both the global and personal levels, is not and cannot itself be an illusion.

Nietzsche, unlike so many of his progeny, was evidently aware of the problem: "This is the mystery: how did the organism arrive at a judgment of Same and Other and Enduring?"[24] But I find no attempt in the Nietzschean corpus to resolve this mystery. This is a fundamental problem for Nietzsche's positive doctrine in addition to being a perception of a riddle in the ultimate scheme of things. Even if we were to grant that formal or mathematical structure is an illusion in Nietzsche's sense of the term, this structure does not lose its indispensable role in the effectivity of the will to power. The structure of an illusion remains a structure, without which the illusion cannot function as an illusion. And the same could be said for the content of the illusion, as Freudian psychoanalysis should have taught us.

It is therefore entirely plausible to argue that Nietzsche's reversal

22. 13:261, 14 [81] and 13:274, 14 [98], both 1888.
23. 12:25, 1 [58], 1885–86.
24. 9:544, 11 [268], 1881. Cf. pp. 434ff., 10 [E93], 10 [E95] and 10 [F100], 1883.

of Platonism is a failure on internal grounds, or stated in a more pro-
vocative way, that Nietzsche, despite himself, remains a Platonist. To
this extent, I would partially rehabilitate Heidegger's interpretation of
Nietzsche. I do not, however, agree that Nietzsche's Platonism consists in an unconscious acceptance of Being as presence. Certainly
there is nothing in the discussion of the will to power to sustain this
thesis. Nietzsche's unconscious Platonism results from an inadequate
analysis of the presence of mathematical structure within illusion
(*Schein*) or perspectival construction. On this ground, Heidegger is
himself a Platonist. Those who avoid Platonism in this sense are, in
my view, entirely incoherent. Or rather, there is no possibility of a
reversal, or indeed of a repudiation, of Platonism at this level, except
by the comprehensive reinstitution of chaos.

Our first attempt to understand Nietzsche's "reversed Platonism" as
the replacement of a mathematical by an artistic metaphysics has
shown that this replacement ends in chaos. The following remark,
made by Nietzsche in 1880 with respect to his earlier thought, would
seem to apply to the later doctrines as well: "The attempts to conduct
an extra-moral meditation on the world were previously too lightly
undertaken by me—aesthetical (the honoring of genius—)"[25] We may
restate our initial result in such a way as to prepare for the next stage
of the investigation. Nietzsche, as we have seen, regularly interprets
Platonism as an essentially moral doctrine. He therefore assumes that
the mathematical or formal structure of the Platonic cosmos is an illusion, namely, a construction or perspective imposed by Plato onto
chaos in order to preserve mankind from the immorality or guilt of
Becoming. So far as I can see, Nietzsche presents no convincing evidence for this interpretation. It is also incompatible with his own
account of philosophy as a whole, and hence of Plato's philosophy,
as the expression of the will to power: "Philosophy is this tyrannical
instinct itself, the spiritual will to power, to the 'creation of the world,'
to the causa prima."[26]

It is not satisfactory to explain this passage and others like it as a
reference to the unconscious motivation of philosophy, and in particular of Platonism. The compelling discussion of the philosophical
nature in part 6 of *Beyond Good and Evil* makes it clear that the genuine

25. 9:31, 1 [120].
26. *Jenseits von Gut und Böse* 5:22, par. 9.

philosopher intentionally creates a new table of values: "*The genuine philosophers are however commanders and lawgivers: they say, 'let it be so!'* ['so soll es sein!']"[27] Nietzsche does exactly the same.

If the invocation "let it be so!" is moral, then Nietzsche is again a Platonist (and not on Heideggerean grounds). At the level of the genuine philosopher or lawgiver, there is no intrinsic difference between morality and tyranny: "Fundamental thought: the new values must first be created—we are not *spared* this! The philosopher must be like a lawgiver."[28] The lust for tyranny characterizes Plato also in his philosophical nature, a lust of which, according to Nietzsche, he was fully aware. Speaking of the instinct of born masters, Nietzsche says: "Beneath each oligarchy lies . . . always concealed the lust for tyranny . . . (so was it for example with the Greeks: Plato points it out in a hundred places, Plato, who knew his own kind—and himself . . .)."[29]

In sum: philosophy is the will to power at both the conscious and the unconscious levels. All values, old as well as new, have been created by fiat—let it be so!—and hence by the conscious intention of the philosopher. Whatever the shortcomings of Platonism,[30] there cannot be any question that Plato was, if moral, an advocate of the morality of masters, exactly like Nietzsche ("Look at Plato: he denies *everything else that is great!*"); both are, like all genuine philosophers, magicians and chimaeras, or in other words, advocates of medicinal or noble lies, an advocacy endorsed by Nietzsche on Plato's authority.[31]

To state the same point in ontological terminology, Socrates' exoteric discussion of the Idea of the good with the young Glaucon in Plato's *Republic* is not a moral repudiation of Becoming but an identification of goodness as intelligibility. That Nietzsche himself understood the exoteric nature of the connection between Platonist moralism, or the ascetic Ideal, and Plato is in my opinion evident in the following passage from *The Genealogy of Morals*:

27. Ibid., 5:211, par. 45. Cf. 11:611ff., 38 [13], 1885.
28. 11:533, 5 [71], 1886–87.
29. *Zur Genealogie der Moral* 5:384, pt. 3, par. 18.
30. See 11:243, 26 [254], 1884 for a remark concerning Plato's naiveté about the rationality and necessity of evil.
31. 10:337, 8 [15], 1883; *Jenseits von Gut und Böse* 5:111, par. 190. Cf. 10:104, 3 [1], 417: "Voller Leidenschaft aber herzlos und schauspielerisch: so waren die Griechen, so waren selbst die griechischen Philosophen, wie Plato"; 13:293, 14 [116], 1888: "Plato: ein grosser Cagliostro." For philosophers and lying, see 11:451f., 34 [96], 1885, and 11:651, 40 [44], 1885, as well as the quotation from Stendhal in 13:19, 11 [33], 312.

The peculiarly world-negating, life-opposing rejection of the senses, the recollective standing to one side of the philosophers, which has been retained until today—it is above all a consequence of the conditions under which philosophy in general arose and endured: that is, insofar as for the longest time it was *indeed not possible* on the earth without an ascetic covering and uniform, without an ascetic self-misunderstanding.[32]

The last words of this paragraph do not negate but supplement the immediately preceding account of asceticism as a conscious disguise.

The question of esotericism or of the philosopher's masks is an important one in Nietzsche. It bears centrally on the nature of Nietzsche's genuine or conscious Platonism, and I will return to it shortly. But first we must restate the nature of Platonism itself. We cannot here engage in a detailed study of Platonism, but it is necessary to ask ourselves what are the essential elements in the philosophical nature as presented in the Platonic dialogues. In order to identify these elements, we cannot merely (and naively) list the attributes assigned to the potential philosopher by Socrates in the *Republic*. The discussion there is political or itself exoteric. On the other hand, we are not forced to make farfetched or textually unsupported assertions.

To take the important case, there can of course be no question that for Plato, the philosopher is a person of the highest morality. But high morality is altogether compatible with tyranny in the original sense of absolute rule, as the *Republic* itself demonstrates. The highest or philosophical (as opposed to the demotic) morality is derived from the identification of virtue as knowledge and of knowledge as wisdom. In the present context, I shall take this as obvious and go on to characterize knowledge as of two general kinds: mathematical and poetical. By mathematical I mean knowledge of formal structure; by poetical I mean knowledge of the human soul.

The poetical element of the philosophical nature is closely connected to the third element I wish to cite. This element is less frequently noticed in Plato than are the other two; I call it *hermeneutical* or *philological* and will support this terminology with references to two representative texts. In the *Symposium* (202e3ff.), Diotima explains to the young Socrates that the daimonic Eros is an intermediary between gods and mortals, "interpreting (*hermēneuon*) and conveying human

32. 5:361, pt. 3, par. 10.

things to the gods and divine things to humans." In the *Phaedrus*, Socrates responds to a threat from his companion that he will be shown no more speeches as follows: "Oh you wretch! You've discovered how to compel a man who loves speeches to do what you command!" (*andra philologō*; 236e4–5).

Socratic philology is hermeneutical in the precise sense that it interprets divine and human speech in order to arrive at an understanding of human nature in its particularity as well as in its generality. As the dialogues themselves exemplify, and as is explicitly recommended in the *Phaedrus*, this understanding and its presentation are perspectival or accommodated to the differences among human beings. These differences correspond very closely to what Nietzsche calls "rank-ordering" (*Rangordnung*). The connection between rank and nature is immediately obvious from the following text: "What concerns me is the problem of rank-ordering within the species mankind, in the progress of which as a totality I do not believe, the problem of rank-ordering between human types, which have always existed and always will exist." [33]

It is true that for Nietzsche, "The quantum of power determines the rank that thou art; the rest is cowardice." [34] Nietzsche, despite the punctual and continuously self-differentiating manifestation of power, accepts something like a statistical regularity of patterns of accumulation of power. Otherwise, the will to power could not exert itself in such-and-such a way. In mankind, these regularities constitute the enduring human types. Their endurance as types is independent of the instability of individual representatives of these types. [35] We may accordingly distinguish three senses of hermeneutics or perspectivalism, although Nietzsche does not do so explicitly: the first is the expression of the micropersonal level, that is, perceptions, instincts, desires, and the like; the second is the expression of the individual person, and the third, of the type. It is to this third type of interpretation that rank-ordering refers. To exaggerate slightly, these types are Nietzsche's equivalents at the human level to Plato's hierarchy of Ideas.

33. 13:481, 15 [120], 1888.
34. 13:20, 11 [36], 1887–88. I retain the second person singular in my translation to bring out the personal level of the statement.
35. Consider here Nietzsche's criticism of Darwin and his explanation of how the powerful individual is usually overcome by the greater strength of the herd. 13:303, 14 [123], 1888.

However these patterns may have established themselves, the perspectival relativity at the personal and micropersonal level is for Nietzsche compatible with universality or duration through historical time at the typical level. His rejection of the Stoic[36] and the Kantian[37] conceptions of nature do not then constitute a complete reversal, let alone a rejection of Platonism. The Platonism of rank-ordering, however, must be distinguished from the Machiavellian or Newtonian motivation of this and other similar passages: "My task: the dehumanizing of nature and then the naturalizing of humanity, after the latter has acquired the pure concept 'nature.'"[38] Nietzsche rejects the conception of a teleological nature in favor of a modern interpretation of nature as amoral, extravagant, merciless, "fertile and barren and uncertain all at once."[39] I note in passing that this is also an anthropomorphic interpretation.

The discontinuity between rank-ordering and the "value-free" dimensions of nature amounts to this: it is man who creates value in his estimation of the patterns of accumulated power manifested by nature. At the same time, these values are natural in that they themselves exemplify the intrinsic expression of the will to power (itself a supreme anthropomorphism). Nietzsche refuses to speak of nature as a standard of value, despite his attribution to it of noble and base qualities. We are presumably to understand that these qualities cancel each other in the totality of the manifestation of power. This leaves mankind, in accord with the reversal of Platonism, free to create new values, and thereby to surpass itself, as is taught at length in *Thus Spoke Zarathustra*.

We thus come face to face once more with the problem of illusion (*Schein*). The free creation of value, precisely as an expression of the will to power, is an illusion. As in Spinoza, with whom Nietzsche felt kinship, freedom is knowledge of necessity, or *amor fati*.[40] It is therefore superficially correct, but at a deeper level profoundly wrong, to say that man creates value. No human being creates anything, despite

36. *Jenseits von Gut und Böse* 5:21, par. 9.
37. *Menschliches, Allzumenschliches* 2:41, pt. 1, par. 19.
38. 9:525, 11 [211], 1881. Cf. 12:482f., 10 [53], 1887, on the "Vernatürlichung des Menschen im 19. Jahrhundert."
39. *Jenseits von Gut und Böse* 5:21, par. 9.
40. 13:492, 16 [32], 1888. For praise of Spinoza, see the letter to Franz Overbeck, 30 July, 1881, in *Nietzsches Werke*, ed. Karl Schlechta (Munich: Carl Hanser Verlag, 1956), 3:1171.

Nietzsche's exoteric rhetoric: the world is a work of art giving birth to itself.[41] It is "the will to power—and nothing beyond that!"[42] Therefore, when Nietzsche warns us that "nature, estimated aesthetically, is not a model. She is . . . chance,"[43] he intends us to understand that, as I would put it, it is the nature of nature to be shaped into a world, but at the same time that the intrinsic natural chaos will both regulate and disrupt our creations.

Paradoxically enough, the best world is the one that remains closest to nature as chaos. This is the world of strength, vitality, ruthlessness, and fecundity, although it is also inevitably the world of decadence and nihilism.[44] We may summarize the preceding line of thought as follows. Nature is chaos,[45] but chaos is what allows creativity.[46] At the microscopic level, the human creator is accordingly also chaos;[47] but from within the dimension of illusion (*Schein*), wherein human life is alone possible, chaos is concealed by the schematizing function of the *dichtende Vernunft*. These schemata not only make life possible; they unfortunately also vitiate life by their very duration. For this reason, Nietzsche has in fact two comprehensive goals. The first, as we have seen, is life within illusion (*das Leben im Schein*). But the second goal is the exact opposite: "My philosophy—to extricate mankind from illusion at any risk! Also no fear in the face of the destruction of life!"[48]

The "destruction of life" is a return to what Nietzsche calls "the innocence of Becoming."[49] Human creativity depends upon the absence of eternal standards or ends in nature; conversely, to say that Becoming is innocent is to justify it in each of its moments.[50] We see here a stage in the affirmation of the eternal return.[51] Nietzsche char-

---

41. 12:119, 2 [114], 1885–86. Cf. 7:111, 5 [79], 1870–71.

42. 11:611, 38 [12], 1885.

43. *Götzen-Dämmerung*, "Streifzüge eines Unzeitgemässen," 7:115, par. 7.

44. On the permanent presence of decadence, see 13:87, 11 [226], 1887–88; 12:468, 10 [22], 1887. For the connection between decadence and nihilism, see 13:265, 14 [86], 1888: nihilism is "die Logik der decadence" and not its cause.

45. "Der Gesammt-Charakter der Welt ist dagegen in alle Ewigkeit Chaos." *Die fröhliche Wissenschaft* 3:468, bk. 3, par. 109.

46. A representative text: 11:654, 40 [53], 1885.

47. 9:434f., 10 [E93]; 9:437, 10 [F100]; 9:428, 10 [D67]: all texts from 1880–81.

48. 9:620, 13 [12], 1881.

49. "Die Unschuld des Werdens." 12:385f., 9 [91], 1887.

50. 13:34f., 11 [72], 1887–88.

51. Representative texts: 11:10f., 25 [7], 1884; 12:213, 5 [71] and 12:312, 7 [54]: both from 1886–87.

acteristically overlooks the fact that the eternal return of the same depends upon the nonillusory or irreducible presence of unity and hence of mathematical or formal structure in each returning element. Without this, sameness would dissolve into chaos. Nietzsche is therefore wrong to maintain that logic is a human product or complete fiction.[52] When Nietzsche says that there is no genuine conceptualization in mathematics, as "we 'conceive' only where we understand motives,"[53] this mistake is of the greatest importance. The mathematical element of Platonism cannot be reduced to the poetical element of Nietzsche's own teaching. And this is a mistake that Nietzsche has transmitted to his progeny. The Ariadne-thread is also the medium of the nihilism from which it seeks to rescue us.

The reduction of mathematics to poetry, one could say, renders unstable the required hermeneutical balance between the two fundamentally different senses of illusion (*Schein*).[54] As life-enhancing or healthy, illusion is good or noble; as decadent or sick, it is evil or base. The difference between health and sickness, however, is a difference of rank-ordering and therefore of types, natures, or unities —in the final instance, of unities as patterns of accumulated power. These patterns are works of art not in themselves but as interpreted or evaluated within a human perspective. On the other hand, human perspectives are works of art only in the metaphorical sense in which the world is described as a work of art giving birth to itself. If nature is then art for Nietzsche, it is equally true that art is nature.

With this in mind, we can see that the celebration of creative art, whatever emotional need it may have satisfied in Nietzsche, is part of his exoteric teaching. Let me restate this somewhat more fully. Art is an interpretation of the will to power. In this perspective, Nietzsche can say, "Art pertains not to nature, but only to human beings,"[55] and

---

52. 11:435, 34 [49] and 11:505, 34 [249]: both from 1885.

53. 10:93, 25 [314], 1884. Cf. *Götzen-Dämmerung*, "Die Vernunft in die Philosophie," 6:76, par. 3.

54. The discussion in *Menschliches Allzumenschliches* 2:31, 35, and 40f., holds good for all periods of Nietzsche's thought. It is not affected by his interest in physics. See *Jenseits von Gut und Böse* 5:28, pt. 1, par. 14: "Es dämmert jetzt vielleicht in fünf, sechs Köpfen, dass Physik auch nur ein Welt-Auslegung und -Zurechtlegung . . . und *nicht* eine Welt-Erklärung ist."

55. 8:458, 23 [150], 1885.

much later, in passages already cited, that art is the greatest stimulus to life and that it is worth more than the truth.[56]

On the other hand, the expression *will to power* is itself the title of an artwork, a metaphor or an interpretation of nature very much in the spirit of modern science, toward which latter Nietzsche expressed conflicting feelings. I agree with Giorgio Colli's acute observation that the will to power is an exoteric doctrine discarded by Nietzsche in the very last stage of his thought, an observation that is sustained by the entries in Nietzsche's last notebooks.[57]

These notebooks show conclusively that Nietzsche abandoned the project of writing a book entitled "The Will to Power" and turned instead to questions of human values, politics included, and in particular to autobiography. This new focus is a sign that Nietzsche recognized the impossibility of a theoretical foundation for his teaching. A theory is a work of art or an interpretation; as such, it cannot be confirmed by nature. The net result, which one finds in contemporary philosophy of the most diverse schools, is that nature becomes a work of art. More specifically, nature is concealed by an artifactual representation of nature. We thus return, despite everything, to the Kantian doctrine of the cognitively inaccessible *Ding an sich selbst*. And thus the nature concealed within the artifact is itself an artifact. Unfortunately, there is no Ariadne-thread to lead us out of this labyrinth: or let us say that the effect of the thread has been reversed.

Allow me to emphasize this conclusion. The failure of Nietzsche's esoteric theory, namely, comprehensive perspectivalism or the schematizing of chaos by itself, leads to the initially paradoxical result that the exoteric doctrine becomes the genuine esoteric doctrine, namely, comprehensive illusion licenses not an ontological toy called "will to power" but the tyrannical or master ethic of the imposition of a rank-ordering by noble lies. There is, however, one qualification, possibly fatal. The informed exotericist, who has been "reversed" and is now the genuine esotericist, knows that he has failed. This, I suggest, accounts for the central role in Nietzsche's writings, from beginning to end to be sure, but with special poignancy in the last stages, of Dionysus: of intoxication and self-forgetting. The poignancy lies in

56. 13:194, 11 [415], 1887–88, and *Götzen-Dämmerung*, "Streifzüge," par. 24; see also 13:227, 14 [21], 1887–88.

57. *Nachwort*, 13:651–55.

the recognition that honesty engenders decadence and the base nihilism, which accordingly requires a noble lie, not simply to the vulgar but to oneself. Herein is to be discerned the difference between the philosophers, who are always decadent, and the masters, who assert their values without philosophizing, that is, without the bourgeois use of "arguments," to employ a term much in favor among those whom Nietzsche called "English flatheads" and their acolytes.

In this section and the next, I want to follow the turn that I have attributed to Nietzsche from the esoteric to the exoteric, and to reexamine the construction of the world of illusion (*Schein*) by the *dichtende Vernunft*. First, however, it will be useful to establish that the distinction between the esoteric and the exoteric is found in all periods of Nietzsche's thought. As a general preface, one could say that this distinction is intrinsic to the fragments of Heraclitus, whom Nietzsche especially admired. It is also obvious in Nietzsche's constant advocacy of an aristocratic rank-ordering.

The classical text containing an explicit discussion of the esoteric-exoteric distinction is to be found in *Beyond Good and Evil*, as well as in an interesting notebook entry from the same period.[58] But Nietzsche is continuously aware of the dual problem faced by the genuine philosopher: how to conceal his superiority and how to present it. In an epigram dating from 1876–77, Nietzsche says: "Last opinion about opinions. — either one conceals his opinions or one conceals oneself behind his opinions. Whoever does otherwise does not understand the course of the world or else belongs to the order of holy foolhardiness."[59] In the same work, Nietzsche indicates his own understanding of prudential writing: "I write in such a way that neither the people, the populi, nor the parties of all kinds can read me. As a consequence, these opinions never become open."[60]

This passage, which is presented in dialogue form, is unmistakably Platonic and should be read together with two later references to Plato concerning lies. The more important passage reads as follows: "Our cultivated contemporaries, our "good persons" do not lie — that is true, but it does *not* redound to their honor! The authentic lie, the

---

58. *Jenseits von Gut und Böse*, esp. par. 30, but see pars. 26–30. See also 13:187, 5 [9], 1886.
59. *Menschliches, Allzumenschliches* 2:517, pt. 1, no. 338.
60. Ibid., 2:584, pt. 2, par. 71.

genuinely resolute "noble" lie (about the worth of which one may listen to Plato) would be for them too severe, too strong."[61]

We may distinguish three motives for esotericism or the noble lie in Nietzsche. The first is the motive of the philosopher as educator: "An educator says not what he himself thinks but never anything other than what he thinks about a matter in relation to the benefit of him whom he educates."[62] The second motive, which is a major theme of the discussion of the philosophical nature in *Beyond Good and Evil*, is the intrinsic hiddenness of the great thinker: "Everything deep loves the mask."[63] On this point also, Nietzsche expresses his kinship to Plato, about whose "hiddenness and Sphinx-nature" he repeatedly comments.[64]

The pedagogical motive may of course combine with the intrinsically concealed nature of the philosopher: "Here the outlook is unrestricted. There are heights of the soul at which a philosopher is silent; there is a kind of love that leads him to contradict himself; there is a politeness of the knower that lies."[65]

And there is also a third motive, a kind of aristocratic playfulness or natural expression of superiority that is required neither by interior depth nor exterior prudence: "A great man . . . when he does not speak to himself, has his mask. He prefers to lie rather than to tell the truth: it takes more spirit and will."[66]

From these three motives, I distinguish the comprehensive human need for illusion, which a fortiori requires the philosopher to lie: "We have need of lies . . . in order to live."[67] To summarize: the "necessary concealment of the wise"[68] not only makes it intrinsically impossible for the many to understand the few but requires the few to accommodate their depths to the superficial yet equally compelling needs of the many. Once again, we see the link between rank-ordering and nature. What Descartes calls the *philosophus larvatus* is not only compatible with, but a direct consequence of, the love of the truth.

61. *Zur Genealogie der Moral*, 5:386, pt. 3, par. 19. See also 11:189, 26 [152], 1884, for the second reference and compare, *inter alia*, 13:187, 5 [9], 1886–87.

62. 11:580, 37 [7], 1885.

63. *Jenseits von Gut und Böse* 5:57f., par. 40.

64. Ibid., 5:47, par. 28; 5:111, par. 90.

65. *Götzen-Dämmerung*, "Streifzüge," 6:148, no. 46.

66. 11:451f., 34 [96], 1885. See especially 11:543, 35 [76].

67. 11:142, 25 [491], 1884.

68. Ibid.

The turn from the esoteric to the exoteric may now be restated as follows. The chaotic essence of Being and the constructive nature of its schematisms make theory, or seeing things as they are, impossible. It is not simply that what we see is a work of art: to see is already to interpret or create, that is, to alter or distort. Chaos and constructivity thus also legitimate an "artistic metaphysics" or reversed Platonism in which the genuine philosopher is free to impose new values by the force of his will: *so soll es sein*.[69] Rhetoric is the power that transforms the *Sollen* into *Sein*. Rhetoric, or exoteric speech, is not in the service of an esoteric theory but rather of a creation *ex nihilo* or prophetic revelation.

Stated as sharply as possible: The fact that Nietzsche cannot sustain his appeal to the Platonic conception of natural aristocracy becomes the basis for the doctrine of creativity. The esoteric truth is then that there is no truth and no theory. The exoteric celebration of human creativity is thus free to step into the void, as it were, and so to become itself the esoteric as well as the exoteric theory. But this means that the distinction between the esoteric and the exoteric collapses. Hence Nietzsche's progressively more blunt, indeed, shrill public announcements, which are not due to the final madness, but in my view constitute an entirely correct tactical judgment by Nietzsche as to what is required in order to enforce his ultimate tyranny.

In place of the distinction between the esoteric and the exoteric, let me suggest that we have instead two levels of exoteric doctrine. These levels will be represented for us by two metaphors, the will to power and the *dichtende Vernunft*. The first metaphor, as we have seen, is the rhetorical expression of a putative theoretical principle, which

69. When Nietzsche says in 1876–77 that he has abandoned the "metaphysisch-künstlerischen Ansichten" of his earlier writings (8:463, 23 [159]), he means that the role of art has been deepened, not abandoned. In fact, the following statement from the later preface to *Die Geburt der Tragödie* does not disown the main insight of the early essay concerning Dionysian intoxication; instead, one could say, it suppresses the Apollonian lucidity that, paradoxically enough, resurfaces in the later teaching as decadence: "der rein aesthetischen Weltauslegung und Welt-Rechtfertigung . . . : denn alles Leben ruht auf Schein, Kunst, Täuschung, Optik, Nothwendigkeit des Perspectivischen und des Irrthums." 1:18. In this connection, see 9:31, 1 [120], 1880: "Versuche einer aussermoralischen Weltbetrachtung früher zu leicht von mir versucht—eine aesthetische (die Verehrung des Genies—)."

does not rise above the metaphorical level and hence descends to the level of artistic construction. There is no theoretical explanation of art, because every explanation is nothing but an interpretation, namely, itself a work of art.[70]

The *dichtende Vernunft*, or poetic reason, is a metaphor for the activity of the production of metaphors, namely, of simulacra of the patterns of chaotic motion by which human existence, in an entirely inexplicable manner, is able to make itself possible. It would be tempting to call poetic reason the Nietzschean equivalent to a Kantian regulative Idea. The least one could say is that Nietzsche's ostensible explanations of the construction of consciousness take place by means of principles that include, or are in their entirety, metaphors of consciousness. The force of these metaphors is to convey the impression that consciousness constructs itself. In fact, there is no explanation for the transition from chaos to consciousness.

In my opinion, the contemporary tendency to search for an ontology, intended or unintended, in Nietzsche is sufficiently strong that one must state over and over again: Nietzsche has no ultimate teaching of a theoretical, constructive nature. The riddle to Nietzsche's consistency cannot be unlocked because it does not exist. If one prefers the formulation, one may say that the riddle is its own resolution. *Die dichtende Vernunft*, however, is an excellent metaphor for the central activity celebrated by Nietzsche, both in what it advocates and in what it does.

As a preliminary step in our inspection of this metaphor, it is worth repeating that poetry in the conventional sense is not at issue here. Nietzsche says, "We defend artists and poets and whoever is a master: but as beings of a higher nature than these merely 'productive men' who only possess know-how, we do not confuse ourselves with them."[71] In a blunt expression, Nietzsche observes that "the poets were always the valets of some moral doctrine or another."[72] They are certainly not, as Shelley claimed, the legislators of society, except in the derivative sense that they present as their own the doctrines of the great lawgivers, thereby serving as instruments for the rhetorical dissemination of these doctrines among a wider audience than would be accessible without them.

70. Cf. 12:39, 1 [121], 1885–86: "Welt-Auslegung, nicht Welt-Erklärung."
71. 11:544, 35 [76], 1885.
72. *Die fröhliche Wissenschaft* 3:371, pt. 1, par. 1.

This point is well made by Nietzsche's Zarathustra, who connects his initial criticism of traditional values to the shameful because poetic expression of the as-yet-unexplained future in images or parables. The future, he says, is a hotter South than artists have dreamed of, "where dancing gods are ashamed of all clothing"; here Zarathustra still speaks "in parables, and limps and stammers like poets: and truly, I am ashamed that I must still be a poet!"[73] The future must be mediated for the decadent present by the shameful clothing of poetic diction. This, I believe, is an essential element in the song of the old magician in part 4 of *Zarathustra*: "A suitor of the *truth*? Thou? . . . No! Only a poet!"[74]

The poet has a servant's consciousness, or in other words does not understand his own function. The same may be said for the innocent child in part 1 of *Zarathustra* into whom the lion metamorphoses: "The child is innocence and forgetting, a new beginning, a game, a self-propelled wheel, a first excitation, a holy Yea-saying."[75] The child, or new and innocent stage of civilization, who thus corresponds to "the innocence of Becoming," is not the servant but the offspring of the philosopher-lawgiver. The philosopher-lawgiver, on the other hand, is necessarily conscious of his own creative activity; hence he says, "Let it be so!"[76] He is therefore also fully conscious of the theoretically incoherent circumstances that initiate and justify his creative activity: in other words, like all philosophers, he is decadent.[77] The lawgiver cannot himself become, but may only procreate, a child: he cannot enter into the promised land.

For this reason we must also distinguish between the philosopher and the *dichtende Vernunft*. The latter is instrumental; the former employs this instrument in order to present a teleology. Let us keep this distinction in mind as we turn now to the passage in which Nietzsche introduces the expression *die dichtende Vernunft*. The passage is entitled *Erleben und Erdichten*, that is, "living through and inventing."[78]

---

73. *Also sprach Zarathustra* "Von alten und neuen Tafeln," 4:247, pt. 3, no. 2.
74. Ibid., "Das Lied der Schwermut," 4:371, no. 3.
75. Ibid., "Von den drei Verwandlungen." 4:31, pt. 1.
76. "Der Philosoph soll *erkennen, was noth thut*, und der Künstler soll es *schaffen*." 7:423, 19 [23], 1872–73.
77. See esp. 13:626, 24 [1], 1888, which corresponds to *Götzen-Dämmerung*, "Was ich den Alten verdanke," 6:157, no. 3. In addition, *Der Fall Wagner* 6:11; 13:260–63, 14 [83], 1888.
78. *Morgenröthe*, 3:111–14, pt. 2, no. 119.

Nietzsche begins with the observation that nothing can be more incomplete, however well we know ourselves, than the comprehensive picture of the desires constituting our essence. These instincts are satisfied by the work of chance, namely, the chaotic processes that we mistakenly regard as the unified activity of a self-identical individual ego or subject. Nietzsche calls these processes *Ereignisse* and *Erlebnisse*, "events" that become one's own by being "lived through." They constitute the level of conscious experience or illusion.

This illusion of self-conscious unity is the surface pattern of the microprocess of needs and satisfactions. Surface and interior are contingent and, at a still deeper level, chaotic. In traditional language, Nietzsche is maintaining that causal and formal order are the product of random motion; this is reminiscent of classical atomism, yet is also not without its Kantian resonances. In place of the transcendental ego is poetic reason. But poetic reason is not an autonomous agent; it is instead a metaphor taken from the vocabulary of illusion to describe the consequences of physiological instinct.

We may regard this entire passage, with all of its materialist elements and anticipations of Freud, as a poetic transformation of German Idealism. There is no causal connection between laws regulating the atomic microprocesses and the emergence of physiological instincts on the one hand, or between these instincts and self-conscious experience on the other. The underlying paradigm is not mathematical but musical. The activity of the construction of personal experience, accordingly, follows no a priori concepts or universal rules: it is hermeneutical.

To return to the details of the text: Nietzsche distinguishes the instincts underlying experience into those like hunger, which cannot be satisfied by any dream-food, and the majority, like the moral drives, which can. In this distinction, self-consciousness is tacitly assigned the status of dreaming; the instincts are divided between *wakefulness* (the physiological level) and *sleeping* (the level of *Erlebniss*). Nietzsche does not say so explicitly, but it is evident that the characteristically human instincts are themselves dreams. The dream of self-consciousness is not disturbed by a recognition of the true nature of wakefulness, namely, its "terrible contingency" (*diese Grausamkeit des Zufalls*), thanks to its capacity to produce its own nourishment. We also note that Nietzsche does not, as one might expect in an ostensibly positivist account, derive dreaming or sleeping as an activity from the microprocesses of physiology. The activity of dreaming produces nourishment for those instincts that have not been satisfied during waking existence. But the instincts do not produce the dreaming or the dreams. Instead, dreams are *inventions* (*Erdichtungen*), "interpretations of our nerve-irritations during sleep, very free, very arbitrary interpretations of excitations of the blood and the intestines," and so forth.

What we may call the text, that is, the tissue of instincts "read" by the dreamer, remains very much the same from one night to the next. It is, however, subjected to continuously varying interpretations by the poetic reason. *Die dichtende Vernunft* is not a philologist in Nietzsche's sense of the term: It engages in interpretation (*Auslegung*), not explanation (*Erklärung*). Philology or *Wissenschaft* would awaken us from our poetic slumbers, thereby initiating the decay of *Erlebnisse*. Which interpretation is produced depends upon which instinct or hunger assumes the role of *souffleur* for the night. This striking image comes from the stage or opera; the metahermeneutical principle is the prompter, hidden from the audience but not from the performers, who whispers cues to assist the aberrant memories of the artists onstage. Although it is of course true that the prompter is reading from the score, the artists do not read his cues; they hear them. The prompter clarifies; the artist interprets. Nietzsche is not yet Jacques Derrida: Writing serves here as the objective or Platonist basis for the spoken improvization of the interpreter.

The meaning of this striking image is at once plain and ambiguous. The artist-interpreter, although regulated by the text, is distinct from it. But the details of the passage give us no basis for a solid inference as to the origin or the nature of the artist or dreamer. Furthermore, we should not be confused by the distinction within the metaphor between dreaming and waking; the dreamer is self-consciousness and the dream is life in its entirety. When Nietzsche says that wakefulness does not have the "freedom of interpretation" characteristic of dreaming, because the former is "less poetic and unreined," he is thinking of the distinction between physiological and moral instincts. The direct continuation of the passage, however, explicitly suppresses this distinction. There is no essential difference between waking and dreaming; the waking instincts are also interpretations of irritations of the nerves. The result, nevertheless, is not materialist determinism. In the most diverse cultural strata, "the freedom of waking interpretation in the one is in no way inferior to the freedom of the other in dreaming."

This last formulation is somewhat ambiguous, but Nietzsche's intention seems to be to establish on the one hand a comprehensive freedom of interpretation within "waking" or moral life (*Erlebniss*), and on the other a connection between moral life and physiology: "Must I amplify . . . that even our moral judgments and evaluations are only images and fantasies about a physiological process that is unknown to us, a kind of speech that is customary for pointing out certain nerve-irritations? That all our so-called consciousness is a more or less fantastic commentary on an unknown, perhaps unknowable, yet felt text?" In the last lines of the passage just cited, Nietzsche becomes more extreme. The image of the *souffleur* is given a Derridean inflection, not to say deconstruction; the result is to weaken the bond between the text of the drama or score of the opera and the freedom of the artist to interpret. The force of the dream virtually suppresses the residue of philology; feeling replaces knowledge, and music triumphs over *Wissenschaft*.

Allow me to repeat that the suppression of the distinction between waking and dreaming does not abolish the separate status of the *dichtende Vernunft* or dreamer. Instead, that status is extended to constitute the totality of human existence. Nietzsche's central contention was succinctly expressed by Shakespeare in *The Tempest*: "We are such stuff as dreams are made on/And our little lives are rounded with a sleep." I am tempted to quote once more from Shakespeare, a line that illuminates our theme from an oblique angle: "If music be the food of love, play on!" Does Nietzsche intend to convey to us that the dreamer, whether lover or musician, artist or prompter, is in all cases nothing more than a dream interpreting itself in response to physiological stimuli? Perhaps, but there is no clear support for this reading in the text. Nietzsche does not argue; he sings and dances. In any case, the song of a reflexive dream is ultimately as Platonist in its invocation of unity, and as Kantian in its invocation of self-consciousness, as is the scientific metaphor of physiology.

We saw previously how Nietzsche attempts to assimilate mathematics into poetry. We can now add that poetry is assimilated into hermeneutics. The more deeply we penetrate into Nietzsche's thought, the more evident it becomes that the ostensible reversal of Platonism is rather a collapse or a dissolution. This assertion, however, needs to be qualified in at least one fundamental way: reversed or collapsed Platonism retains a rhetorical form of presentation that is directly bound up with a Platonist rank-ordering, and to that extent, with a Platonist conception of nature. For Nietzsche, however, there is no theoretical account of rank or nature. Thus, whereas for Plato an esoteric teaching demands an exoteric presentation, there is for Nietzsche finally no difference between the esoteric teaching and the exoteric presentation. Interpretation triumphs entirely over explanation. The distinction between the *souffleur* and the artist disappears; the replacement of cognition with feeling leads to the unraveling of the text into an unending Ariadne-thread, or to an unendingly unraveling Ariadne-thread, which leads deeper into the labyrinth.

Despite Nietzsche's frequent expressions of praise for philology in the *wissenschaftliche* sense, in which explanation determines the precise meaning of the text without falsifying it through interpretation,[79] Nietzsche's underlying and in his last period explicitly dominant position is rather this: "The same text permits countless interpretations; there is no 'correct' interpretation."[80] In the series of notes from which I cite here, Nietzsche goes on to identify "the essential element in the organic nature" with "a new interpretation of the event, the perspectival inner multiplicity that is itself the event."[81]

This is the same as the doctrine we have just inspected in the earlier passage from *Dawn* on poetic reason. Each point of the will to power is an interpretation, but the converse is also true: "In truth, interpretation is itself a means toward becoming master over something."[82] In an important passage: "The world that concerns us is false, that is, is not something found but rather a creation from or rounding-off of a small sum of observations; it is 'in flux' as something in Becoming, as a falsehood that is continuously displacing itself anew, that never approaches to the truth: for—there is no 'truth.'"[83]

Poeticizing (*Dichten*) is "creating from" (*Ausdichten*), a process of interpretation by selection from the unending, intrinsically chaotic flow of perceptions, sensations, representations, instincts, collisions, and intersections of microelements of Becoming. Lies thus become truths by the honesty and passion with which they are expressed: the

---

79. *Der Antichrist* 6:233, par. 52. Cf. *Menschliches, Allzumenschliches* 12:29, pt. 1, no. 8 and 2:442, pt. 1, no. 153; also 13:456, 15 [82], 1888.
80. 12:39, 1 [120] and 1 [121], 1885–86.
81. 12:41, 1 [128]; cf. 12:100, 2 [82]: both 1885–86.
82. 12:140, 2 [148], 1885–86.
83. 12:114, 2 [108], 1885–86.

will to power is a rhetorical expression for rhetoric. Art is worth more than the truth because it *is* the truth (which incidentally refutes the maxim).

The doctrine encapsulated within the goal of "life within illusion" is once more unmasked as itself an illusion. To repeat an earlier citation, "Being satisfies itself in complete illusion." [84] This early remark may be interpreted in the light of a much later fragment: "to evaluate Being itself: but evaluation is itself this very Being." [85] The hermeneutical circle is effectively closed with the addition of the following fragment: "There is nothing of value in life beyond the degree of power —granted of course that life itself is the will to power." [86] Mathematics is reduced to poetry, and this in turn to interpretation. To be sure, interpretation is identified as will to power, but this is itself merely a metaphor or interpretation of the schematizing of chaos.

Very far, then, from representing Nietzsche's ultimate groping toward ontology, the will to power is the point of implosion into which the esoteric dissolves, thereby to be transformed into the exoteric. Everything deep loves a mask, but only because there is nothing behind the mask. A doctrine generated by the profound anguish of spiritual depth in an age of superficiality has the terrible result of accelerating the exteriorization of depth and the consequently inevitable rejection of interiority. The ego, the subject, *homo sapiens*—all follow God into the abyss of deconstruction.

These extreme consequences, today known as "liberation," follow from Nietzsche's extreme formulation of the critical modern doctrine that we know only what we make. From Descartes to Kant, Fichte, and Hegel (and in an isolated post-Nietzschean example, the early Husserl), if in different ways and with different degrees of success, the identification of knowledge as construction or projection is regulated by the mathematical conception of identity and order but therefore implicitly by the Platonist doctrine of formal unity. Nietzsche abolishes the regulatory function of mathematics. He plays a major role in the historical process that led the proponents of mathematics to insist that it is constitutive as well as regulative, substance as well as form. In so doing, unfortunately, the proponents of mathematics themselves became Nietzscheans.

84. 7:200, 7 [157], 1870–71.
85. 13:45, 11 [96], 1887–88.
86. 12:215, 5 [71], 1886–87.

The difference between Nietzsche and his modern predecessors comes to this: whereas the earlier thinkers say that knowing is making, Nietzsche asserts that it *ought* to be: "One *shall not* [*sollte*] thus any longer know anything of an object [*Sache*] that one could not create. Besides, this is itself the only means to know anything truly, namely, to attempt to make it."[87] The reversal of Platonism, even though mathematics becomes the art of interpretation, leaves intact the Platonic conception of the philosopher as a warrior-king. As a direct consequence of political art (not the art of politics), Nietzsche secularizes, or more precisely takes onto himself, the creative labor of the Judaeo-Christian God: "In sum and good, very good indeed: after the old God has been destroyed, I am ready *to rule the world.*"[88] This statement, written when Nietzsche was about to lapse into the silence of madness, is the same as the "sober" remark made thirteen years previously: "My religion . . . lies in the labor of creating genius; education is all that is to be hoped for; everything that consoles is called art."[89] Or again, "My challenge: to produce natures that are superior to the entire species 'humanity': and to this end to sacrifice myself and 'those who are closest' to me."[90] This is the goal to which *Thus Spoke Zarathustra* is devoted.[91]

In bringing this chapter to a close, I do not wish to leave the reader with the impression that my sole intention was to demonstrate the self-contradictory nature of Nietzsche's thought. Nothing could be farther from the truth. I have indeed attempted to show that Nietzsche's reversal of Platonism is a circle, and in that sense a labyrinth, which can be called the eternal return of the same if and only if *the same* is understood as chaos. But it may be true that all philosophical teachings are circles, even though regulated by mathematics.

Although Nietzsche has given to his followers the gift of chaos, this does not lessen the purity of his intention to be our benefactor.

87. 8:89, 5 [167], 1875.
88. 13:646, 25 [19], 1888–89. Cf. Nietzsche's "mad" letter of January 6, 1889, to Jacob Burckhardt, which begins as follows: "Lieber Herr Professor, zuletzt wäre ich sehr veil lieber Basler Professor als Gott; aber ich habe es nicht gewagt, meinen Privat-Egoismus so weit zu treiben, um seinetwegen die Schaffung der Welt zu unterlassen," in Schlechta, *Werke*, 3:1351.
89. 8:46, 5 [22], 1875. Cf. 8:43, 5 [11].
90. 10:244, 7 [21], 1883.
91. See the indispensable study by Lawrence Lampert: *Nietzsche's Teaching* (New Haven: Yale University Press, 1986).

We may benefit from Nietzsche's purity or nobility only by asking ourselves how it is possible for bad consequences to follow from good intentions. Nietzsche was himself well aware of the dangers of his experiment in divinity and believed them to be justified: "We make an experiment with truth! Perhaps mankind will accordingly be destroyed! So be it! [*Wohlan!*]"[92] I will risk the suggestion that whether Nietzsche's experiment was justified depends in large part upon whether the Enlightenment could have been suppressed without engendering consequences far worse than those of the failure of the French Revolution.

On this point, I prefer Nietzsche's remarks about crab-men to his attack on modernity:

> Whispered into the ear of a conservative. —What one did not know previously, what one knows today, is able to know —, a *retrograde formation,* a reversal in any sense and to any degree is surely not possible. . . . No one is free to be a crab. There is no getting round it: one must go forward, that is to say *step by step further into decadence.*[93]

92. 11:88, 25 [305], 1884. This fragment refers explicitly to Zarathustra. Cf. *Morgenröthe* 3:274, pt. 5, par. 453, and 13:492, 16 [32], 1888.
93. *Götzen-Dämmerung,* "Streifzüge," 6:144, par. 43. Cf. 13:20, 11 [39], 1887–88.

Index

Alembert, J. de, 71
Aristotle: and conservatism, 7f.,
    10, 65; and Plato, 18, 41, 106;
    and the arts, 70; and Hegel, 83,
    111, 116; and justice, 92f.; and
    noncontradiction, 147f., 155;
    and intuition, 161f., 164; and
    nonbeing, 166

Cantor, G., 156
Charmides, 94–96, 102f.
Colli, G., 222
Critias, 96f., 99f., 102

Derrida, J., 19, 229
Descartes, R.: and mathematical
    ideas, 22–36; and freedom, 71f.;
    and method, 135–39; and dualism,
    154; and the modern revolution,
    160f.
Dewey, J., 180

Eleatic Stranger: 60f., 62, 67, 166–68
Euripides, 86

Fichte, J. G.: and freedom, 65–82;
    and Plato, 84f., 90, 97, 106; and
    Rorty, 180
Fraenkel, A. A., 34

Gentzen, G., 155

Hacking, I., 120f., 126
Hegel, G. W. F.: and Enlightenment,
    vii–x, 1, 16f., 1–21; and Plato,
    62, 83–106; and freedom, 66f.,
    69, 72–75, 79f.; and Aristotle, 83;

theory and practice in, 107–17;
    and dialectical logic, 118, 122–25;
    and negation, 169; and Rorty, 181,
    183; and Nietzsche, 190, 201, 211,
    214
Heidegger, M.: and Plato, 19, 35, 58;
    and language, 164f.; and Rorty,
    176, 178, 187f.; and poetry, 209;
    and Nietzsche, 215–16
Hobbes, T., 87
Homer, 86
Hume, D., 169
Husserl, E., 35, 161–64

Kant, I.: and Plato, 37–64, 84f.,
    105; and Fichte, 70–81, 90; and
    postmodernism, 164f.; and Rorty,
    179f., 184–87; and Nietzsche,
    211–13
Kelkel, A., 164
Klein, J., 26
Kojève, A., 114

Lakatos, I., 140–45
Locke, J., 76–78

Marx, K., 117, 190, 205

Nietzsche, F.: and Enlightenment,
    2, 22; and Plato, 54, 77, 199, 203,
    210, 214–19, 224–25; and Fichte,
    76, 81; and postmodernism, 165;
    and revolutionary politics, 189–
    208; and Hegel, 190, 201, 211, 214;
    and Marx, 190, 205; and poetic
    reason, 209–34; and Kant, 211–
    13; and Heidegger, 215–16; and
    Socrates, 216–18; and Spinoza, 219